£ 10 50

A REGIONAL HISTORY OF
THE RAILWAYS OF GREAT BRITAIN

General Editors: DAVID ST JOHN THOMAS and J. ALLAN PATMORE

VOLUME III
GREATER LONDON

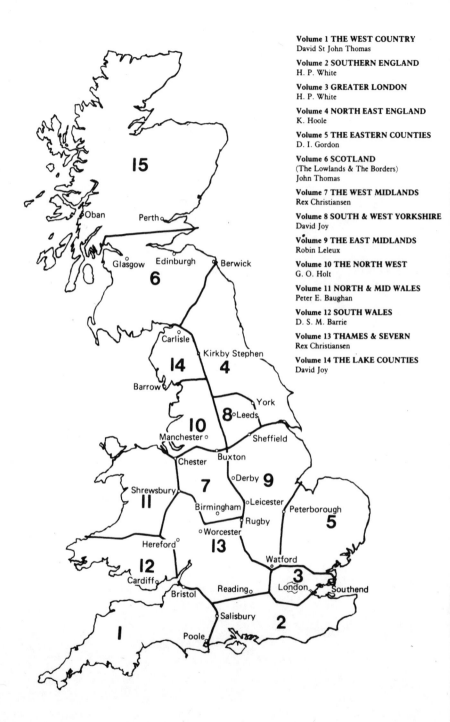

Volume 1 THE WEST COUNTRY
David St John Thomas

Volume 2 SOUTHERN ENGLAND
H. P. White

Volume 3 GREATER LONDON
H. P. White

Volume 4 NORTH EAST ENGLAND
K. Hoole

Volume 5 THE EASTERN COUNTIES
D. I. Gordon

Volume 6 SCOTLAND
(The Lowlands & The Borders)
John Thomas

Volume 7 THE WEST MIDLANDS
Rex Christiansen

Volume 8 SOUTH & WEST YORKSHIRE
David Joy

Volume 9 THE EAST MIDLANDS
Robin Leleux

Volume 10 THE NORTH WEST
G. O. Holt

Volume 11 NORTH & MID WALES
Peter E. Baughan

Volume 12 SOUTH WALES
D. S. M. Barrie

Volume 13 THAMES & SEVERN
Rex Christiansen

Volume 14 THE LAKE COUNTIES
David Joy

Frontispiece London at the dawn of the railway age was small and compact. The changes about to take place, largely brought about by the new means of transport, can be appreciated by comparing this 1838 view of the London & Croydon Railway with the present scene from the Vesta Road overbridge (SE4) 3 miles from London Bridge. New Cross Gate station is in the middle distance with the London & Greenwich viaduct beyond. (*Guildhall Museum*)

A REGIONAL HISTORY OF
THE RAILWAYS OF GREAT BRITAIN

Volume III

GREATER LONDON

by

H. P. White

WITH 45 PLATES
20 ILLUSTRATIONS IN THE TEXT
AND FOLDING MAP

DAVID ST JOHN THOMAS
DAVID & CHARLES

First edition published by David & Charles 1963
Second, revised edition published by David & Charles 1971
This third, revised edition published by
David St John Thomas 1987
and distributed by David & Charles

British Library Cataloguing in Publication Data

White, H. P.
    Great London. – 3rd ed. – (A Regional
history of the railways of Great Britain;
V. 3).
    1. Railroads – England – London
– History.
    I. Title   II. Series
    388.4'2'09421   HE3019.L8

    ISBN 0-946537-39-9

Phototypeset by Typesetters (Birmingham) Ltd
Smethwick, West Midlands
and printed in Great Britain by
Redwood Burn Ltd, Trowbridge, Wiltshire
for David St John Thomas

Distributed by David & Charles Publishers plc
Brunel House   Newton Abbot   Devon

Distributed in the United States of America
by David & Charles Inc
North Pomfret   Vermont 05053   USA

Contents

I   LONDON AND ITS PARTS   *page* 9

II THE SOUTHERN TERMINI AND THEIR APPROACHES   27
London Bridge and the Charing Cross Extension
· Victoria · the 'City Line' · Waterloo

III THE SOUTHERN SUBURBS   52
The South Eastern Railway · the London,
Chatham & Dover Railway · the South Eastern
& Chatham Railway Companies Managing
Committee · the London, Brighton & South
Coast Railway · the London & South Western
Railway · 'Southern Electric': beginnings ·
'Southern Electric': fruition · the post-war period
· the social consequences of electrification

IV CENTRAL LONDON   80
The North London Railway · the post-war years ·
the Metropolitan · the Widened Lines · the
District · the Inner Circle · train services on the
Inner Circle · the East London Line

V THE TUBES   103
The City & South London · the Central London ·
the Hampstead Tube · the Bakerloo · the Piccadilly · the Great Northern & City · the Victoria
and Jubilee Lines · UndergrounD · the London

Passenger Transport Board · London Transport
in the post-war era

VI   MAIN LINES AND MIDDLESEX   117
The Great Western Railway · Paddington · the
Great Western & Great Central Joint Line ·
branches from the Great Western · the London &
North Western Railway · Euston · the main line
from Euston · Willesden Junction · suburban
growth · branches from the London & North
Western · the West London and West London
Extension · the North & South Western Junction
and its associated lines

VII   CLAY, HOUSES AND ELECTRIC TRACTION IN MIDDLESEX   139
The District and the Piccadilly in West London ·
the Metropolitan 'Extension' · 'Metroland' ·
developments on the Extension · Uxbridge · the
Great Central · decline, fall and rise at Marylebone · Metropolitan and Great Central branches

VIII   THE MIDLAND AND THE GREAT NORTHERN   153
The coming of the Midland · St Pancras · the
main line · the Tottenham & Hampstead Junction · suburban services and suburban growth ·
the Great Northern Railway · King's Cross ·
main-line developments: King's Cross to Finsbury Park · main-line developments: Finsbury
Park to Welwyn Garden City · suburban growth
along the main lines · Enfield and Hertford · the
Great Northern Electric · the Northern Heights ·
the Piccadilly Extension · the Tube to Edgware

IX   SUBURBAN TRAFFIC EXTRAORDINARY: THE GREAT   178
EASTERN
The Lea Valley and Hackney Downs group of
lines · train services and suburban development ·
industrial development · the Loughton group of
lines · the Romford line · Stratford · electrification
· Liverpool Street

X DOCKLAND AND SUBURBIA ON NORTH THAMES-SIDE 200
The Blackwall Railway · the Docklands Light
Railway · the North Woolwich Line and its
branches · the genesis of the London, Tilbury &
Southend Railway · traffic growth and economic
development in south Essex · Southend · sub-
urban growth · the dock and industrial traffic ·
Fenchurch Street

XI RAILWAYS AND MEGAPOLIS: A CONCLUSION 219

BIBLIOGRAPHY AND ACKNOWLEDGEMENTS 225

INDEX 229

CHAPTER I

London and its Parts

One Briton in four now lives in London and the Home Counties. But London's dominance is far from new. Ever since Roman times it has been the largest city in Britain; for almost the whole of the period it has been the country's commercial heart; for at least half the time it has been the political capital; today it is the centre of the main industrial area; and its role as a social centre has increased its attraction.

Of course there have always been many who would agree with William Cobbett's castigation of its growth as draining the Provinces of wealth, culture and talent. In the 1820s when the city numbered over 1.25 million inhabitants he wrote of 'the increase of London, the swellings of the immortal Wen'. But his great Wen was even then on the threshold of unparalleled expansion in terms of population and even more in terms of area. In 1831 the densely peopled urban area occupied some 18 square miles (about the area of present-day Brighton and Hove) and housed about 1.65 million souls. By 1961 it had exploded into a sprawling mass, covering over 700 square miles and numbering 8 million inhabitants.

Subsequently the trend has been a decline in the population of the built-up area (6.8 million in 1985), accompanied by discontinuous development in the towns and villages far beyond the 'Green Belt', which so far has mercifully constrained unlimited spread of the vast urban area.

The causes of this explosive expansion have been numerous, including the Industrial Revolution which affected London as well as Manchester; the expansion of trade and commerce in the imperial years of the nineteenth century; and the increasing geographical separation, for individuals, of work and home. Of these causal factors, one of the most

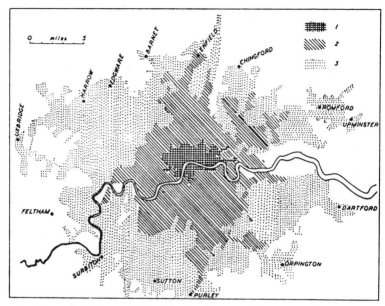

FIG 1 The suburban sprawl – London's growth in terms of area: 1 the built-up area in 1801; 2 the built-up area in 1914; 3 the built-up area in 1951.

important was the steam railway, which allowed not only the more wealthy a wider choice of where to live, but as the century advanced, clerks and skilled artisans as well. The turn of the century brought other modes of transport, the electric railway, surface and underground, the electric tram and the motor bus.

World War I brought about fundamental changes and after 1920 expansion of the built-up area was much more marked than population growth. The causes were again numerous: the development of 'light' industry maintained a high level of employment with increasing demand for labour; and other factors were a reduction in building costs, the availability of cheap mortgage money, and the implementation of slum-clearance plans. But again a very powerful permissive factor was the electric railway, in coordination or competition with the bus and the declining tramway system.

The post-1945 period has been characterised by the establishment of the Green Belt and the land-use planning system, which included, at least until 1976, vigorous decentralisation policies. Again transport has had fundamental consequences, but since 1950, while it has been the private car which has predominated, the electric and diesel railway has still played a vital part.

Suburban growth therefore provides both a significant and a unifying theme in the complex story of Greater London and its railways. It is the main purpose of the book to examine the effects of expanding railways on London's growth and, conversely, the consequences of that growth on the network and its traffic.

But first, just as an artist, to understand the face he or she is painting, must be aware of the bone structure beneath, to understand London we must in imagination strip away the streets and buildings and consider what lies beneath. For us the story begins at least sixty million years ago – when the London Basin, a great downfold in the sheet of chalk covering southern Britain, began to be filled up with clays, gravels and sands, a process which took up all but the last million of the sixty. Then ice sheets swept southward to the line of the Thames. Subsequently, the river has created a series of bordering gravel terraces as it has cut down through the soft rocks of the Basin.

The outer rim of the London Basin is formed by two divergent ridges of chalk hill extending eastward from Salisbury Plain. The southerly one is the North Downs, which extend unbroken to the White Cliffs of Dover. The Chilterns run north-easterly until they peter out in the heart of East Anglia. Each ridge is in effect a plateau with a steep outward face. The reverse slopes dip away, imperceptibly for the most part, towards London. They are seamed with valleys, some of which lead back to gaps through the summit of the ridges.

It is these gaps which have enabled the main-line railways radiating from London to cross the chalk barriers by moderate gradients, and so have controlled the alignment of the trunk lines. For example, from Paddington the line to Swindon follows the Thames through the Goring Gap beyond Reading, the West Coast Main Line from Euston climbs the Gade/ Bulbourne valley to the Tring Gap, and the Brighton line uses the dry valleys south of Croydon to reach the Merstham Gap.

Between the North Downs and the rather narrow river terraces south of the Thames and east of Croydon is a wide area of gravel-capped hills, interspersed with tracts of clay. The distribution of sands and gravels on the one hand and of clay on the other had important consequences for early suburban development. Until the latter part of the nineteenth century sewerage was very restricted. G. A. Sekon, an early historian of transport, wrote that the Hammersmith house in which he lived during the 1870s depended on well and cesspit. Thus subsoil influenced settlement, sand and gravels being favoured as soakaway was easier, and clays avoided. These low hills nearest the river extend from Blackheath through Denmark Hill and Herne Hill. The heights extend southward through Chislehurst, Hayes and Crystal Palace. Westward they are less extensive, but form the high ground of Wimbledon Common/Richmond Park.

The northern part of the Basin is more complex. The Chiltern Plateau, descending gradually southward, is clearly bounded by a low-lying vale on the slopes of which lie Uxbridge, Watford, St Albans and Hatfield. Within this arc most of south Hertfordshire is occupied by a clay plateau about 400ft high, which incidentally leads to the many tunnels on the East Coast Main Line from King's Cross. Long fingers of high ground, usually capped with gravel, reach south-westward. The longest, most southerly and best known is the Hampstead Ridge from Finchley through Highgate and Hampstead to Ealing. The plateau descends steeply onto the flat clay plain of Middlesex, approximately bounded by the main lines from Euston and Paddington.

East of the River Lea the rolling clay country of Epping Forest, Chigwell and Ongar has a similar abrupt southern slope and similar southward sand-and-gravel-capped ridges in the areas of Brentwood, Ockenden and Laindon. But there is no corresponding clay plain.

The gravel terraces north of the Thames are several miles wide. On them both the City and West End grew up. Westward they extend continuously to the great loop of the river within which are Heathrow Airport and the Staines Reservoirs. Eastward from the City they extend through Stratford, Ilford and Romford to the low hills of south Essex.

This is the landscape on which London grew up, a city that has, with some truth, been described as a collection of villages. In fact London has never been a single political entity save in the short period between the creation of the Greater London Council in 1965 and its abolition twenty years later. But the 'collection of villages' goes deeper. A variety of communities can be found in close proximity. Nowhere is this better seen than on a Sunday morning at Aldgate Pump. To the west the sabbath calm of the City remains unbroken, but eastward Aldgate High Street and Middlesex Street (Petticoat Lane) teem with life. A few minutes' walk takes one from the bourgeois exclusiveness of Bayswater to the racial *mélange* of Notting Hill, while Camden Town and Holloway pass with dramatic suddenness into Hampstead and Highgate.

Lest it be assumed these frontiers belong to the older parts and that suburban sprawl results in monotonous uniformity, it must be added that even here distinctions are clear enough. First, the outward spread swamped existing communities which still survive. This is particularly noticeable in the Thames-side towns and villages such as Richmond, Kew and Twickenham, but also in Harrow, Romford and Bromley (Kent). Secondly, housing densities, house size and the presence or absence of industry result in adjoining areas being socially distinct, Woodford from Walthamstow, Sudbury from Alperton, Chislehurst from Sidcup, while at Carpenders Park tracks of the West Coast Main Line, in traditional style, separate post-war local authority housing from that provided by speculative builders.

The various functions of London are also important. It is not only the administrative capital of the United Kingdom, it is also the commercial heart and a world money and commodity market. It is the main social centre and the chief tourist magnet and it also remains the hub of the greatest concentration of industry. Throughout its long history it has also been a major port, though revolutionary changes since 1970 in shipping and the port industry have led to a decline in activity in Greater London itself as operations have become concentrated downstream on Tilbury. But in times past the port has helped to shape the railway system.

To assist in appreciating the complexities of Greater London, a regional division has been attempted of this seemingly amorphous sprawl extending some 25 miles northward from Purley to Enfield and eastward for a similar distance from Southall to Dagenham.

In many ways Greater London still bears traces of its dual origin in the twin cities of London and Westminster. London, the present City, grew up on the terrace gravels which overlooked the river on the inside of a bend, where water was deep. Here on the site of the Roman town the medieval city grew up within walls which can be traced in a few remains, street patterns and street names. Today bankers and merchants are in virtually sole possession in their giant office blocks which soared phoenix-like from war's ashes to share the skyline with St Paul's Cathedral. At ground level are shops, restaurants and pubs catering for City workers. In 1981 some 300,000 people worked within the 'square mile' during the day, but the total residential population numbered only 5,864, and by 1985 it had fallen even further to an estimated 5,100.

Westminster grew up on Thorney Island in the marshy estuary of the Tyburn where it joins the Thames. Here the royal court was established and with it grew up the machinery of government which still remains centred on the Palace of Westminster (popularly the Houses of Parliament). In 1985 some 179,000 people lived in the City of Westminster (which includes some of the West End). This is many more than are resident in the City, but the difference between the daytime working population and the night residential one still remains enormous. Just as finance is localised within the City, so administration is localised here.

Of later date and clearly distinguishable from Westminster (though not so clearly in the popular mind) is the West End. This grew up in the eighteenth century as a residential area between Westminster and the Euston Road, and expanded during the nineteenth century into Belgravia and Marylebone. Streets and squares were laid out which still retain examples of Georgian and Victorian architecture. Yet behind the mansions squalid slums were once apt to lurk, such as the notorious Seven Dials (off Shaftesbury Avenue).

The character of the West End is much changed. It has become the main social centre of the country, its shops, restaurants and theatres catering for the whole of southern England. Since 1920 commerce has been spilling over from the City. Not only are office blocks going up, the terrace houses have become offices or flats. The West End mansion is now as anachronistic as the slums of Central London. Bloomsbury is now largely occupied by the University of London. Employment in Westminster and the West End exceeds 600,000.

These three entities, the City, Westminster and the West End, with the former slums separating them, we may call *Central London*. For London Transport its limits are at Hyde Park Corner, Euston Road and City Road and for the Greater London Council it included the Cities of London and Westminster and parts of the Boroughs of Camden and Islington. But all would agree that as far as transport is concerned it is characterised by the daily tidal flow created by the journey to work. In 1985 over a million people entered Central London between 07.00 and 10.00 hours. Of these, 765,000 or 71.8 per cent came by train – 364,000 (34.1 per cent) by Underground and 401,000 (37.6 per cent) by British Rail; 89,000 (8.3 per cent) by bus; 26,000 (2.5 per cent by cycle and motor-cycle and the remaining 180,000 (17.4 per cent) in cars, despite the fearful congestion they caused.

In the quarter-century since 1960 there has been much change. Total numbers entering Central London have declined by 16.4 per cent from 1.27 million. This has resulted from a decline in employment due to outward migration of firms, the microchip revolution, and recession. Numbers arriving by BR fell by 38,000 but its share of the total rose slightly. Numbers by Underground also showed little change. The share of the car increased from about 7 per cent. But the bus share showed a catastrophic decline, relatively from 17.4 per cent to 8.3 per cent and absolutely from 222,000 to 89,000.

This immense daily tide, flowing between 07.00 and 10.00 and ebbing between 16.00 and 19.00, together with its causes and the trends within it, is the main theme of our story. It is no new phenomenon. In 1905 the Royal Commission on Locomotion in London stated that 'one of the most important . . . problems of London locomotion is the movement of population from the suburbs towards the centre every morning and back again in the afternoon and evening'. It has tremendous social implications and is vital to the economy and operation of the transport system.

Encircling Central London from Camden Town eastward and then southward as far as Lambeth is the *Inner Arc*, a zone of suburban development which preceded the railways. Some parts, such as Islington, date from the late eighteenth and the early nineteenth centuries, but others, Spitalfields among them, grew up as early as the sixteenth. Though a variety of social classes first colonised them, the whole area by 1914 had become uncompromisingly working class and industry had become inextricably mixed up with housing. After 1960, however, the surviving Georgian terraces of Barnsbury and Islington attracted the process of 'gentrification'. In the late 1970s this spilled over into neighbouring Victorian areas – Kentish Town, Holloway and Hackney. These are being recolonised by the professional classes.

Once the home of a teeming, overcrowded population, the zone included many of the horrifying slums portrayed by Dickens and later by Mayhew. In 1901 nearly 150,000 people lived in Stepney. A full half of the area was occupied by factories and roads, so the real population density was 300 per acre – and an acre is about half the size of a football pitch. But rising living standards and slum clearances, accelerated by bombing, have meant that, while the zone is by no means universally salubrious, there are few slums in the sense there were even in 1950.

Population therefore declined steadily after 1900 and rapidly after 1940. Thus in 1961 Stepney had shrunk to 91,940. Similarly Bethnal Green, stationary at 129,000 in 1891 and 1901, had fallen to 47,018 in 1961, and Bermondsey, which numbered 119,452 in 1921, housed but 51,815. The reorganisation of the local-authority areas in 1965 obscures direct comparison in later years, but depopulation continued apace. Between 1961 and 1981 the population of the area covered by the London Borough of Islington declined from 261,232 to 160,890, and that covered by Tower Hamlets in the same period from 205,682 to 142,841. But the 1980s have seen a tendency to stabilisation. The Registrar General's estimates for 1985 show a 1.1 per cent increase over 1981 for Islington and 1.3 per cent for Tower Hamlets.

The suburban ring which grew up for the most part between 1870 and 1914 may be termed the *Inner Suburban Zone*. It varies so greatly in social structure, appearance and housing densities that it is difficult to generalise about it. Places like Blackheath, Dulwich, Putney and Swiss Cottage

Plate 1   London Bridge LBSC station and forecourt in about 1905; the LBSC offices, formerly the Terminus Hotel, are seen at the right.

Plate 2   The Brighton side at London Bridge. In 1880 the intensive local services were handled by trains of uncomfortable four-wheelers, hauled by small, well-kept tank engines. (*Locomotive & General Railway Photographs*).

Plate 3   The same scene in 1983. (*Allan C. Mott*).

Plate 4   In 1900 Charing Cross was a gateway to the Continent. Boat-trains for both Dover and Folkestone are loading at adjacent platforms. The photograph was taken before the collapse of the arched roof. (*National Railway Museum*).

Plate 5   Brighton Baroque at Victoria. The much smaller SE&C station can just be seen on the left. (*Allan C. Mott*).

Plate 6   Steam was very much in evidence at Waterloo in 1950. Viewed from its rail approach, Waterloo is even less impressive than the façade, except for the complexity of the track work and simplicity of the signalling. (*British Rail*)

TABLE 1

PASSENGERS AT LONDON TERMINI – 1960
WEEKDAY AVERAGES*
(Figures in thousands)

Station	Arrivals			Departures			Total 24 hrs	Two peak hours as percentage of total
	24 hrs	07.00– 10.00	Peak hour	24 hrs	16.00– 20.00	Peak hour		
S. Region								
Cannon St	37	35	23	38	36	25	75	64%
Charing Cross	61	44	26	64	45	25	125	41%
Holborn (1)	37	33	19	30	26	17	67	54%
London Bridge	104	74	42	95	67	38	199	40%
Victoria (2)	81	55	33	82	59	33	163	40%
Waterloo (3)	99	72	45	97	70	38	196	42%
TOTAL	419	313	188	406	303	176	825	44%
W. Region								
Paddington	32	7	6	32	NA	6	64	19%
L.M. Region								
Broad St	NA	6	4	NA	4	3	NA	—
Euston (4)	NA	5	4	NA	4	3	NA	—
St Pancras	16	6	4	17	6	3	33	21%
Marylebone	6	5	4	6	5	3	12	58%
E. Region								
Fenchurch St	21	18	12	21	18	13	42	60%
King's Cross	15	6	3	15	6	3	30	20%
Liverpool St	90	61	44	91	67	42	181	48%
London Transport								
Baker St	NA	15	8	NA	15	9	NA	—
Moorgate	NA	19	12	NA	15	11	NA	—

* Based on censuses carried out on selected days at each station.
(1) Including Blackfriars and Elephant & Castle.
(2) Excluding continental passengers.
(3) South Western Division station only.
(4) Suburban passengers only.
NA Not available.
Peak hour – the heaviest sixty minutes.

were characterised by large villas in large gardens. Lewisham, Battersea, Hornsey and Leyton consisted largely of small terrace or semi-detached houses occupied by clerks, small tradesmen and skilled artisans. In places like West Ham, Tottenham and the mushrooming old towns of Deptford and

Woolwich, working-class housing was frequently sub-standard and jerry-built, while factories were too closely interspersed by modern standards. But the gross overcrowding and appalling slums of the Inner Arc were absent save in a few areas, the North Woolwich and Poplar docklands among them.

Great changes have occurred over the years. Mr Pooter, hero of G. and W. Grossmith's *Diary of a Nobody*, a respectable managing clerk, who today might live in Barnet, in 1888 had quite a large house in Holloway and kept a maid. Considerable social contrasts still remain within the large new boroughs of Wandsworth, Lewisham and Newham, though there has been considerable urban renewal.

Outside this zone is another, the *Middle Suburban Zone*, characterised by rapid expansion during the interwar period, especially in the 1929–39 decade. Again, house types and environment show wide variety, stemming from and causing differences in social composition. But times had changed and the very large villas of pre-1914 were no longer wanted. The medium-sized detached houses and general 'desirability' of such places as Chislehurst, Sanderstead and Pinner contrasted with the small semi-detached villas which proliferated elsewhere. We must not forget too that there is a hierarchy even among the semi-detached. There were also the estates, large towns in themselves, built by the London County Council (predecessor of the Greater London Council) for slum clearance purposes at Grove Park, St Helier, Becontree and elsewhere.

These new suburbs had housing densities lower than those general in the Inner Suburban Zone and much lower than in the Inner Arc. In 1951 Chislehurst and Sidcup housed 18 persons to the acre, Croydon 26.3, Barking 20.9 and Finchley 20.1. This compared with 76.8 persons per acre in Bethnal Green and 86 in Islington. But lest it be thought that these were special cases of overcrowding, it should be noted that Chelsea had a density of 77 per acre and Kensington 71.9. The mean for the whole of Greater London was 18.1.

South of the Thames the trend was for the new suburbs to grow up around and to transform erstwhile villages such as Bexley, Orpington and Sutton, or former outer suburbs created by the steam railway such as Sidcup, Shortlands and

Surbiton. There are also plenty of examples of this process in the northern suburbs, where Harrow, Edgware, Finchley and Upminster suffered a similar fate. But here the real nucleating force was the railway station rather than old settlements. South of London the country had by 1900 been covered with a close network of lines provided with numerous stations. On the other hand, in the north and north-west, a number of branches were pushed out at dates subsequent to 1900 into open country in anticipation of housing development. Around the stations on these lines large communities grew up where previously there had been no more than a farm or two. Examples are Cockfosters, Arnos Grove and Oakwood on the Piccadilly extension, Queensbury and Kingsbury on the

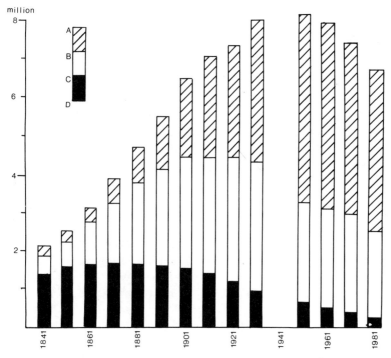

FIG 2 The population explosion – London's growth in terms of population. In each column A–D represents the total population of the area now covered by Greater London, C–D that of the Central Area and surrounding district, and B–D that of the area of the former County of London. Broadly, B–C can be equated with the Inner Suburban Zone and A–B with the Middle Suburban Zone.

Stanmore line and Rayners Lane and Eastcote on that to Uxbridge. In the south this happened only along the 1939 line to Chessington and around a few newly opened stations such as Petts Wood, Albany Park and Stoneleigh.

Whatever their origin, the growth of these suburbs between 1921 – or more particularly 1931 – and 1939 was enormous. A few examples only must suffice here. Hornchurch (Essex) more than doubled its population from 17,489 in 1931 to 39,398 in 1951 (there was no 1941 census). Near-by, Romford expanded from 19,442 in 1921 to 88,002 in 1951. Enfield had grown only from 60,738 in 1921 to 67,752 in 1931, but reached 110,465 over the next twenty years. In the north-west growth was even more spectacular. Edgware grew from 1,516 in 1921 to 17,513 in 1951, and Ruislip from 9,112 to 16,035 between 1921 and 1931 and to 68,288 by 1951.

After 1951 growth in the Middle Suburban Zone rapidly declined or ceased. Between 1951 and 1961 Ruislip–Northwood increased by only 6.2 per cent, while Hendon and Enfield declined by 2.8 and 0.9 per cent respectively. Romford's increase of 30.2 per cent was largely due to the establishment of the LCC Harold Wood overspill estate. Between 1961 and 1981 population has remained virtually stationary. Of the twenty Outer London Boroughs, four, Bromley, Bexley, Hillingdon and Sutton, have shown insignificant increases, though for all 1971 was a peak. The rest showed slight decreases over the twenty years. Subsequent trends have shown little change. In twelve of the boroughs the 1985 estimates show less than a 1 per cent change up or down over 1981, which can be ignored as the 1985 position is only an estimate. There is no pattern in the other eight, Ealing increasing by 3.6 per cent and Barnet by 2 per cent while Hounslow showed a fall of 4.1 per cent and Barking a fall of 2 per cent.

With the rigid interpretation of the Green Belt since the War, the edge of the continuously built-up area, the 'conurbation', has remained remarkably stationary at least at the time of writing. But expansion has taken place discontinuously far beyond. We can therefore define an *Outer Suburban Zone* which by 1960 could be said to have reached out as far as Clacton, Thanet and the West Sussex coast and up the Thames valley at least to Henley. Northward, however, the edge of the Chilterns still marked the northern frontier. But improved communications, including rail electrification, were both the cause and the effect of the subsequent extension of that frontier.

To take two random examples, the initial timetable after electrification in 1966 showed four electric-multiple-unit departures for Northampton (65¾ miles) between 16.30 and 18.30. By 1986 there were six departures, three of them of locomotive-hauled trains. At Huntingdon (58¾ miles) passengers to London at the peak period grew from a daily average of 604 in 1981 to 1,040 in 1986. In contrast all services north of Aylesbury (37¾ miles) ceased in 1963 and there has been much more limited expansion north thereof.

This has been the zone of more recent population growth. New towns such as Basildon, Harlow and Crawley have been established and speculative building has taken place wherever planning permission can be obtained. The 1951–61 population increase in Dartford Rural District was 41.9 per cent, in Burgess Hill (East Sussex) 64.1 per cent and in Rayleigh (Essex) 103.9 per cent. Subsequent boundary changes make direct comparison difficult, but in the 1961–81 period, though growth was less spectacular, it was well above the national average. Thus Sevenoaks District (Kent) grew by 26 per cent, Rochford (Essex) by 49.5 per cent, North Herts by 26.6 per cent and Stevenage by 73.3 per cent. Differences between the 1981 Census and the 1985 estimates show wide divergencies in trends. The population of Sevenoaks actually declined by 1.5 per cent, while that of Rochford increased by the same amount and that of North Herts by 3.1 per cent.

As is to be expected, the outer termini of intensive suburban services on through lines normally lie around the edges of the conurbation. But since 1960 the tendency has been for these termini to be pushed further out. 'Intensive' has been taken for this purpose to imply a regular-interval service from Central London of at least three suburban trains per hour by one or more routes (1986 timetables). These are set out in Table 2. The exception is the Western Region, which still does not have an intensive service from Paddington to the inner-suburban stations, so Slough has been arbitrarily selected. (In fact, like several outer-suburban stations, it has three services an hour to Paddington, but this is by chance.)

TABLE 2

TERMINALS OF 'INTENSIVE' SERVICES ON THROUGH LINES

Region		1961				1986	
		A	*B*			*A*	*B*
SR	Dartford	18.25	9	Gravesend		25.5	4
	Bickley	13.25	4	Swanley		18.25	4
	Orpington	13.75	4	Sevenoaks		22.0	5
	Purley	13.25	6	Purley		13.25	6
	Dorking North	26.75	3	Leatherhead		22.25	3
	Surbiton	12.0	6	Surbiton		12.0	8
	Twickenham	11.25	8	Staines		19.0	4
WR	West Drayton	13.25	*	Slough		18.5	3
WR/LRT	West Ruislip	13.5	6	West Ruislip		13.5	5
LMR/LRT	Rickmansworth	17.0	3	Moor Park		15.0	6
LMR	Watford Jct	17.25	6	Watford Jct		17.25	3
	Elstree	12.25	*	St Albans		20.25	4†
ER	Potters Bar	12.25	*	Welwyn Garden C.		20.25	5
	Broxbourne	17.25	3	Broxbourne		17.25	5
	Shenfield	20.25	3	Shenfield		20.25	5
ER/LRT	Upminster	15.25	10	Upminster		15.25	7‡

'Intensive' is defined as three or more stopping and semi-fast services to London by one or more routes per hour off-peak.

A   Miles from the nearest London terminus.
B   Trains per hour.
*   Arbitrary selection, as less than three trains per hour.
†   Includes two trains per hour first stop St Pancras.
‡   Terminus of LRT services, but note Shoeburyness (39.5 miles) has three trains per off-peak hour to Fenchurch St.
Source: Public timetables.

Because of this somewhat close coincidence, the area bounded by these termini is the area selected for consideration in this book. But it will also be necessary to include the dead-end branches such as the Ongar line where London Transport reaches out into rural Essex. The activities of two companies, the London, Tilbury & Southend and the Metropolitan, must be considered as a whole, both being as essentially London railways as the North London and the District. Finally there must be some recognition of the extension of outer suburban operations.

Greater London owes its present social and economic structure largely to railway development, but each region stands in a different relationship to the railways serving it. Central London had taken shape before the Railway Age, but its present functions and economic structure were the result of the daily inflow of workers, made possible only by railway development. Movement within Central London, too, is made tolerable only by diverting a considerable portion of the traffic to railways below the streets.

The Inner Arc, though largely antedating the railways, was largely influenced by them, not always for good. But over the years it came near to abandoning them. Here is a story of closed stations and forgotten services equal to that of rural England. The few years since 1980, however, have seen something of a revival.

The Inner Suburban Zone was the creation of the steam railway. Where services were adequate and fares reasonable, as on the Great Eastern, the suburbs spread rapidly outward. Where suburban traffic was neglected, notably by the Great Western and the London and North Western, open country could soon be reached. After 1900 tram and bus competition became acute, especially for short journeys, and led to rail electrification, which restored competitiveness. However, since about 1960 the area has become something of a problem one, particularly for Southern Region. Declining population has led to declining traffic.

The Middle Suburban Zone was similarly the creation of the electric railway. Rail maintained advantages, notably of speed, for longer journeys, particularly to and from Central London. In 1951 the average speed of buses was 11.4mph and of suburban trains 20.4. Average journey lengths were 2.2 miles by bus, 5.6 by Underground, and 10 by BR. This zone is the principal source of the peak traffics, for between 20 and 30 per cent of the employed population resident in places such as Orpington, Sutton and Harrow work in Central London. There was always a certain amount of short-distance traffic, especially as suburban retailing and commercial centres such as Croydon developed, but after 1950 car and television cut deeply into off-peak traffic.

In the Outer Suburban Zone commuter traffic developed from certain places between the Wars. By 1960 Tonbridge and Tunbridge Wells had 3,000 season-ticket holders and there were stations in outer Surrey, the Chilterns and South Essex almost equally busy. But the great growth has been since 1960, even during the 1970s when fares increased faster than inflation. For the most part there has been little competition; the Shenfield electrification (1949) quickly reduced the large volume of traffic on parallel Green Line routes. As the time factor is important, long-distance commuting by car has not reached large proportions, except among those whose motoring costs are paid for by their firms and who have a parking space provided. Deregulation initiated by the 1980 Transport Act has had, as yet, patchy consequences. Commuter coaches have proliferated on routes where train services are perceived to be slow and unreliable, on the North Kent route to Gillingham and beyond, and also interestingly to Southend, but are virtually absent on routes paralleling the 'Great Northern' electric system. Information is scarce but in 1986 it was estimated that the new coaches were carrying less than 1 per cent of peak-hour traffic – about 5,000 commuters.

While commuting traffic must remain the principal theme, it is possible to distinguish other traffic currents in the bewildering complexity of London's rail system.

Passenger
1. Long-distance traffic to and from London.
2. Through traffic. Long-distance services over the country as a whole have always chiefly been concentrated on London, so through traffic has always been heavy. In the past it was specifically catered for. Eventually, however, save for the suitcases and rucksacks with which it encumbers tube trains, it became almost indistinguishable from the urban. The completion of the orbital M25, however, frightened BR into reviving past efforts.
3. Urban traffic, ie movement within Central London.
4. Suburban traffic, ie movement not only to and from Central London, but between suburbs. This latter includes the decline and partial revival of peripheral routes.

Freight
It must always be remembered that London is a very important industrial centre. Industrial growth for many years depended on the railways. Since the War, however, freight traffic has declined catastrophically, as a result of road competition and the decline in coal consumption, and also, surprisingly, of policies of the Railways Board as well as

government. By 1977 only 5 per cent of freight entering and leaving London was carried by rail. The main themes in the story of freight by rail are:

1. Long-distance traffic to and from London.
2. The 'water outlet'. Port traffic has been a prize, but owing to the organisation of the Port of London, where until recently a large portion of cargo loaded on or discharged from ships was moved off or onto lighters to be taken to wharves anywhere along the Thames, access to the river was as much sought after as direct access to the docks.
3. As with passenger traffic, interchange traffic between the northern and southern lines.
4. Local traffic. But this has always been limited, as it has always been mostly handled by road.

The relative importance of suburban, long-distance and freight traffic naturally varied widely between companies. But only the District and the Tubes handled no freight at all. In other respects in their early days both the Metropolitan and the District were orthodox steam railways, which until the turn of the century handled the bulk of the traffic.

After 1900 the steam services were gradually electrified, but until 1967 for suburban traffic only, the exception being the Southern Railway's extensions of its suburban system. The main-line companies continued to intermingle electric suburban trains with steam-hauled outer-suburban, long-distance and freight trains. Between 1958 and 1962 all remaining steam suburban services were converted to diesel traction and with electrification to Bournemouth in 1967 the last main-line steam workings into London ceased. Continued electrification after 1960 has meant that by 1983 Paddington shared with Marylebone the dubious distinction of being the only London terminus from which there are no BR electric trains.

With their early electrification the development of the Metropolitan and the District diverged from that of other companies. They assumed the functions of 'rapid transit', specialising in the mass movement of urban and suburban traffic by intensive services of multiple-unit electric trains. However, with the drastic decline since 1965 in the number of freight terminals, before which date almost all stations had freight facilities, most BR lines have become specialised short-distance passenger handlers.

The Tubes have a somewhat different history. Built to deal with urban traffic, they originally reached out only to the inmost suburbs and from the very first were rapid-transit lines. But with the projection of Bakerloo trains over the LNW to Watford in 1917 they entered a new phase of extension into the middle zone. These extensions were sometimes over new lines, but often were along existing routes, either taken over completely or on new lines parallel to the main lines.

It is notable that but one Tube line ever penetrated far south of the river. The dense pre-existing rail network and its early and universal electrification forestalled others. The story of the southern lines offers a number of such contrasts with those to the north. They can also be logically dealt with as a unit.

CHAPTER II

The Southern Termini and Their Approaches

London's first railway was opened in 1836. At that time orchards and market gardens occupied the gravel terraces westward from Chelsea, around Barking and up the Lea valley. On the claylands large fields grew grain, hay for London's horses and pasture for cattle. Parks of country houses crowned the gravel-capped hills.

But the outward suburban spread, which the new railways were to facilitate, had already begun. Since 1800 St John's Wood, Camden Town and Islington had grown up with good-class housing. Southward, pleasant squares, interspersed with sordid slums, which the railways were to empty impartially, extended to the City and Westminster. To the east houses were invading the fields of Bethnal Green and Stepney. Between Commercial Road and the river, building extended to Limehouse church, while master mariners lived in the neat villas of Wapping and Shadwell.

On the south bank continuous building connected Rother-hithe with Lambeth. For the most part it was an area of noisome slums. But away from the river middle-class housing had filled in the area up to the New Kent Road and was reaching out into Walworth and Kennington and even out to Camberwell.

To the west Pimlico and Belgravia had recently linked Chelsea village with Westminster, though along the river bank the latter still petered out in the Millbank slums. Park Lane and the first section of Edgware Road still defined London's north-western limits.

Along the Bath Road, the villages of Kensington, Hammer-smith and Turnham Green were linked with London by ribbon development, but along the Uxbridge Road open country was soon reached. Only the small villages of Kilburn and Edgware interrupted the rural solitudes along the Edgware Road. A ribbon of building extended through Tottenham to Upper Edmonton, while beyond, unusually for Middlesex and south Essex, the villages along the Enfield Road were large and closely spaced. Along the Colchester Road desultory building reached out to Bow. Along the roads leading southward ribbon development reached Brixton Hill and Upper Tooting. The environs of London were sparsely peopled, villages small and scattered and towns few.

In 1831 the City still housed a tenth of Greater London's population, but the wealthier merchants and professional men had already moved out to the West End or the rural seclusion of Sydenham, Clapham or Stoke Newington. Cobbett sneered: '. . . between Sutton and the Wen there is, in fact, little beside houses, gardens, grass plots and other matters to accommodate the Jews and Jobbers and their mistresses'. Mr Wemmick (*Great Expectations*) walked into the City from Walworth. Their chief clerks were seeking new houses in Pentonville or Islington. Lowten, Mr Perker's clerk (*The Pickwick Papers*), lived in Camden Town and walked to Gray's Inn. But many thousands of poorer folk lived in Holborn, Smithfield and Moorgate. The industrial suburbs of Spitalfields and Shoreditch were becoming increasingly overcrowded. But evil though the slums of the East End were, they were never so bad as those of Central London. In 1849 Calmel Buildings in Orchard Street (the south end of Baker Street) housed 944 human beings in twenty-six three-storey houses.

Even in 1836, therefore, separation of work and home had begun, though people could still walk to and fro. The 1846 Royal Commission on London Traffic found the greater number of commuters from the Surrey side. In 1836, 75,000 pedestrians crossed Blackfriars Bridge and 100,000 London Bridge daily. But the southern suburbs were nevertheless not so extensive and property values were lower. Thus the southern lines had a large traffic potential and they could reach convenient bridgeheads without undue cost.

Eventually there were four southern companies and each would seek both a City and a West End terminus. Three threads thus run through this chapter: a dogged and costly progress toward the heart of both City and West End; inter-

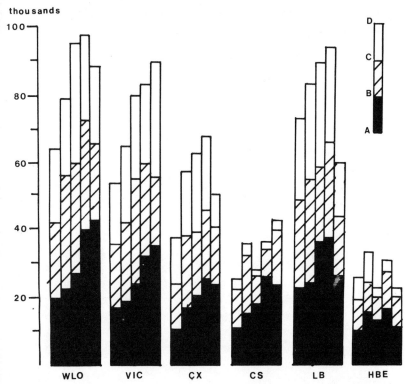

FIG 3 Passengers arriving at the Southern Region's London termini, based on annual censuses recording the average number of passengers on an ordinary weekday during the census period, usually over two weeks in February. For each station the columns represent the figures for (left to right) 1930, 1939, 1948, 1960 and 1978. In each column A–D represents 24 hours, A–C 07.00–10.00 and A–B the busiest hour. WLO Waterloo (Western), VIC Victoria, CX Charing Cross, CS Cannon Street, LB London Bridge, HBE Holborn, Blackfriars and Elephant.

company rivalry; and successive enlargements of stations and rail approaches to deal with constant traffic increases.

LONDON BRIDGE AND THE CHARING CROSS EXTENSION

London Bridge is the oldest London Terminus and eventually became the busiest. Its nucleus was the simple two-platformed structure of the London & Greenwich, officially opened on 14 December 1836. Col. George Landmann, the Company's engineer, suggested a viaduct to cross the dozen or so lanes of the Bermondsey slums – 'One of the most abominable [suburbs] in the environs of London' (says an 1858 guide) – and the market-gardens beyond. Even the promoters realised that revenue from suburban traffic on this 3.75 mile line would be inadequate, so they envisaged letting off arches as dwellings, shops and warehouses, reached by toll paths alongside. Understandably the arches proved unpopular for houses, but are still widely used as premises for small businesses.

Because of a continued addiction to walking, receipts were disappointing until tolls could be levied on 'foreign' users. Eventually there were three such users, the Croydon, the Brighton and the South Eastern. The London & Croydon was formally opened on 1 June 1839 from Corbett's Lane Junction to West Croydon, 10.25 miles from London Bridge. It passed through sparsely peopled countryside. In default of nearby villages two of its stations were named after inns, Dartmouth Arms (Forest Hill) and Jolly Sailor (Norwood Junction). Anerley, another, was named after a villa owned by a Scots merchant (the name means 'lonely'). The Company's policy was to encourage tourist traffic amidst this long-vanished Arcady.

In 1853 Measom's *Guide* described Anerley as a 'holiday resort', but by then the area around the new Crystal Palace was becoming fashionable for suburban villas. A guide of 1858 stated that the area around Sydenham was rapidly being built over and at Penge half-finished streets were enveloping Beulah Spa.

The original London Bridge station would thus have become quite inadequate, and even before it had opened the Croydon obtained powers for a separate station, on the *north* side. Then, on 7 August 1840, the Greenwich was authorised to widen its viaduct on the *south* side for the use of its tenants. This came into use on 10 May 1842. Consequently the terminal stations were exchanged and the former Greenwich station was now administered by a Joint Committee of the Brighton, Croydon and SE.

The Greenwich tolls were high and the SE hatched a scheme to break the stranglehold. On 4 July 1843 it obtained powers

TABLE 3

THE 'USER' OF TRACKS ON THE EASTERN APPROACH TO LONDON BRIDGE

	July 1975	17 June 1928	1901	13 August 1866	24 February 1850	10 May 1842	14 December 1836
North side of viaduct							
1	E Down	E Down No 1	SEC Down No 1	SEC Up	G Up		
2	Reversible	E Down No 2	SEC Down No 2	SEC Down	Down		
3	E Up	E Down No 3	SEC Down No 3	SEC Up	Down		
4	E Down	E Up No 2	SEC Up No 2	G/SE Down	G/NK Down		
5	E Down	E Up No 1	SEC Up No 1	SE Up	NK Down	G Down	G Down
6	E Up	E Down local	LBSC Down	LBSC/SE Down	Up	G Up	G Up
7	E Up PL	E Down through	LBSC Up	LBSC/SE Up	LBSC/SE Down	SE/LC/LB Down	
8	C Down main	C Up through	LBSC Up	LBSC/SE Up	LBSC/SE Up	SE/LC/LB Up	
9	C Up main	C Up local	SL* Down	SL Down	LBSC/SE Up Croydon local		
South side of viaduct							
10	SL Down	SL Down	SL Up	SL Up			
11	SL Up	SL Up	SL Up	SL Up			

c Central. e Eastern. g Greenwich. lb London & Brighton. lbsc London, Brighton & South Coast. lc London & Croydon. nk North Kent. pl Passenger loop. se South Eastern. sec South Eastern & Chatham. sl South London. * Reversible 1909–28.

for a mile-long branch from Bricklayers' Arms Junction on the Croydon to a 'Grand West End Terminus'.

Sir William Cubitt, engineer to the SE, selected a site on the Old Kent Road as being clear of building and 'near the Bricklayers' Arms, a travellers' resting place'. Westminster Bridge could, in fact, be more conveniently reached than from London Bridge. BRICKLAYERS' ARMS was opened on 1 May 1844, but, though later connected to the North Kent at North Kent East Junction, it was never a success as a passenger station. Regular services ceased in 1852 and it became a goods depot. The locomotive shed closed in 1961 and in 1969 a centralised parcel depot opened. The line was eventually abandoned on 29 August 1981.

The SE had achieved its purpose, for the Greenwich reduced the tolls from 3d to 1¼d per passenger and in 1845 leased the line to the larger company, which now controlled the London Bridge approach. On this, traffic was rapidly growing and in 1847 powers were obtained for two more lines, on the north

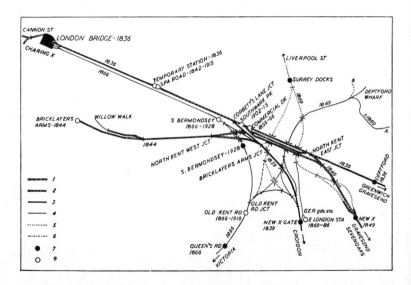

FIG 4 The approaches to London Bridge: 1 London & Greenwich; 2 South Eastern; 3 London & Croydon, 4 London, Brighton & South Coast; 5 East London; 6 East London (abandoned); 7 passenger stations; 8 closed passenger stations, A Foreign Cattle Market; B Surrey Commercial Docks.

Plates 7 and 8 THE CHANGING SCENE AT GROVE PARK. The widening of lines in response to increased traffic has brought great changes to the railway scene. In the upper picture, a down goods train passes Grove Park on the SE main line in about 1900. In the lower, a ten-coach train leaves for Orpington in 1958. Both photographs were taken from the now demolished signal box. (*Upper, L&GRP; lower, author*)

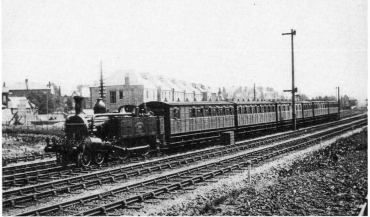

Plate 9   A North London train from Broad Street climbs the heavy grades of the GN's 'Northern Heights' line in about 1900. (*L&GRP*)

Plate 10   A Metropolitan train of the same period near Willesden Green gives an impression of even greater antiquity. But speculative building is going up fast in anticipation of imminent electrification. (*L&GRP*)

Plate 11   In about 1925 a small ex-GE 2–4–2 tank drags its long train of six-wheelers up Brentwood bank. Today electric trains speed up the quadrupled track. (*L&GRP*)

side. It will be seen from Table 3 that down Greenwich and up North Kent trains shared a single down line. This was the origin of right-hand running on the Greenwich, then with a self-contained and frequent shuttle service. After 1850, and especially with the opening of the Crystal Palace, traffic continued to grow.

In 1846, 625,000 passengers used London Bridge station; in 1850, 5.6 million; and in 1854, 10.8 million. By 1858 about 7.5 million were using the SE side and 6 million the Brighton. To accommodate this traffic, most of which was to and from the West End, a new station was designed by Samuel Beazley, architect of the principal North Kent stations. But after a quarrel the Brighton left the joint station and built its own to the south, just in time to deal with the Crystal Palace traffic.

The *Illustrated London News* of 24 July 1858 thus described the new stations and their traffic:

> The Greenwich traffic, which seldom includes any luggage, is connected by two lines of rail . . . Next to the right are the North Kent rails [both these parts were obliterated by the High Level] . . . Its neighbour group [later the Low Level] belongs to the Dover line, three rails, two platforms and a carriage road. The Brighton, Croydon and Crystal Palace series of lines comes last, chumming together under one span of roof, but sociably contriving matters so that special pairs of rails are appropriated for the long and short trains [ie long distance and local].
>
> Of ordinary trains during the month of July there start to Greenwich 49 *per diem*, on the North Kent line 29, to Dover and Margate 15, to Brighton and the South Coast 14, to Croydon and Epsom 24, to Beckenham and other short stations 11 and to the Crystal Palace etc. 25, total 167. This catalogue does not include the excursion trains nor the 'special trains' which convey grand ambassadors on their missions or bring up Royal visitors *en route* to Buckingham Palace.

On 30 June 1862 the London, Brighton & South Coast obtained its South London Act for a line from London Bridge to Victoria. In connection with this, three more tracks, Brighton property, were brought into use on the south side of the viaduct on 13 August 1866, together with (until 1978) platforms 19–23. On 1 January 1880 the lines were continued on to Bricklayers' Arms Junction on a separate viaduct and called the South Bermondsey spur (see Figure 4).

TABLE 4

THE EVENING RUSH HOUR THROUGH LONDON BRIDGE
HIGH LEVEL — OCTOBER 1906

Charing Cross	Cannon Street	London Bridge	
17.02	17.11	17.14	Dartford via Greenwich
17.08	17.17	17.20	Redhill and Reading
	17.18	17.21	Mid-Kent
17.11	17.20	17.23	Erith via Bexleyheath
		17.27*	Dartford Loop
	17.25	17.28	Dartford via Blackheath and North Kent
17.17	17.25	17.29	Caterham
	17.30	17.32	Bromley North
17.21	17.31	17.34	Erith via Greenwich
	17.34	17.37	Mid-Kent
17.27	17.37	17.40	Maidstone via Dartford Loop
17.30	17.38	17.42	Bexhill via Orpington
17.33	17.42	17.45	Plumstead via Blackheath
	17.42	17.45	Gillingham via Dartford Loop
17.37	17.46	17.49	Wadhurst via Orpington
		17.51	Mid-Kent
	17.50	17.53	Dartford via Blackheath and North Kent
	17.50	17.53	Orpington
17.42	17.52	17.55	Plumstead via Greenwich
17.46	17.56	17.59	Mid-Kent
17.50	17.58	18.01	Redhill and Gomshall
17.53	—	18.01	Plumstead via Blackheath
	18.00	18.02	Bromley North
	18.03	18.06	Dartford via Bexleyheath
17.59	18.08	18.11	Dartford via Greenwich
	18.10	18.13	Mid-Kent
18.07	—	18.14	Blackheath
15	23	27	trains

* From Low Level.

Summary of Destinations

	1906	1962	1984
Main line	3	14	25
Bromley North	2	4	3
North Kent via Greenwich	4	5	7
North Kent via Blackheath	5	4	4
Bexleyheath	2	7	10
Dartford Loop (Sidcup line)	3	8	10
Mid-Kent	5	9	7
Croydon line	3	0	0
Totals	27	51	66

The six through platforms of the High Level station date from the Charing Cross extension, when the Dover (Low Level) station became the continental freight depot. In 1901 Southwark Depot was opened for this traffic, which was transferred to Hither Green in 1960. It was then used for parcels until 1969 when it was closed and demolished. From 2 June 1902 the Low Level was used for passengers, this time with four platforms.

By the twentieth century London Bridge had essentially become the station of the Common Man and it is hard to imagine 'grand ambassadors' ever using it. After 1950 excursionists and hop-pickers no longer came either. But by 1902, 23.7 million passengers were using the Brighton side and 6 million the SE. Ninety-six trains arrived before 10.30. On an average 1961 weekday 104,000 passengers arrived, an 18.6 per cent increase over 1939, 71 per cent coming between 07.00 and 10.00. Crowds poured across the river to the City or streamed through the 'hole in the wall' up to the High Level to insert themselves somehow into overcrowded Charing Cross trains. During the evening peak hour 38,000 would return. But outside peak hours there was but a trickle of short-distance travellers. By 1978 arrivals had fallen to 58,020; 75.8 per cent in the morning peak. The evening peak-hour traffic had fallen to 22,685. By 1985 the daily 'user' figure was 121,000, showing an upturn over 1984. The front of the station was badly damaged during World War II, but the new station was not officially reopened until 15 December 1978. The bus-stands in front are now covered over, and any façade has disappeared behind this and the surrounding office blocks. But the circulating area and offices are pleasantly modern. In the years since the War Brighton traffic, especially from the Inner Suburban Zone, has declined and that from the SE section increased. So the station, spanned by its broad bridge equipped with train departure indicators, is only part of a total rearrangement. The 'Mound', as the postal platform served by the line at No 6 platform was called, was abolished and the Low Level reduced to two platforms to allow an extra up line to be provided for non-stopping trains. The Low Level was incorporated into the Brighton station, and the number of platforms under the three great arches reduced from twelve to eight. At the same time, to the east of the station the tracks were again rearranged (Table 3).

Schemes for a 'Grand Terminal Station' on the noisome alleys of the Hungerford Market were mooted in 1845. But not until 8 August 1859 was the Charing Cross Railway incorporated, the SE being spurred on by proposals for Victoria. The 1.9 miles over the crowded roof-tops cost £4 million and the new terminus was opened on 11 January 1864 for local traffic (using the Villiers Street entrance) and on 1 May for all traffic. An intermediate station at Blackfriars Road was closed when Waterloo Junction (Waterloo from 7 July 1935) was opened on 1 January 1869. Today about 30,500 passengers use the former Waterloo Junction's four platforms, at which all trains stop. Half the passengers come during peak hours; for the rest of the day most of them are going to and from the main Waterloo station.

A City terminus on Cannon Street was authorised on 28 June 1861 and opened on 1 September 1866. It had a triangular approach from the double-tracked Charing Cross line, but later a third track was laid for a five-minute shuttle service between the two stations, a reflection of the chronic congestion in the Strand and Fleet Street. The service disappeared as other trains became more numerous.

Until the end of 1916 the majority of trains were reversed in Cannon Street before continuing on to Charing Cross. But by 1900 the situation on the triangle had become chaotic. The sides were too short for increased train lengths and according to a South Eastern & Chatham report it would sometimes become completely blocked by trains fouling each other. It was the main cause of the SE&C's bad time-keeping record. In 1904 between 17.00 and 18.00 on weekdays twenty-five down trains and almost as many up passed through London Bridge and all but two or three had to be reversed in Cannon Street. By 1902 a widening programme had been completed, but it left a legacy of so many flat junctions that operating even the present service is a real tour de force. The side of the triangle carrying all the Charing Cross trains remains only double.

By 1902, 13.5 million passengers a year were using Cannon Street and 10.2 million Charing Cross. Traffic continued to grow, particularly after 1918 and delays were as bad as ever. But no more widening was attempted and it was left to the Southern to deal with the situation by electrification and by the installation of power signalling.

N. Hawkshaw, engineer to the Charing Cross Railway, designed magnificent single-arched roofs for both stations. At 15.40 on 5 December 1905 a heavy beam fell from Charing Cross roof. Passengers were hastily cleared from the 15.50 for Hastings. A few minutes later the two outer bays of the roof collapsed, much of the wreckage falling through the roof of the adjacent theatre. About thirty men were working on the station roof and a hundred more in the theatre, but casualties were mercifully light. Seven workmen were killed, but no railwayman or passenger. The arched roof was replaced by the present flat one.

In 1926 Cannon Street's nine platforms, five short and narrow, were rebuilt to provide eight faces and a large circulating area. In 1956 a start was made on complete rebuilding. The arched roof was taken down, the platforms were extended across the circulating area and a new one was provided under the rather featureless new office block which replaced the flamboyant former hotel building. Completion, because of a dispute with the Corporation of London over design, was delayed until 1965.

With the outward spread of commerce and more frequent journeys from the suburbs to the West End for shopping or theatre, Charing Cross, with six platforms, is now very much busier than Cannon Street with eight, about three times as many passengers using it as did in 1902. In 1960, 322 trains arrived daily, 89 before 10.30 as opposed to 45 in 1902. An average of 125,000 passengers a day passed through the station, an 11 per cent increase over 1939. During the six busiest hours 90,000 arrived and left, but because of its convenience for the West End, there was a constant flow of suburban travellers. In season, holiday crowds were conspicuous. On summer Saturdays in 1960, 8,000 or more left by Dover line trains between 08.30 and 15.00 and about half as many by those to Hastings.

In the period since, total electrification was achieved in 1986 with electrification to Hastings. The number of long-distance outer-suburban trains has increased, but the off-peak suburban services are fewer. Peak-hour arrivals have remained stable. Charing Cross, which lost its continental role after World War I, regained it during the 1970s, though it took the form of foot passengers for the Eastern Docks ferries and the hovercraft using the normal services to Dover Priory and connecting bus services. By 1978 the number of peak-period trains had remained much the same, 84 arriving before 10.30, but the average daily use had fallen to 113,500, 80,250 arriving and leaving during the two peaks. In 1985 the number of passengers handled daily was 112,500, very little change over 1978. The 1986 timetable showed twenty-five departures between 10.00 and 15.59 for stations beyond Tonbridge compared with eight in 1955.

There is less variety in Cannon Street's traffic, as it is used virtually exclusively by commuters, albeit from as far afield as Thanet, Ashford and Hastings. With the rebuilding of the war-damaged City, this traffic more than recovered from the low level to which it fell in 1946. Thus while 4,600 fewer passengers arrived daily in 1960 compared with 1939, peak-hour arrivals were *up* by a similar figure. Of the 36,700 passengers arriving on an average 1960 day all but 2,200 came in between 07.00 and 10.00, and 23,100 came during the busiest hour. Outside peak hours only a skeleton service was provided, chiefly to terminate trains which could not be accommodated at Charing Cross. From 1936 to 1939 and after 1960 until full electrification to Dover, Cannon Street was used by relief continental services. In 1978 daily traffic had reached 76,576, with a peak-period concentration of 92.5 per cent. By 1985 daily use had fallen to 74,500, but since the station now has only an infrequent shuttle service to London Bridge outside peak hours and the last train leaves at 19.50, peak traffic has in fact increased.

Cannon Street and London Bridge formerly were important for parcels, mail and newspapers. In 1961 the latter des-patched eight parcels trains during the night hours. By 1984 these had been reduced to five, Cannon Street was out of the business and motor luggage vans made two daily visits to Charing Cross.

VICTORIA

The Brighton also cherished ideas for a West End terminus, but nothing happened until the Crystal Palace was moved from Hyde Park to Sydenham after the 1851 Exhibition. In expectation of consequent excursion traffic the West End of London & Crystal Palace Railway obtained powers on 4 August 1853 for a 5.75 mile line from the London & South Western to an end-on junction with the LBSC's spur from Sydenham. Powers were also obtained for short extensions: to the Thames at New Chelsea Bridge; and to Norwood Junction. In 1854 another branch was sanctioned from Bromley Junction (0.8 miles beyond Crystal Palace on the Norwood line) to Farnborough (Kent).

The lines traversed a rural area and local traffic would be sparse. But the Brighton was interested as an approach to Waterloo and, when the LSW proved uncooperative, to a Thames-side terminus, Pimlico. Wandsworth Common to Crystal Palace was opened for public traffic on 1 December 1856 and worked by the Brighton. The Norwood extension opened on 1 October 1857 and Pimlico station on 29 March 1858. Pimlico portions were now detached from London Bridge trains at East Croydon.

Although the West End line crossed under the LSW it was not until 1863, when the district was rapidly being built over, that an interchange station was opened. Although in Battersea, this has always been CLAPHAM JUNCTION. Its seventeen platforms are in a 'V' shape, enclosing Clapham Yard, the main carriage depot for Waterloo. Over 2,500 trains now pass through in the day, making it one of the busiest traffic junctions in the world. Traditionally it was little used for passenger interchange, but after 1975 more and more outer-suburban and main-line trains called, leading to an increase in passengers changing and passing the barriers.

The West End line also attracted the interest of the London, Chatham & Dover, anxious for an approach to London independent of the South Eastern (Vol 2, Chapter III). The former's Farnborough Extension was opened on 3 May 1858 to Bromley (now Shortlands). At Beckenham Junction the SE made connection from their Addiscombe line.

The Extension never got any further. Instead it was continued by the Mid-Kent (Bromley to St Mary Cray), incorporated on 21 July 1856. It opened to Southborough Road (now Bickley) on 5 July 1858 and was linked to the LCD's line from Rochester on 3 December, when the latter's through trains reached Victoria. The LBSC bought the West End line on 11 July 1859 and a year later the Farnborough Extension became part of the LCD.

Meanwhile on 23 July 1858 the Victoria Station & Pimlico had been incorporated to build a 73 chain line from what is now Stewart's Lane Junction to a new terminus across the river. It was sited on the Grosvenor Canal basin, the lowest-cost land in this rapidly developing area. Victoria Street had been completed as recently as 1851 and Belgravia newly laid out by Sir Thomas Cubitt. Subscribing half the capital, the LBSC became entitled to half the station. This part was opened on 1 October 1860, Pimlico being closed and absorbed into Battersea goods depot, now a coach park. The other half was leased to the LCD and GW. The LCD used a temporary station until the main one was ready on 25 August 1862.

The circuitous and steeply graded approaches to Victoria were unsatisfactory to both companies. The LBSC obtained powers in 1860 for a cut-off from Windmill Bridge Junction (where the lines from West and East Croydon meet) to Balham Junction, thus avoiding Crystal Palace. It was first used on 1 December 1862 and quadrupled by 1903. On 29 July 1862 a high-level line was authorised between Pouparts Junction (east of Clapham Junction), over instead of under the LSW, to the south end of Grosvenor Bridge, and this opened on 1 December 1867.

By the Metropolitan Extensions Act of 6 August 1869 the LCD in its turn obtained an independent and easier access from Penge Junction (Beckenham) to Stewarts Lane, again by-passing Crystal Palace, now left with only local traffic, albeit growing along with housing development.

The LCD then obtained powers in its 1864 New Lines Act for a high-level line from Factory Junction (west of Wandsworth Road) to Grosvenor Bridge, avoiding the steep dip through Stewarts Lane. The observant traveller can still distinguish the old approach through the maze of tracks below.

The GW came by way of the West London Extension (p. 133), opened on 2 March 1863. From Latchmere Junction on the WLE, connections facing west led to the Windsor and Brighton sides at Clapham Junction and facing eastward to the WE&CP and the LCD at Longhedge Junctions (named after a nearby farm). Mixed gauge was provided and on 1 April 1863 a service from Southall started. By October 1866 this

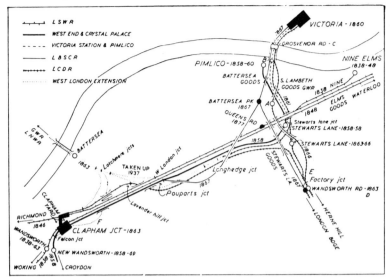

FIG 5 The Clapham Junction area: A Battersea Park Road 1867–1916; B Battersea Park & Steamboat Pier 1860–70; C opened 1870, LBSC side closed 1907, LCD side closed 1911; D LCD side closed 1916; E Wandsworth Road Goods (Midland); F Falcon Lane Goods (LNWR).

was provided solely by narrow-gauge trains until it ceased on 22 March 1915, though the GW remained a lessee of Victoria until 1933. From 1911 it also maintained a large goods depot, now closed, at South Lambeth.

The complex history of stations in the area is summarised in Figure 5. Initially Grosvenor Bridge had only a double line of mixed gauge, but in 1866 it was widened to seven tracks. The Brighton had the use of the two original ones, now solely narrow gauge, and a third new one. The other four included two mixed tracks. Under its 1898–9 Acts the Brighton obtained powers to add two further tracks, making nine in all.

The Victoria Street frontage of the station was temporary and ramshackle, but the LCD provided the plain, but not unpleasant range of buildings along Wilton Road. There were seven platforms and ten tracks on the Brighton side, and eight platforms and six tracks on the Chatham.

The 1898–9 Acts also authorised the Brighton to rebuild its side. There being no room to provide extra platforms, the existing ones were lengthened and recessed at the outer end to allow trains to reach the inner ends while the outer ones were occupied. A more impressive frontage was provided in 'Brighton Baroque' style and the station formally reopened on 1 July 1908. The next year the SE&C completed its Victoria Street frontage in the form of a wide arch inscribed 'The Gateway to the Continent'. Appropriately it includes the 1914–18 war memorial as through it so many troops left for France.

In 1924 the Southern knocked a wide opening in the party wall. But though it administered the stations as one, duplicate facilities were still provided. The refurbishing begun in 1978 included, as with all other Southern termini, a new barrier line supporting new departure/arrival indicators; an enlarged concourse for the Brighton side; the filling in of the recessed platform ends; and the concentration of local booking on the Brighton side and the Continental Travel Centre on the Chatham.

On the Chatham side cross-Channel traffic remains heavy, though Kent Coast holidaymakers are less numerous. In 1962 sixteen trains left for Margate and Ramsgate between 08.00 and 12.00 on summer Saturdays with some 10,000 passengers, but in off-peak periods it was – and is – quiet. In 1985 there were eight departures per hour, two for Orpington, two via Maidstone East and four via Chatham.

In contrast the Brighton side is always busy. In 1962 the basic service was 10 suburban departures, 8 main-line and a solitary steam or diesel for the Oxted line. By 1987 all 21 departures were electric. In 1985 there were 28 departures between 17.00 and 17.59.

In 1902, 29.4 million passengers used Victoria, 18.6 million the Brighton side. On an average 1960 weekday 81,286 passengers (excluding continental) arrived, an increase of 35.5 per cent over 1939; 54,556 came between 07.00 and 10.00, an increase of 56.1 per cent over 1939, a measure of the growing commercial role of the West End. The proportion of passengers arriving in the morning peak was 67 per cent of the total, nevertheless the lowest concentration of all southern termini apart from Waterloo. Subsequent growth has been less spectacular, but declining short-distance traffic has been compensated by increasing long-distance to make it the second busiest of all BR stations. In 1978 the daily arrivals had increased to 89,000, with 63,500 using the Brighton side and 25,600 the Chatham. Total daily traffic was 180,393 with a peak-period concentration of 63.2 per cent. By 1985 peak-period arrivals were 49,398, of which 33,400 were at the Brighton side (37,637 in 1978) and 15,998 at the South Eastern (17,580 in 1978). Nevertheless the 1985 figures represent an 8.6 per cent increase over 1984. The daily total of 169,000 is exceeded only by Waterloo.

Victoria serves the Continent, the Sussex and Thanet resorts, prosperous inland towns and middle-class suburbs stretching continuously from Dulwich and Streatham to the North Downs. After 1962 it entered the Air Age with the erection of an air terminal over platforms 15/16. This was greatly enlarged by 1987 as part of the Victoria Plaza over platforms 9–19. In 1967 some 750,000 used the rail link with Gatwick Airport. In 1984 the fifteen-minute Gatwick Express was inaugurated, the only Inter-City service on Southern Region. In 1985, 2,448,000 passengers were carried by the new service, generating £6.9 million in point-to-point revenue; this is the third highest in Inter-City services, exceeded only by Euston–Manchester and Euston–Liverpool. Victoria's links with the West End were improved beyond recognition with the opening of the Victoria Line in 1969 (Chapter V).

THE 'CITY LINE'

The 1860 Metropolitan Extensions Act, perhaps the most important in the LCD's history, also gave it access to the City, authorising a 4.5 mile line from Herne Hill to join the Metropolitan Railway at Farringdon Street (Chapter IV). The scheme involved the demolition of houses north of Camberwell accommodating some 3,000 souls. Because a further Act of 25 July 1864 entailed even more demolitions, Clause 134 required the LCD to 'run a train every morning of the week from their Loughborough Park and Peckham Junction stations to their Ludgate station' and back in the evening at 'one penny per journey' to convey workmen who, it was presumed, would now be rehoused further out. H. J. Dyos, writing in the *Journal of Transport History* in 1955, showed that unskilled workmen were dependent on casual employment and were unable to live away from the work they had to

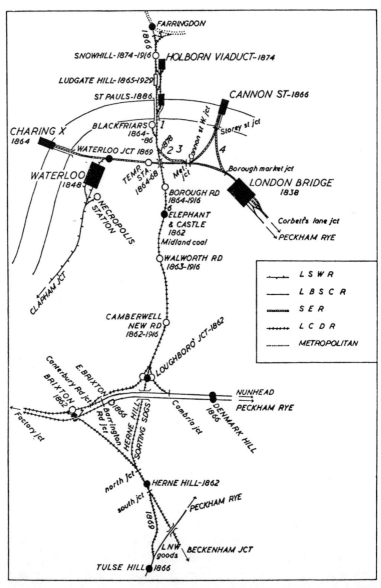

FIG 6 The LCD and SE approaches to the City and West End. The ownership of lines through Brixton and Denmark Hill is shown as it was when they were built; on completion the northern pair were taken over by the LCD and the southern by the LBSC. 1 Blackfriars Goods, 2 Southwark continental depot, 3 Ewer Street locomotive depot, 4 Cannon Street locomotive depot, 5 West Street junction, 6 GN coal depot, 7 Midland coal depot.

compete for daily. Railway building through the inner suburbs thus increased overcrowding and only the better paid could afford to move out to better housing. The workmen's trains began in 1865, leaving Ludgate Hill and Victoria for the other terminus via Herne Hill at 04.55, returning at 18.15 (14.30 Saturdays).

The 'City Line' was more than the Chatham could cope with financially. It was soon afloat on and then awash in a sea of speculation. But the possibilities for through traffic were vast. To the north the Great Northern and the Midland could be reached and linked with the LBSC and the LSW at Clapham Junction, while from there the West London led to the GW and LNW. All these companies were invited to participate financially and all profited, even if the Chatham did not. Among their gains was the right to work trains to their own goods and coal depots in South London.

From Herne Hill to the Elephant & Castle the line was opened on 6 October 1862 and thence to Blackfriars on 1 June 1864. The station was on the south bank of the river and its building (on the up side) became part of Blackfriars goods depot, which specialised in fruit and vegetable traffic from Kent and which had a wharf on the river. Closed in 1965, carriage sidings replaced it. The site was so limited that the marshalling of freight trains, hitherto normally done at goods depots, had to be carried out at Herne Hill Sorting Sidings, one of the earliest marshalling yards.

The Thames was bridged (removed 1985) and by 21 December 1864 a temporary station at Ludgate Hill was in use, a permanent station opening on 1 June 1865. Gloomy and inconvenient, it had two narrow island platforms, replaced by a single one in 1910. At the time of writing the retaining walls of the roof still survive.

On 1 January 1866 LCD passenger trains began running into the Metropolitan's Farringdon Street station, and there was soon a wide variety of passenger and freight services. Then, by an Act of 13 July 1871, the Chatham became committed to yet another grandiose project, a 292yd branch from the Ludgate–Farringdon line to a terminus, complete with hotel, on the new 1869 thoroughfare of Holborn Viaduct. It opened on 2 March 1874. On 1 August a low-level station, Snow Hill, was opened at the foot of the 1 in 39 incline.

Finally, on 10 May 1886 a parallel bridge across the Thames was opened with yet another new station at its northern end. The original Blackfriars was closed, but, just to complicate the story, on 1 February 1937 St Paul's became Blackfriars. When Ludgate Hill was rebuilt the rear wall of the present Blackfriars was pierced to make two of its five platforms through ones.

The existing layout was completed on 1 June 1878 by the SE opening the Union Street spur up from the Charing Cross line to allow it to share in the through traffic. Inevitably there was trouble over bookings on the SE–GN service, but the spur has remained a useful link.

Less than 700yd separate the inner end of Holborn from the country end of Blackfriars, and Ludgate Hill became increasingly redundant. The Wimbledon trains were the last to call and with their electrification it was closed on 3 March 1929.

Inter-terminal transfer through the congested streets of Victorian London was difficult. Holborn was easily the nearest southern terminus to King's Cross and St Pancras and thus attracted a considerable transfer traffic. All LCD main-line trains, including boat-trains, carried a City portion attached or detached at Herne Hill.

But by 1899 E. L. Ahrons, the great railway writer, was saying of Holborn Viaduct: '. . . no London Station may be said to have had such an ephemeral existence'. Watching the thin trickle of humanity at 17.15 we cannot but agree. In 1963 the bombed frontage was replaced by a soulless office block. Behind are but three platforms; the other three, too short for electric trains, were removed after the decline of the formerly important parcels traffic. The basic service consists of but four departures in the hour, in 1986 two to Sanderstead via Streatham Common and two via the Catford Loop, one to Orpington and one to Sevenoaks. The whole line from Herne Hill is closed at weekends. Just as the Underground destroyed the through services, trams and buses ate into the revenue of the Metropolitan Extensions and of fifteen stations but six remain. The intensive Ludgate–Victoria service perished in World War I and even since electrification there have been successive reductions in services.

In 1902, 19.2 million passengers used Holborn, Ludgate and St Paul's. Use declined with the loss of Inner Zone traffic.

But the growth of LCC estates at Bellingham and St Paul's
Cray and of private building at St Mary Cray and Swanley
increased numbers until in 1960 they were back to 1902 levels.
On an average day 37,000 passengers arrived at Holborn,
Blackfriars and Elephant, 87.7 per cent in the morning peak.
Total arrivals were 5,000 a day up on 1939, but 6,000 more
came during the busiest hour alone. Since then there has been
a considerable decline. Arrivals in 1978 were 23,000, again 87
per cent in the morning peak. In 1985 total traffic at the three
stations was 42,000 daily, 20,000 at Holborn Viaduct, 15,000
at Blackfriars and 7,000 at Elephant & Castle.

In 1978 the exterior of Blackfriars was rebuilt and
incorporated into office blocks. The names carved into stone
blocks at the entrance have been preserved. 'Baden-Baden',
'Nice' and 'Constantinople' evoke the ghosts of a vanished
age. But after its long decline the City Line entered a new
future with the restoration of the Snow Hill link (Chapter IV).
In the long term this will probably lead to Holborn's closure
and possibly to Blackfriars assuming an Inter-City role.

WATERLOO

Compared with previous complexities the story of Waterloo is
straightforward. The original proposal came from a company
projecting a line to Richmond. This awoke the LSW to the
possibility of developing suburban traffic. Their Nine Elms
terminus had been opened on 21 May 1838 on a riverside site
in South Lambeth at the edge of the built-up area. Easily
reached by steamer, it was however much too remote to
encourage short-distance travellers.

So the LSW persuaded the Richmond Company to build its
line from what is now Clapham Junction and to leave the rest
to them. Parliamentary powers were obtained on 31 July 1845
for a 2 mile extension to the south end of Waterloo Bridge. In
their new-found enthusiasm the LSW directors pressed for
further extensions. A scheme was presented to the 1846
London Traffic Commission for a joint station in Union Street
(Southwark) with the projected London, Chatham & North
Kent. But this foundered with the rejection of the latter's Bill.
A proposal to share in the SE's Hungerford Market terminus
also died.

The Richmond Company opened its 6 mile line on 27 July 1846 and sold out to the LSW a year later. In 1847 the Windsor, Staines & South Western (Richmond to Windsor) was incorporated to extend the line from Richmond, the first of a number of piecemeal extensions into the Thames valley that ensured that the 'Windsor Line' fed an increasing volume of traffic into Waterloo. From the latter to the site of Clapham Junction four tracks were provided, two each for the Main and the Windsor Lines, so from the first the two traffic streams were segregated.

The terminus had four platforms, the buildings designed by Sir Francis Tite, who had built Nine Elms, Southampton Terminus and Gosport. It was opened on 11 July 1848 and Nine Elms was given over to goods traffic until closure in 1968. Traffic was diverted to South Lambeth and the new Covent Garden Market built on part of the site. The approach lines were on a viaduct of sweeping curves to avoid the grounds of Lambeth Palace.

Over the years Waterloo grew into a hideous labyrinth of wooden sheds covering odd groups of platforms with a locomotive depot in their midst. A foot or two below its general level the concourse was crossed by the mercifully little-used line to the SE. The station was pilloried in Jerome K. Jerome's *Three Men in a Boat* and was properly swept into oblivion with the old century.

In 1866 an extension was built on the north side to deal with Windsor-Line traffic. At that time forty-eight up Main and fifty-four up Windsor trains were arriving daily, many of them being fly-shunted into their platform. Then, when the Charing Cross Railway was opened in 1864, the siding between platforms 2 and 3 was extended across the concourse to join it. Never of great value, the extension disappeared with the rebuilding, though traces of the platform can be seen at the bottom of the footway up to the South Eastern station.

In 1879 two more platforms came into full use. Officially the 'South Station', the railwaymen called them 'Cyprus', the island being acquired that year. In September 1885 another extension was completed, the existing Windsor Line platforms, Nos 16–21. Kitchener then being active, it was dubbed 'Khartoum'. Simultaneously two extra approach lines were supplied to provide six roads, considered sufficient 'for all time'. Some 700 trains a day were now being dealt with.

On 9 August 1899 powers were obtained for what was virtually a new station. The first platforms, on the south side, were ready by 1909 and by 1914 the present Nos 1–11 were in use. Meanwhile in 1902, 31 million passengers passed amid the turmoil of rebuilding. The new station was formally inaugurated by Queen Mary on 21 March 1922. By that time it was dealing with a weekday total of 707 electric and 326 steam trains. In connection with the rebuilding the viaduct was again widened to take five Main and three Windsor tracks as far as Vauxhall, with four tracks each on to Clapham Junction save for their being a single down Windsor road through Queen's Road (now Queenstown Road) station. The new Waterloo housed the offices of the Southern Railway/ Region, but had no hotel. By 1900 it was in the wrong part of London.

Waterloo is just old enough to be receiving attention from the architectural critics now extolling St Pancras, but their comments are rather less flattering. As a station, however, it is superb, and handsome is as handsome does. Its concourse is spacious (though unfortunately cluttered with a plethora of bothies) and save at times of extreme pressure allows convenient access to the line of platform entrances below the Solari train indicators. Because the station is built on transverse arches a tunnel allows peak-hour crowds to reach the centre part of the platforms direct from the City Tube and the Underground, while a parallel tunnel allows mail and parcels to be kept clear of the concourse.

Platforms 1–6 deal with main-line suburban trains. Formerly longer-distance departures were from 7–11 and arrivals at 12–15, but the distinction between longer- and shorter-distance became blurred with the passing of steam. Between 11 and 12 is a broad taxi-road, of less significance with the decline of the Ocean Liner specials and the accompanying mountains of baggage. The Windsor Line platforms, 16–21, are separated by the office block known as the 'Village'. Outside the north wall are carriage sidings on the site of a proposed extension abandoned as a result of reduced platform congestion consequent on electrification. Here also is the hoist used to bring up Waterloo & City stock for overhaul and down which an M7 0–4–4 tank once plunged. The York Road frontage beyond was developed for offices in the 1960s, and in recent years the concourse has been given white terrazzo flooring, a new barrier line, numerous shop units and a restaurant in the part previously reserved for the sole use of gentlemen. Unfortunately the concourse still remains some-what cluttered.

In 1961 the annual census figures showed an increase of 2,000 arriving passengers a day over the previous year and an 11,000 increase on 1956. A total of 640 trains brought in 100,514 passengers. The concentration into the three-hour peak period was 71.6 per cent, but that was low for a Southern terminus and reflected the amount of long-distance traffic. But even here use in slack hours was down on the pre-war figures. The 1978 census showed a slight decline to 93,245 arriving passengers, 71,621 at the Main Line and 21,624 at the Windsor Line platforms. The 1986 daily total of 180,000 shows only a very slight decline over the 1978 total of 187,000. Plans, at the time of writing, for making Waterloo the terminus for Channel Tunnel traffic would make it even busier.

Its trains serve the more spacious inner and middle suburbs of south-west London, and there are not the jostling peak-hour mobs of Charing Cross and Liverpool Street, though this may be more a reflection of Waterloo's large concourse than of more gracious living by its commuters. As a gateway to the Isle of Wight, Bournemouth and the West Country, Waterloo had a very large holiday traffic and some still remains. The highest number of holidaymakers leaving in a day in the years immediately after World War II was 45,386 in 119 trains. In the summer of 1955 three overnight trains were advertised on Friday nights/Saturday mornings. Even in 1960 on a summer Saturday forty-one crowded trains left between 08.00 and 12.00 with about 20,000 passengers. But this traffic was already in decline and on 6 September 1964 all trains ceased to run beyond Exeter, except for the night newspaper train, which continued for a while. At the time no long-term future was seen for the line west of Salisbury, but patronage has been buoyant in spite of early efforts to run the service down, and in 1986 there were twelve departures for stations beyond Salisbury compared with eight in 1965.

By chance Waterloo was the last London terminus to be

served by main-line steam, for the Bournemouth line passed straight from steam to electric traction in 1967. Today Waterloo is all-electric except for trains to Salisbury and Exeter.

Waterloo has always been noted for the large numbers of special trains, often improvised at short notice: Ocean Liner specials (the Queen Mary needed up to four) and specials for race, military, naval and schools traffic. They are less than formerly but in 1986 the author was astonished at the numbers of large hats and morning coats converging on a train for Ascot on Ladies' Day.

Waterloo is convenient for the West End, especially since it was connected thereto by both the Bakerloo and Northern Lines, but it is remote from the City, which goal the LSW made two serious attempts to reach. First, it subscribed to the Chatham's 'City Line', and obtained running powers. Thus Ludgate Hill was reached from Wimbledon via Herne Hill in 1869.

But much more successful was the floating of the WATERLOO & CITY Electric Railway to build a 2 mile Tube from beneath Waterloo to the Bank. The 'Drain' was opened on 8 August 1898 and absorbed by the LSW in 1907. It has always been worked as an extension of Waterloo's suburban system and through ticketing is available. Recently its ticketing has also been integrated with London Transport.

Peak-hour traffic is very heavy and at the Bank in the mornings the platforms are scarcely cleared before the next train arrives. But the travolators installed in 1960 have done much to increase the capacity of the long slope to the surface. In 1960 its users averaged 41,200 on a weekday, 84.7 per cent in the two peak periods and 53.3 per cent in the busiest morning and evening hour. The years since have seen some decline. In 1982 the daily total was 31,500, 49.5 per cent in the two busiest hours. The line's continuing importance, however, is shown by the 11,532 commuters leaving the Bank during the evening peak, being 19.3 per cent of the Waterloo departures. Five-car trains are run in peaks, reduced off-peak to a single car.

CHAPTER III

The Southern Suburbs

THE SOUTH EASTERN RAILWAY

The service on the London & Greenwich, leased by the SE in 1845, was suburban and intensive. The SE thus had suburban interests almost from its beginning. These were reinforced by the building of its NORTH KENT lines, on which grew up an extensive local traffic between London and the Thames-side towns.

The Admiralty refused to sanction an extension of the Greenwich line on the grounds of upset to the Royal Observatory's instruments. So when in 1845 a line to Gravesend was authorised, the junction was at North Kent East, where the line from Bricklayers' Arms came in, and thence through Lewisham, Woolwich and Dartford, 22.5 miles. Samuel Beazley, architect of London Bridge, designed the principal stations. His Erith, Blackheath and Gravesend have survived, the two last recently having been well restored.

The North Kent was opened on 30 July 1849. It abounded in sharp curves and short but steep grades. New Cross was on the outer fringe of London, but Woolwich, Dartford and Gravesend were among the largest Kentish towns and hitherto had been served by steamer. By 1868 there were 46 down weekday trains to Greenwich and 34 over the North Kent. Only 15 of the latter went beyond Plumstead, described in 1876 as a 'new district of workers' houses and small villas'. By 1906, 49 down trains ran via Greenwich, no longer a terminus, and 40 via Lewisham, 39 continuing beyond Plumstead.

After 1870 Thames-side began to be industrialised. Woolwich had grown from 25,785 inhabitants in 1841 to 146,397 by 1961, and Dartford from 5,619 to 45,643. In 1841 Erith's

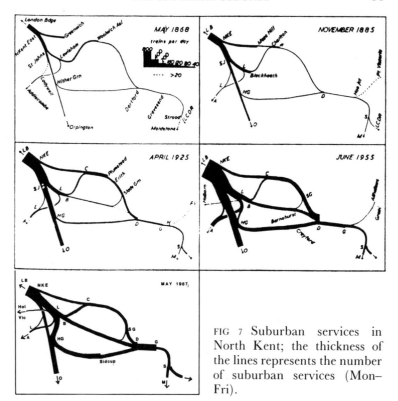

FIG 7 Suburban services in North Kent; the thickness of the lines represents the number of suburban services (Mon–Fri).

population of 2,082 included 221 harvest labourers. During the present century, with the establishment of large engineering works, it grew to 45,043 in 1961.

Apart from Woolwich Arsenal, active until the end of World War II, there is a wide variety of industries: paint, plaster, glass, chemicals, and grain-milling to name a few. Below Dartford are paper mills and cement plants as well. At North End (Erith), coal was imported coastwise and several daily trains were run to gas-works at Lower Sydenham. In 1961, twenty-eight daily freight trains passed Erith. The years since have seen the closure of many private sidings and all freight depots except Plumstead.

On the passenger side, the daily peak of London commuters is less than on many lines, but the large new town of the 1970s, Thamesmead on Plumstead marshes, has brought new traffic and the resiting of Abbey Wood station.

In 1855 the MID-KENT Railway was authorised, and it opened on 1 January 1857 as a 4.75 mile line from Lewisham on the North Kent to the Farnborough Extension at Beckenham Junction. In 1862 a 3.5 mile extension was sanctioned from New Beckenham to Croydon (Addiscombe Road) – Addiscombe after 1925 – on the far outskirts of the town. This was opened on 1 April 1864, the year the SE absorbed the Mid-Kent. Later branches were built from Elmers End to Hayes (1882) and Woodside to Selsdon (1885). The Ladywell Loop, bypassing Lewisham, opened in 1865.

Trains from London were divided at New Beckenham, one part rounding the curve to Beckenham Junction, the other being for Addiscombe; there were shuttle services from Elmers End on the branches. For some time the area remained rural, but between 1880 and 1910 rows of terrace houses grew up round the stations. New Beckenham was the exception, the surrounding villas being large.

Consequently traffic did not develop until after 1900 and present densities were not attained until after electrification. In 1868, 19 down trains passed Ladywell on weekdays. The June 1904 timetable shows 27 trains splitting at New Beckenham, 3 more for Beckenham Junction only and 1 for Addiscombe. There were 10 connections for Selsdon and 19 for Hayes.

The MAIN LINE to Tonbridge was opened to Chislehurst on 1 July 1865 and throughout on 1 May 1868 (Vol 2, Chapter III). In the early days there was no suburban service as such. Later some trains ran to Bromley, on the branch from Grove Park. Otherwise the few stations were served by slow trains for Tonbridge and beyond. In the early 1900s a speculative builder laid out Hither Green with small houses, offering free season tickets from the newly opened station. But until 1920 there was scarcely any building beyond, except of the very large houses around Chislehurst and Elmstead Woods (opened 1904) stations. By 1939 the built-up area had spread to beyond Orpington, and after 1960 there was much building around the stations further out. In 1868 Chislehurst was the only station between New Cross and Orpington. There are now six.

On 30 June 1862 the SE obtained powers for a 10 mile line from a junction with the proposed main line at Hither Green to the North Kent at Dartford Junction. The DARTFORD LOOP opened on 1 September 1866, cutting the distance to Dartford by 3 miles and allowing higher speeds. Fast trains without a Woolwich stop were thus diverted from the North Kent. Through freight traffic greatly increased after Hither Green Yards were laid out in 1899 and a spur thither to Lee Junction was laid in. In 1961 21 regular and 5 conditional trains used the Loop daily. Unusually, by 1986 it was even busier with 28 regular trains and 19 conditional or on certain days only. Staff and passengers have always known the line as the Loop Line, but it has become officially the Sidcup Line.

Deaf as usual to public opinion, the SE refused to promote any line between the North Kent and the Loop. The task was left to local enterprise in the shape of the BEXLEY HEATH (*sic*) Company, incorporated on 20 August 1883. The route was eventually from Blackheath on the North Kent to a triangular junction with that line east of Slade Green.

The grudging cooperation of the SE was obtained but money was short and progress slow, opening being delayed until 1 May 1895. There was no collation, though there was music from a temperance band. England had come a long way since the roaring forties. The SE, learning of building developments at Bexleyheath bought, as was their habit, the now bankrupt company at a large discount.

Both the Loop and the Bexleyheath enjoyed a remarkably good service, and consequently by 1904 clusters of prosperous villas had sprung up round the stations and new settlements had emerged at Bexleyheath, Eltham Park, Mottingham and Sidcup. But farm land remained between stations. There were twenty-seven down weekday trains on the Loop and thirty-two on the Bexleyheath.

It remains to list the other SE branches. The 2 mile gap between GREENWICH and CHARLTON was not finally closed until 1878. In 1865 a Bill was deposited, but the Act only authorised 1.25 miles from Charlton Junction to Maze Hill. There was no incentive to complete this appendix, not opened until 1 January 1873. The remaining 0.75 miles was finally built by 1 February 1878 and from 4 March long-distance trains were diverted through Greenwich and the local service was extended thence to Plumstead.

From Charlton Junction a mile-long branch runs to the

Thames at ANGERSTEIN WHARF, the SE's 'water outlet'. It was built by a local industrialist, John Angerstein, and opened in August 1852. Line and wharf were leased to the SE, who bought them in 1898. Sea-dredged aggregates are now landed and railed. Mention must also be made of the former Woolwich Arsenal system, which was linked with the main line at Plumstead.

The WEST WICKHAM & HAYES Company was incorporated in 1880 to build a 3.5 mile branch from the Mid-Kent at Elmers End to the small village of Hayes. The SE purchased it the next year and it opened on 29 May 1882; it was the successful scheme of a number promoted to develop the thinly peopled country between the Mid-Kent and the Chatham lines. In view of the thousands of houses built since, particularly in the 1930s, and the 1,414 season-ticket holders at West Wickham alone in 1957, it seems strange that the original justification for the branch was to increase access to countryside much favoured by Londoners for day outings.

The WOODSIDE & SOUTH CROYDON, a 2.5 mile link between the Mid-Kent at Woodside and the Oxted line at Selsdon Road (Selsdon from 1935), was opened on 10 August 1885 as part of the Croydon & Oxted joint scheme (Vol 2, Chapter IV). It had a very chequered career for both through and local traffic. The BROMLEY DIRECT Company promoted a 1.5 mile branch from the main line at Grove Park, which opened on 1 January 1878, being absorbed by the SE on 21 July 1879. The old market-town was described in an 1876 guide as being 'easy of access and consequently much in favour with City merchants'. The SE was interested in the potential suburban traffic, monopolised by the Chatham. In 1958, 404,000 ordinary tickets and 32,000 seasons were issued at Bromley North. In recent years there has been the all-too-frequent downward spiral of reduced traffic and service. Off-peak there is now only a half-hourly shuttle from Grove Park.

THE LONDON, CHATHAM & DOVER RAILWAY

The LCD at first concentrated on reaching Victoria and Ludgate Hill and on establishing a frequent service between, for this was then the only section within the built-up area. By

1885 there were over eighty trains each way daily.

By its 1864 New Lines Act the Chatham became involved in the Brighton's South London scheme. Two more tracks were built alongside its existing Victoria Line between Wandsworth Road and Barrington Road Junction (Brixton). The Brighton would continue these four lines eastward to a point just beyond Peckham Rye. On completion the Chatham took over exclusive use of the northern pair and the Brighton that of the southern. Today the stations betray the original building company, the Brighton Baroque palaces of Denmark Hill and Peckham Rye (restored 1986) contrasting with the mean Chatham slums of Clapham and Wandsworth Road. Two curves were built from the northern pair of lines to Loughborough Junction on the City Line. The west-facing allowed the Ludgate Hill–Victoria service to be diverted from Herne Hill and increased.

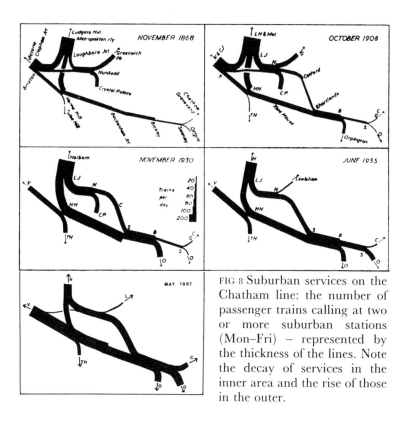

FIG 8 Suburban services on the Chatham line: the number of passenger trains calling at two or more suburban stations (Mon–Fri) – represented by the thickness of the lines. Note the decay of services in the inner area and the rise of those in the outer.

The CRYSTAL PALACE & SOUTH LONDON JUNCTION Company was authorised on 17 July 1862 to build on from Peckham Rye to a vast terminus with a cavernous roof at Crystal Palace. As was so often the case, the Chatham was too late, for Palace excursion traffic was falling. But the district was beginning to develop and intermediate stations were later built. The houses were of the *nouveaux riches* in very large grounds and traffic was limited. Services were suspended during both World Wars and on 20 September 1954 the line beyond Nunhead was finally closed to passengers.

On 28 July 1863 the branch from the Crystal Palace line where Nunhead station opened on 1 September 1871 to GREENWICH PARK was authorised. It was opened to Blackheath Hill on 18 September 1871 and throughout on 1 October 1888. But the route was circuitous and Greenwich had lost its former importance. However, at a time when for the majority a day by the sea was at best an annual event, 'outings' to Greenwich Park were popular. In 1904 there were fifty-seven daily down trains, many of them shuttle services from Nunhead. The branch, along with most of the Chatham's inner suburban services, succumbed to tramway competition, and was closed on 1 January 1917.

On 12 August 1889 a nominally independent Shortlands & Nunhead Company was incorporated to build a 5 mile connection. The CATFORD LOOP was opened on 1 July 1892 and has always been regarded as a relief to the main line, incapable of widening because of Penge Tunnel. But in addition there was an intensive suburban service to Catford, the 1910 limit of the built-up area, and a much sparser one on to Bickley. The Ravensbourne valley above Catford remained unbuilt over and Beckenham Hill was reputedly the quietest suburban station until the edge of the Bellingham LCC estate reached it. In 1924 about 425 tickets were sold daily, traffic doubling by 1934.

It is perhaps not realised that, save for the inner areas, where road competition is keenest, the ex-Chatham lines even today traverse districts mainly of low housing densities. This, added to the comparative inconvenience of Holborn Viaduct and formerly of Victoria, largely explains the limited traffic on this section.

Almost all the housing development so far described took place after 1870 and most of it after 1900. The 1899 Fusion of the SE and the Chatham Railways thus left the new Managing Committee to deal with the rapidly expanding traffic. Accordingly a suburban service was provided on the SE's Tonbridge line (quadrupled to Orpington by 1904) as far as Orpington. This also became the terminus of LCD trains, extended from Bickley over new connections and increased in number. Locomotive and carriage workings were altered so they could be based on suburban depots. Locomotive sheds and carriage sidings were built at Slades Green (in 1954 BR dropped the 's'), Orpington and Purley. But financial difficulties and the onset of war prevented them from tackling the problem more seriously. Traffic in 1921 was 26 per cent up on that of 1914, while shorter hours had intensified the peak. By 1923 the situation had got out of hand and the new Southern Company was left with the task of bringing some order out of chaos.

THE LONDON, BRIGHTON & SOUTH COAST RAILWAY

In describing the Brighton's approach to London many of its lines have been mentioned. The last major link was the 10.5 mile line from PECKHAM RYE to SUTTON opened on 1 October 1868. Three-quarters of a mile north of Tulse Hill the LCD's main line was crossed and the latter company provided a spur from Herne Hill (1 January 1869). South of Tulse Hill the West End line crossed overhead and connecting spurs were built to allow through running to Crystal Palace (1 November 1870) and to Clapham Junction (1 August 1871). South of Streatham the Brighton main line was crossed and spurs were laid in to allow through running from Victoria to Sutton (1 October 1868) and from Tulse Hill to Selhurst (1 January 1886). Finally, severe curves took the line into and out of the West Croydon and Wimbledon line at Mitcham Junction, and the West Croydon and Epsom line was joined outside Sutton.

Study of a map reveals that within the angle of the main lines from London Bridge and Victoria converging on East

Croydon there are no dead-end branches. Instead there is a maze of intersecting lines and connecting spurs which allow an almost limitless combination of routes. Three connect London Bridge and Victoria: the South London via Denmark Hill; a middle loop via Crystal Palace; and an outer one via the Norwood–Selhurst spur (1 December 1862). In addition the Peckham–Sutton line intersects and is connected to the middle and outer loops, creating yet a fourth route via Tulse Hill and Streatham Hill. 'Roundabout' services were also possible from London Bridge and back either via Crystal Palace or via Selhurst. Finally there were numerous possible routes to destinations beyond the outer loop, via East and West Croydon and via Mitcham Junction.

TABLE 5

LBSCR PEAK-HOUR DEPARTURES FROM LONDON BRIDGE –

JUNE 1904

17.30	London Bridge via Norwood Selhurst and Tulse Hill
17.31	Victoria via South London Line
17.36	Victoria via Sydenham and Crystal Palace
17.43	Stoat's Nest (Coulsdon North) via Norwood
17.46	Sutton via Norwood
17.46	Dorking via Tulse Hill and Mitcham Junction
17.50	West Croydon via Norwood
17.50	Battersea Park via South London Line
17.53	Victoria via Sydenham and Crystal Palace
18.00	Brighton
18.00	Horsham via Tulse Hill and Mitcham Junction
18.02	Victoria via Tulse Hill and Streatham Hill
18.05	Brighton
18.07	Crystal Palace via Sydenham
18.10	Sutton via Norwood
18.13	Streatham Common via Norwood and Selhurst
18.15	Wimbledon via Tulse Hill and Tooting
18.16	Victoria via Norwood and Selhurst
18.18	Battersea Park via South London Line
18.25	Victoria via Sydenham and Crystal Palace
18.30	Victoria via Tulse Hill and Streatham Hill
18.30	Stoat's Nest via Norwood
22	Departures (43 in 1962, 30 in 1984)

While existing off-peak services have been greatly simplified, the fullest use of all these routes has been made, especially at peaks. For reasons of space examples from 1904 must suffice. On weekdays there were 95 departures from London Bridge to Victoria, 59 over the South London Line,

23 via Crystal Palace, 2 via Tulse Hill and Streatham, and 11 via Selhurst. These have all disappeared, at least outside peak hours.

It is difficult to describe South London concisely owing to the apparently random distribution of neighbourhoods as exclusive as Dulwich or as slummy as parts of Brixton and Peckham, or of areas of small terrace houses as in Balham and Thornton Heath, but two generalisations may be made which provide some enlightenment. First, the higher ground, especially if gravel-capped, was the most sought-after. The most expensive houses were on the heights of Forest Hill, Crystal Palace and Tulse Hill. Rows of small houses filled the surrounding low ground in Balham, Tooting and Norbury. Second, the wealthier tended to move outward as the poorer moved in, forced from the inmost areas by overcrowding and clearances. In 1902 Charles Booth wrote, 'Southwark is moving to Walworth, Walworth to North Brixton and Stockwell, while the servant-keepers of outer South London go to Croydon.' In recent years partial 'gentrification' has led to small houses around Wandsworth Common and other neighbourhoods fetching alarmingly high prices.

Between 1841 and 1871 the area within the arc of the South London Line had become built over, and growing suburbs reached out to Balham, Norwood and Streatham, the last described in 1871 as 'a suburb of mansions, villas and genteel residences'. By 1914 the area along and within the South London Line had become exclusively working class, while suburban development had filled the triangle within the London Bridge–Selhurst–Victoria loop.

A good service to the City and West End was provided from all stations in the built-up area. Sets of austere four-wheelers survived until electrification, although seven-coach bogie sets were coming in after 1900. Tram, bus and tube competition was severe, but early electrification, frequent trains and competitive fares, together with road congestion, retained traffic and forestalled closures. But in recent years the trains have been much less crowded at peak periods than outer-suburban and long-distance trains.

Most of the London Bridge–East Croydon–Purley traffic was carried in South Eastern trains, though on 5 November 1899 the Brighton started a suburban service to Coulsdon

North and built there a large terminal (last train 30 September 1983) and depot. They also ran by various routes to Sutton and beyond, but the outer suburban services did not really develop until after 1923.

There remain some other lines to mention. The SOUTH LONDON, already referred to, was opened between London Bridge and Loughborough Park (later East Brixton) on 13 August 1866 and the remainder on 1 May 1867. At first traffic disappointed, but with the introduction of the famous 'Terrier' 0–6–0 tanks hauling close-coupled four-wheelers at fifteen-minute intervals, it soon improved to such an extent that eleven or twelve coaches were needed.

The DEPTFORD WHARF branch was opened from New Cross Gate on 2 July 1849 and was always freight only. Deptford and Battersea were the Brighton's 'water outlet' and at the former the Brighton built up a large traffic in coal, distributing as far as Brighton, while it was also landed for railing to power-stations and gas-works at Croydon until the branch was closed on 1 January 1964.

In the mid nineteenth century the country west of Croydon was very thinly peopled, but there was a demand for a line to Wimbledon along part of the abandoned route of the Surrey Iron Railway. The WIMBLEDON & CROYDON Company was incorporated in 1853, promoted by local enterprise personified in G. P. Bidder, the famous railway contractor. The line was opened on 22 October 1855 and worked by Bidder until leased to the Brighton the next year. It still wears a curiously rural air. Though electrified, it is largely single track, while at Waddon Marsh and Beddington Lane the signalman issues the tickets. Passenger traffic remains steady, though the once-heavy freight traffic has gone.

The line from West Croydon to EPSOM opened on 10 May 1847 and the EPSOM DOWNS branch from Sutton on 22 May 1865. The CATERHAM RAILWAY from Purley, which figured so largely in the quarrels between the Brighton and the SE, was opened on 5 August 1856, and the CHIPSTEAD VALLEY from Purley to Tattenham Corner in stages between 2 November 1897 and 4 June 1900. Both these last were SE lines in the heart of Brighton territory. The history of all four has been dealt with in Vol 2.

All these lines were pushed out into the rather poor farming country of the North Downs. Some commuters moved out over the years, but building did not really get under way until the 1920s and was resumed after 1950. Services were therefore sparse until electrification and for long a rail-motor dealt with the normal traffic on the Epsom Downs branch.

THE LONDON & SOUTH WESTERN RAILWAY

The suburban services of the South Western have always fallen into two parts, those down the Main and those down the Windsor Line. From the former the two most important branches were probably the New Guildford, dealt with later, and that to Epsom, which the LSW was anxious to reach, for once the Brighton got there, Surbiton would no longer be rail-head for the racing. It was thwarted, however, until the WIMBLEDON & DORKING Company was incorporated on 27 July 1857 with powers to build a 5.75 mile branch from Epsom Junction (the site of Raynes Park station of 1871). Opened on 4 April 1859, it was worked by the LSW, which absorbed it in 1862. There was no intermediate place of any importance other than the market-town and former spa of Epsom.

Turning to the Windsor Line, Richmond was reached on 17 July 1846 and Datchet on 22 August 1848 (Vol 2, Chapter V). The 1847 Act of incorporation empowered the Windsor, Staines & South Western (Richmond to Windsor) also to build a 7.25 mile line from Barnes to a triangular junction with the Windsor Line beyond Whitton. The HOUNSLOW LOOP, after what was then the only place of consequence other than Brentford, opened to Isleworth on 22 August 1849 and to Feltham Junction on 1 February 1850, the curve to Whitton Junction opening for passengers on 1 January 1833. Passenger traffic has always been purely local, and since 1900 has suffered severely from trams, buses and the District Line, but the Loop has been an essential link for through freight (Chapter VI), formerly marshalled at the now closed Feltham Yard of 1919.

Further up the river, Kingston-on-Thames, where Saxon kings were crowned, with 8,147 inhabitants in 1841, was the second largest Surrey town. Opposition, especially by coaching interests, had kept early main lines away and the consequences were becoming serious. Coaching was dead, the maltings were suffering from grain being railed direct to London instead of reaching Kingston by water, and retail trade had been hit. Kingston-on-Railway (Surbiton) was growing fast and Richmond was benefiting from the Windsor Line.

There was local satisfaction in 1859 when a branch from the latter at Twickenham was authorised. Opened on 1 July 1863, it did little to assuage Kingston's ambitions, for the route to London was slow and circuitous. In 1865 powers were obtained for an extension to the main line at Malden (now New Malden), opened on 1 January 1869. To cross the High Street involved the building of a new high-level through station, itself completely rebuilt in 1934–5. From Twickenham to Malden has always been known as the KINGSTON LOOP.

Measom's *Guide* of 1856 mentions housing development in the Battersea area, but the site of Clapham Junction was on the outskirts of London and open country lay between it and the town of Wandsworth and the village of Wimbledon. Far into the country were the market-towns of Hounslow, Richmond, Teddington and Kingston, the objectives of railway development. They prospered amidst fertile market-gardens, those of Isleworth being described by Measom as justly famed for raspberries and strawberries.

But London was now within easy reach and this salubrious region was sought by businessmen following the footsteps of more leisured eighteenth-century Londoners. 'Barnes has nearly doubled in size in the last ten or twelve years', says a guide of 1876. By 1914 continuous building had spread along the Main and Windsor Lines to Wimbledon and Richmond respectively.

All this attracted the envy of the District. It backed the Kingston & London Company, which obtained powers in 1881 for a line from the District terminus at Putney Bridge to Kingston and thence to Guildford via Cobham. The LSW, forgetful of its fighting youth, or saving its enmity for the arch-enemy at Paddington, met these proposals with sweet reason, which paid off in the 1882 Transfer Act.

The LSW agreed to build the NEW GUILDFORD line between Guildford and Surbiton (opened 2 February 1885), but linked it with their own main line at Hampton Court Junction. A line from Kingston to Putney Bridge was to be built jointly by the LSW and the District, but ultimately this was diverted from the LSW's stronghold to Wimbledon and promoted solely as a South Western concern.

The 3.5 mile WIMBLEDON & PUTNEY line opened on 3 June 1889, and on 1 July a flying junction was completed up from the Windsor Line at Point Pleasant to East Putney. A virtually separate terminus was provided at Wimbledon. District trains were projected from Putney Bridge and the LSW provided a service from Waterloo via East Putney (ceased 1941). The Southern Region still finds the line useful for stock movement and to reach Longhedge Junction from the main line. Although their trains never call, the intermediate stations are staffed by BR. Wimbledon station was rebuilt in 1929. Its ten platforms deal with about 50,000 passengers a day. In 1961 the goods department dealt with some 93,000 wagons a year, but it closed in 1970.

The pattern of the LSW's surburban services differed from those of other southern companies. The residential area beyond Wandsworth and Earlsfield had the reputation of being more exclusive, and certainly housing densities were generally lower. Commuters tended to travel in from further afield. Thus there never were intensive inner-suburban services. Nor were there, apart from the 'roundabouts' on the Kingston and Hounslow Loops and the Hampton Court trains, the equivalents of the Crystal Palace, Bickley or Dartford services. Suburban stations were mainly served by stopping trains bound for distant terminals, Windsor, Reading, Guildford and Dorking. These ran through heathlands, past golf-courses, villas in large grounds, and pleasant Thames backwaters. There was thus an attention to passenger comfort that must have driven South Eastern or Great Eastern users apoplectic with envy.

The 1904 timetables show 31 down trains over the Hounslow Loop and as many on the Kingston Loop via Twickenham. There were 22 down trains to Wimbledon via East Putney, 29 to Hampton Court and 22 to Epsom.

A few other branches remain to be mentioned. That to HAMPTON COURT was the earliest: 1.75 miles, it opened from Hampton Court Junction (west of Surbiton) on 1

February 1849. W. J. Chaplin, the LSW's Chairman, was unenthusiastic, but considered the line a public necessity. But in true Victorian tradition, virtue was rewarded and the LSW did handsomely from visitors and residents. In 1865 thirteen of the forty-seven Main Line departures from Waterloo were for Hampton Court. In 1955, 300,000 tickets were collected and 10,000 seasons issued.

The THAMES VALLEY Company was incorporated in 1862 to build a branch from Strawberry Hill on the Kingston Loop. Opened on 1 November 1864, it ran for 6.5 miles through market-gardens to Shepperton. Even today the district beyond Hampton is not fully built up and race meetings at Kempton Park have provided the heaviest traffic. In 1894 a triangular junction was completed, and through running from Kingston began in 1901.

The TOOTING, MERTON & WIMBLEDON was authorised in 1864 to build a connecting line from Streatham Junction on the Peckham–Tulse Hill–Sutton line. In the next year it was jointly taken over by the LSW and the Brighton and opened on 1 October 1868. At Tooting the line forked, one branch reaching Wimbledon via Haydons Road, the other joining the Wimbledon & Croydon, the last 0.75 miles of which also came under joint ownership. On 1 January 1869 the LSW inaugurated its Wimbledon and Ludgate Hill service, and there were also LBSC trains. The Tooting–Merton Park section closed to passengers on 3 March 1929 and completely on 5 August 1968.

'SOUTHERN ELECTRIC': BEGINNINGS*

By 1900 separation of work and residence had become general for the middle class. But though it was also becoming common for many workmen, the 1905 Royal Commission was convinced that lower fares were necessary to encourage outward migration of the working class to reduce overcrowding. This was not achieved until the 1930–60 period and then mainly because fares rose more slowly than the real value of wages. But even so 'journey-to-work' was steadily increasing in volume and length. Journeys per head by local railway increased from 10 a year in 1867 to 30 in 1895 and 42 in 1902.

But the tram had become a rival mass-transporter, at least

* See also Vol 2, Chapter 9.

for short journeys. Journeys by tram had increased from twelve per head a year in 1880 to fifty-two in 1902. By 1901 the London County Council had become an operator. As a social policy, very low fares were charged to reduce housing congestion by migration. Electrification began in 1901 and was accompanied by extensions far into the suburbs. By 1911 journeys per head had leapt to 113.

During the same decade rail traffic stagnated, while on some lines there had been a drastic decline in traffic and an even more alarming contraction in revenue. The choice was closure or electrification, which would reduce operating costs and permit increased service at competitive fares. Conversely, on lines with increasing traffic the greater acceleration now possible after the frequent stops would permit more trains without the expense of widening.

However, C. E. Lee has pointed out (*Railway Magazine*, Vol 105) that the LBSC adopted its electrification policy to counter projects for an electric railway to Brighton. Electrification powers were obtained in 1903 and in the following year it was decided to provide a test section on the South London line between Peckham Rye and Battersea Park. But it was not until 1906 that the competing tramways in the area were electrified.

But whatever the reason, electrification was timely. The LBSC told the 1905 Royal Commission that it had lost 1.25 million passengers in the previous six months to and from 'the Croydon direction', and between 1903 and 1908 passenger journeys over the South London fell from 8 million to 3.5 million. At Peckham Rye bookings fell from 1,213,281 in 1902 to 526,273 in 1909. Electrification, at 6,600V alternating current with overhead pick-up, was extended to London Bridge and Victoria (8.6 miles in all) and the new service began on 1 December 1909 with doubled frequency and reduced times. By 1910 the line was again carrying 8 million passengers, and in 1922 the figure was 12 million.

Since then Tube extension and improved bus services have cut deeply into the regained traffic. A 1960 survey found that between 07.00 and 09.00 only 71 passengers joined trains at East Brixton (closed 1976) for Victoria and 46 for London Bridge. At Queen's Road comparable figures were 54 and 606. Off-peak trains have been of two cars only since at least 1938, and from 1984 the half-hourly service was reduced to peak only.

On 12 May 1911 an electric service was inaugurated between Victoria and Crystal Palace, involving the conversion of 7.5 route miles of the old West End line from Battersea Park. In March 1912, to economise coal during a miners' strike, a service from London Bridge was started after electrification of the section from Peckham Rye and the Tulse Hill spurs, the full service beginning on 1 June. On that day trains were extended from the Palace to Norwood Junction, which meant conversion of a further 5.5 miles. Plans were prepared for extensions to Cheam and Coulsdon North, the latter being the first step to Brighton, but war delayed completion until 1922.

By 1901 electric trams from Hammersmith had reached Hounslow, and they reached Kingston soon after. Competition from these and the rejuvenated District (Chapter IV) rapidly eroded the LSW's suburban traffic. In 1908 the Chairman complained that 1.25 million passengers had been lost to trams and buses in the previous six months. In 1913 the LSW announced plans for electrification of lines on which traffic worth £100,000 a year had been lost. In contrast with the Brighton it adopted the third-rail system using direct current at 600V. But like the Brighton it used multiple-unit trains.

Work continued in spite of the War and a Waterloo–Wimbledon via East Putney service was inaugurated on 25 October 1915. On 30 January 1916 the Kingston 'round-abouts' were converted, together with the Shepperton service, and on 12 March trains over the Hounslow Loop. Electric trains ran to Hampton Court from 18 June and on 20 November down the New Guildford line to Claygate with pull-and-push connections beyond. But owing to stock shortage the Claygate trains soon reverted to steam.

A total of 56.8 miles had so far been converted. Timetables were arranged on a basis of regular intervals, which became standard practice on the Southern and later on BR as a whole. In 1913, 25 million passengers had been carried on all these services, but by 1918 carryings had risen to 40 million and two years later to 52.6 million.

In south-east London there had been no real penetration by

the Underground. But by 1908 trams were running through Woolwich to Abbey Wood and in 1911 a bus service began between Oxford Circus and Sidcup. The SE&C services were hard hit, especially those on the North Kent and the Metropolitan Extensions. The Managing Committee sought electrification powers, and in 1920 announced plans to electrify to Gillingham, Tonbridge and Redhill on a 1,500V dc fourth-rail system.

'SOUTHERN ELECTRIC': FRUITION

In 1923 the Southern Railway inherited 58.3 route miles of third-rail electrification from the LSW (including the Wimbledon & Croydon) and 24.6 of overhead from the Brighton, 82.9 miles in all. They pressed ahead with their predecessors' plans and developing their own.

On the Western Section conversion was completed of the remainder of the New Guildford Line, together with those from Raynes Park to Dorking North and from Leatherhead to the New Guildford at Effingham Junction. These totalled 31.9 route miles and trains began running on 12 July 1925. The area was rural and still is one of discontinuous settlement beyond Hinchley Wood and Ashtead, but the inner area was built up in the 1930s. At all stations a considerable season-ticket traffic built up. At Dorking North 669 seasons were sold in 1924, but by 1932 the figure had reached 2,737. Between 1927 and 1937 there was a tenfold increase at Motspur Park and Worcester Park.

On the Central Section work continued on the overhead conversion of 18.25 route miles, and services were inaugurated on 1 April 1925. The sections involved were from Balham Junction to Sutton via Selhurst, Selhurst to Coulsdon North, and Tulse Hill to Streatham Junction, with the connecting spurs.

There were no further extensions, however, and on 9 August 1926 the Southern announced that it was standardising on third rail. This LSW system had already been adopted for the extensive conversions on the Eastern Section where the Southern was desperately making up lost time.

These new services were inaugurated in three stages. The first covered 31 route miles and affected the services from

Victoria and Holborn to Orpington both by the main line and the Catford Loop, together with the Crystal Palace branch. Working on the latter began on 1 April 1925 for staff training and the full service on 12 July. At first six trains an hour were provided between Herne Hill and Shortlands, but over the years, in response to off-peak traffic decline, the frequency declined to two an hour in 1960. In a 1960 census 882 people joined up trains at Catford between 07.00 and 09.00, while at the adjoining Catford Bridge on the Mid-Kent the figure was 4,152. Further up the Catford Loop the figures were 1,087 and 554 at Crofton Park and Nunhead respectively. On the other hand traffic at the rebuilt St Mary Cray and Swanley had vastly increased.

The second stage was inaugurated on 28 February 1926 and covered the line from Charing Cross and Cannon Street to Orpington, together with the Bromley North branch and the Mid-Kent to Addiscombe with the short spur to Beckenham Junction. The Hayes branch had been worked by an electric shuttle since 21 September 1925 to provide crew training. In all 27.5 route miles were involved.

The final stage, 33.5 miles, consisted of the four routes to Dartford – the North Kent via Blackheath and via Greenwich, and the Bexleyheath and Loop lines. A few electric trains ran during the General Strike, and the full public service began on 19 July 1926.

Timetables were on a fixed-interval basis, generally with twenty-minute and thirty-minute intervals on the ex-LCD and ex-SE lines respectively. But in about 1935 intervals on the Mid-Kent, Bexleyheath and Loop services became fifteen minutes. By then new building had made these by far the busiest, and peak crowding was already serious.

As yet the main line from London Bridge was not converted, as so much of the traffic was carried in SE trains. But now electric trains began running in steam schedules on 25 March 1928 to Crystal Palace via Sydenham, to Caterham and to Tadworth. Meanwhile work was going ahead laying third rail on the overhead routes and on the planned extensions from Streatham Junction to Epsom Downs via Mitcham Junction and from Crystal Palace to Beckenham Junction.

On 17 June 1928 interval electric services were inaugurated

on these latter routes. The Caterham and Tadworth trains were also put on an interval basis and the latter were extended to Tattenham Corner. The alternating-current trains were withdrawn gradually, the last leaving Victoria at 00.30 on 22 September 1929. Eventually, overcrowding on services to East Croydon and beyond became as bad as on the notorious north-west Kent lines, while traffic in the Sutton area was increasing fast.

However, the services in the area between Wimbledon and Croydon were lagging badly and passengers were rapidly deserting. The old LSW service from Wimbledon to the City was converted to electric traction on 3 March 1929. Suspended during World War I, it was hastily restored in 1923 in reply to the threat from the Tube extension to Morden, but it was scarcely flourishing. In 1928 receipts at Haydons Road were £300. In 1933, four years after electrification, they had reached £5,000.

In 1910 a group of landowners had obtained powers for a 4.75 mile line from Wimbledon to Sutton, over which District trains would run. These lay dormant until 1922, when there were proposals to link the line with the Morden Extension (Chapter V). The Southern, sensitive to this thrust into its territory, admittedly the part with the worst services in the Inner Suburban Zone, strongly resisted the move. In the end it was agreed that there should be no physical connection with the Tube and that the Southern should build and work the WIMBLEDON & SUTTON, for which powers were obtained in 1924.

The line opened to South Merton on 7 July 1929 and on to Sutton on 5 January 1930. It was worked by the electric service from Holborn, projected on from Wimbledon to West Croydon, until 1986 when it was included in a London Bridge 'roundabout' via Norwood, West Croydon, Wimbledon and Tulse Hill (and the other way). At St Helier the LCC built a large overspill estate (1960 population 30,692) and by 1939 private housing had spread over the rest of the district.

On 6 July 1930 the programme was completed when a self-contained electric service of increased frequency replaced steam pull-and-push trains on the Wimbledon & Croydon. On the same date electric services began to Windsor over the 12.75 miles from Whitton Junction through Staines.

In 1935 a short but very important extension came into use. The Chatham's Greenwich Park branch had lain derelict since 1917, but in 1929 a connection from it to Lewisham was opened, together with a spur thence from the Mid-Kent to the main line. The remainder of the Greenwich branch was then torn up. The purpose of this was to enable transfer freights from all parts of London to reach Hither Green. Later the spur and the line from Lewisham to Nunhead were electrified. On 30 September a peak service began between the Bexley-heath and Loop lines and Blackfriars. Suspended during World War II, they were reinstated in August 1946. Most of them ran to Holborn, and after 1985 they reached Victoria.

This was an attempt to relieve the gross overcrowding, as more trains could be run as far up as Lewisham, but not beyond as the London Bridge approaches were now saturated. Commuters, however, long preferred the discomforts of the trains to Charing Cross and Cannon Street.

On 30 September 1935 the Woodside & South Croydon was reopened to local traffic and an electric service was inaug-urated between Charing Cross and Sanderstead. Because of limited paths available this was achieved by diverting the Beckenham Junction trains, but the spur to that station remained in occasional use especially when Clock House flooded after heavy rain. The service was later reduced to a peak-period shuttle with a two-car set from Elmers End. A 1980 passenger count revealed 116 passengers using Bingham Road daily, and 50 and 36 at Coombe Road and Selsdon respectively. Not surprisingly, the service ceased on 12 May 1981. Electric trains now reach Sanderstead from Holborn via Tulse Hill and East Croydon, which involved converting the 0.25 miles between South Croydon and Selsdon.

Finally, a new line was opened from Motspur Park, on the Raynes Park–Epsom line, to Tolworth on 29 May 1938, and on 28 May 1939 to CHESSINGTON SOUTH. The four stations on the 3.75 miles are the centre of entirely new communities. But for World War II it would have been extended to Leatherhead; afterwards the Green Belt made the extension redundant.

By 1939 all the Southern's lines in Greater London had been electrified. Post-war main-line extensions followed, and that to East Grinstead in 1988 meant that a few peak services to Uckfield from Victoria and between Clapham Junction and Olympia, together with the trains to Salisbury and Exeter from Waterloo, were the only diesel operations on Southern Region in Greater London.

THE POST-WAR PERIOD

The system had thus taken shape by the outbreak of World War II, so post-war changes have not been so fundamental as in other parts of London. Nevertheless they have been extensive. Summing them up is difficult, but we can perceive two contradictory trends, positive and negative, as the Southern strove to react to traffic change and to provide improved services.

On the negative side, falling off-peak traffic after 1960 was countered by the lengthening of service intervals, so that by 1985 services on the Sidcup and Bexleyheath lines had been reduced from 15 to 30 minute intervals, and on the Tattenham Corner branch beyond Smitham from 20 to 60 minutes, while Teddington has three trains an hour to Waterloo instead of six. These are random examples typical of the whole picture and should be contrasted with the eight trains an hour each way from Alexandra Palace. It is a policy which is probably self-defeating, the small cost saving being outweighed by revenue loss due to declining convenience.

Vacillation by successive governments in providing support as they pursued the chimera of financial profitability resulted in long delays in re-equipping. The system therefore suffered periods during which stock and operating methods became increasingly obsolescent. In 1986 services on the South Eastern lines were being maintained by stock at least twenty years old and of an outdated design even when new.

In addition there was a long period of decline in relationships between management, staff and, most unfortunately, the passengers, who became the victims of conflict between the first two, as go-slows and strikes led to increasing unreliability. The loss of the esprit de corps, the mark of the Southern Railway, was to be deplored as it must be the mark of a service such as the Southern's. Restoration must be a prime objective of the new Network South East (p. 223).

On the positive side, under the circumstances outlined, was

a remarkably steady replacement of ageing rolling stock. Gradually the Class 405 (4-SUB) units became standard on the inner-suburban services. They were reliable, if old-fashioned. But after a number of years of trials, in 1981 the Class 508 units with their revolutionary sliding doors were introduced on the western lines. They were replaced after 1983 by the similar 455s which at the time of writing provide the bulk of the inner-suburban services on the western and central lines.

There has also been a renewal of signalling, with control from large centres, such as London Bridge, which was commissioned in 1975 and controls 47.3 route and 147.5 track miles. As we have seen, all the London termini have been rebuilt or refurbished. Many of the other larger stations were rebuilt before the War. Apart from the restoration of war damage, further progress was slow until after 1960, when many stations such as Dartford and Maze Hill were rebuilt. The present tendency is toward preservation rather than destruction, Denmark Hill, Peckham Rye, Blackheath and Norbiton being among the stations preserved. Through the long years of increasing traffic, however, East Croydon at the time of writing remains unimproved. Above all, Southern Electric remains indispensable to London's social and economic well-being.

THE SOCIAL CONSEQUENCES OF ELECTRIFICATION

Electrification was one of the means of satisfying the social urge towards better and less-congested housing which characterised the period after 1920 and which was fulfilled at the cost of an increase in the length of the average journey to work and in the proportion of total income spent on it. In the inter-war years the Inner Zone tended to empty into the semi-detached new Middle Zone. It was the land required for low-density housing that resulted in the phenomenal spread of London.

In the Inner Zone there was much building of council flats and conversion of larger houses to flats. But rebuilding did not really make its mark until the febrile activity of rebuilding in the 1960s and the gentrification of the 1980s.

In the Middle Zone the LCC laid out its vast overspill

estates at Mottingham, Downham, Bellingham and St Helier, for the most part connecting them by tramway extensions. But near-by stations were much used, particularly after post-war fare equalisation, when rail's superior speed told. But the majority of houses were built on large estates by speculative builders, taking advantage of reduced building costs and offering cheap mortgages. In the 1930s a down payment of £50 and weekly repayments of £1 5s would secure a small but adequate house. Properties were invariably advertised as being served by electric lines. The 1950s saw virtually all land taken up and the 1970s the replacement of large houses and their gardens by high-density maisonettes.

It would be tedious to detail the growth of all Greater London south of the Thames, so North-West Kent has been selected as typical. The area can be defined by the London Boroughs of Bexley and Bromley. In 1925 the built-up area extended only to Penge, Catford, Lee and Blackheath, with two projecting prongs. One of these linked Penge with Beckenham, Bromley and Bickley along the ex-LCD main line, and consisted mainly of high-class housing. The other extended along the bank of the Thames as far as Abbey Wood and was composed of small houses intermingled with in-dustry, served more by trams than the North Kent Line. Beyond the built-up area towns and villages were growing fast, but were still separated by farmland.

The 1931 population figure was 232,801 but by 1951 it had grown to 449,230, after which it tended to stagnate. Housing densities were low, varying from 3 per acre in the Urban District of Orpington to 18.2 in the old Borough of Bexley. There was no comparable growth of local industry, though decentralisation of offices had some effect on local employ-ment, particularly after 1960. Job ratios (the proportion of daytime jobs to actively employed population) have always been low, those of 1951 varying from 29 per 100 in Bexley to 73 in the former Borough of Erith. Many would have travelled to neighbouring industrial areas such as Woolwich, but a quarter or more (in the case of Beckenham in 1951, 37 per cent) travelled to Central London at peak periods.

The area of the former Chislehurst and Sidcup Urban District had a 1921 population of 16,920. In the year of electrification, 1926, the estimated number was 18,500, a 9 per

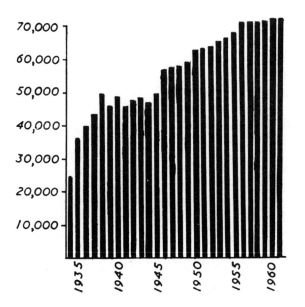

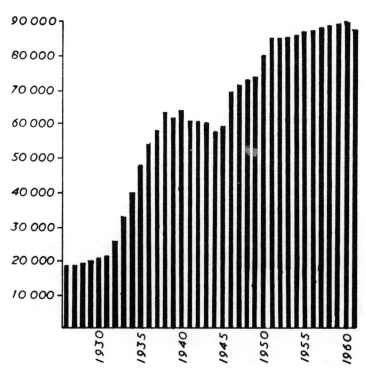

cent increase in five years. The 1931 census recorded 21,680, an increase of 17 per cent in the succeeding five years. But in the next five years, to 1936, the increase was one of *155 per cent.* The War saw a slight decline, but after 1945 growth was resumed, reaching a peak census figure of 86,907 in 1961, four times that of 1931.

There were a few factories, but otherwise only service industries, and the 1951 job ratio was 44 per cent. Over half the working population of 24,795 were employed outside the area. Of these 2,931 went to Woolwich and 1,113 to Greenwich, but 8,955 travelled daily to the Central area. This story of growth and the subsequent social structure is repeated with few exceptions throughout the Middle Zone.

Thus villages mushroomed into large towns, with corresponding expansions in passenger traffic. In 1925, 1.1 million tickets were sold at Sidcup, Welling and Bexleyheath. Ten years later the figure stood at 4.8 million. In the same period season-ticket issues swelled from 8,959 to 57,000. In 1957 there were 2,950 season-ticket holders travelling from Sidcup and 2,235 from Welling. The average 1961 month saw 10,000 cheap-day tickets to Central London sold at Sidcup and in that year sales of 743,792 tickets and 55,772 seasons were recorded.

In 1924 Grove Park was in a semi-rural area and large numbers of first-class seasons were issued. In that year 771,133 ordinary tickets and 1,088 seasons were sold. In 1934 comparable figures were 917,585 and 12,041. The Downham Estate (1960 population 25,464) was even then incomplete and by 1938 the harassed booking clerks were issuing 3,000 workmen's tickets daily. Even at Charlton the author was selling 500 daily. Since then social custom and fare structures have brought change. No longer do junior office workers crowd the 'last workmen's' train to while away the time in coffee shops until their City offices open.

Again the list of examples of expansion could be extended ad nauseam. But to preserve balance some examples from other representative 'Southern Electric' stations are recorded in Table 6.

FIG 9 Population growth in the south-eastern suburbs: *above* Orpington; *below* Chislehurst and Sidcup. (Note: Boundary changes prevent the figures being continued.)

Throughout the inter-war years wage rates remained stable, though the value of money tended to *increase*, while unemployment in the South East was lower than average. The increasing length of the average journey to work, however, especially when coupled with the higher rentals of better housing, bore heavily on the less well paid. But low fares and cheap mortgages benefited the middle class. The 'quarterly special' season-ticket rate from Sidcup to Charing Cross, 12

TABLE 6

COMMERCIAL RESULTS OF ELECTRIFICATION — BOOKINGS AT SELECTED SUBURBAN STATIONS

		1927		*1937*
			Seasons	
Malden		12,043		31,643
Surbiton		16,061		45,607
Motspur Park		2,061		12,808
Worcester Park		3,201		31,984
		1924		*1932*
Dorking North		669		2,737
		1927		*1935*
			Ordinary	
Banstead, Belmont and Epsom Downs		329,778		859,794

	1927		*1934*	
	Ordinary	*Season*	*Ordinary*	*Season*
Lordship Lane*	30,043	870	57,019	1,742
Beckenham Junction	277,338	5,345	394,804	14,680
Crofton Park	242,115	5,019	338,753	7,115
Bellingham	164,025	2,727	313,743	4,832
Ravensbourne	9,151	145	24,887	882
Orpington	272,060	2,677	403,451	13,378
	1928		*1935*	
Kenley	28,000	600	68,000	1,200
	1925		*1935*	
Woolwich Dockyard	85,272	537	99,138	517
Woolwich Arsenal	849,815	6,696	884,200	8,160
	1925		*1934*	
Eden Park	8,358	61	75,841	4,188
West Wickham	46,984	336	251,024	18,711
Hayes	21,856	159	177,424	5,831
	1924		*1934*	
Grove Park	71,133	1,088	917,585	12,041

		1938	*1946*	*1961*
Sidcup	Ordinary	733,010	772,163	743,792
	Seasons	21,523	25,509	55,772

* Now closed.

miles, worked out at under 11d per working day, while the workmen's fare from Charlton to Charing Cross was 7½d.

By the end of the 1940s wages were rising faster than travel costs. In 1939 our worker from Charlton would have spent 3s 9d a week getting to Charing Cross out of a wage of about £2 10s to £3. By 1949 the average weekly wage was £10 19s 4d, while in Greater London south of the river the average expenditure on public transport was 4s 2d, and 5s 6d in the outer area. This trend was not reversed until the 1970s, when fares increased faster than the general cost of living, due to greater wage inflation in public transport. Though even in 1980, when the annual second-class season from East Croydon to London was £294, to drive would have incurred petrol costs alone of £204. The decline in inflation after 1980 together with greater cost-effectiveness in transport has probably restored the previous situation of faster growth in real income than in fares.

CHAPTER IV

Central London

THE NORTH LONDON RAILWAY

Complex in detail, railway development south of the Thames is comparatively straightforward in outline. But to the north there are two complications. First, an otherwise simple pattern of radiating trunk-lines, supplemented by the two compact systems of the Great Eastern and the Tilbury in the east have been overlaid and obscured by the elaborate and virtually independent system of the Underground. Second, there are at least two important peripheral routes.

It has been said that London lacks a 'belt line', but it must be remembered that a regular freight service developed from Hither Green right round to Ripple Lane (Barking). Only across the Thames in a direct line between the two was the ring incomplete. Over the southern part there has never been a single route, but several streams converged on the North & South Western Junction and the West London lines to pass over them to Willesden. Thence the trunk stream traversed the Hampstead Junction line to Gospel Oak. Here it divided, one branch making for South Tottenham and thence to the Temple Mills and Ripple Lane yards and the Royal and Tilbury Docks, the other making for the City and for Poplar and Millwall Docks over the North London Line.

From 1860 to 1910 this route, in whole or in part, was a principal artery for passengers. But while passenger traffic still rather remarkably survives over much of it, this movement amounts to only minor eddies in the great rivers of present-day passenger flow. On the other hand the once constant procession of freight trains, though in some decline since the 1960s, still remains at what is now for BR a high level.

The second peripheral route, at one time of equal import-

Plate 12 Commuting clerks of the early 1900s rode home from the City on the GN. Here a train from Moorgate climbs out of King's Cross past Holloway station.
(*L&GRP*)

Plate 13 But the wealthy commuters on the LSW were provided with the latest bogie coaches. A train of two four-coach 'bogie block' sets from Waterloo passes Surbiton.
(*L&GRP*)

Plate 14 The LT&S also had the reputation of providing very good rolling stock. This train is from Ealing to Southend and is of special coaches for that service. (*L&GRP*)

Plate 15 This contemporary engraving gives an excellent idea of the 'cut and cover' method of building the Inner Circle. Here is Pentonville Road with Euston Road on its original line in the background. King's Cross station can be seen, but St Pancras was not yet built. (*London Transport Museum*)

Plate 16 Baker Street in 1986 had been restored to its original state, though the crinolined ladies of 1863 are no longer to be seen. (*London Transport Museum*)

ance, was from Paddington and King's Cross over the Metropolitan to Ludgate Hill and thence to South London. This suffered decline and, in the cross-river aspect, eventual extinction. But in recent years it has experienced a revival. We must therefore break with a chronological approach and deal with the North London Railway, the nucleus of the first route, and then with the Metropolitan, that of the second.

The genesis of the North London lay in the desire of the London & Birmingham to connect with the waterborne traffic of the lower Thames. This diversion of through traffic peripherally around London has been a continuing feature, reflected in the New Road (Marylebone, Euston and City Roads) of 1756–7, the North Circular Road and the M25.

The East and West India Docks & Birmingham Junction Railway was incorporated on 26 August 1846 to build 8 miles of line from Camden to the West India Docks. The prospectus stated that shippers were complaining of delays to goods and that 'the expense of forwarding goods between Camden Town . . . and shipping on the river, now so expensive, may be reduced 50 to 70 per cent'.

It was successful largely because it fitted the recommendations of the 1846 Commission on London Traffic set up in the 'Mania' to consider the nineteen Bills affecting Central London. The Commission decided that the advantages of building railways up to Central London were overrated for long-distance travellers and unjustified for short-distance ones. The southern termini could be sited close to the river as disturbance to property would be less and it was of low value, but the northern termini should be located on the New Road and a 'belt line' provided to link them.

The company became the North London on 1 January 1853. Nominally independent, it was popularly accorded the degree of freedom now ascribed to the satellite states of Eastern Europe. The LNW subscribed 67 per cent of the capital and nominated one third of the directors, while the Secretary's office was at Euston.

Post-Mania money was tight and the first section, the 5 miles from Bow Junction (on the Blackwall) to Islington, was not open until 26 September 1850. Some authorities say that passenger traffic was not originally envisaged, but the 1846 prospectus says: '. . . income from Passenger Traffic will be very great both from suburban travellers and those making steamer connections from Brunswick Wharf'. At first passengers were the only resource and a fifteen-minute service from Fenchurch Street was put on. Extensions went into service to Camden Town (Camden Road 1853–70 and from 1950) on 7 December 1850 and to Hampstead Road (Chalk Farm from 1862, Primrose Hill from 1950) on 9 June 1851. A junction with the LNW remained unused for regular traffic.

Though the line was peripheral, traffic was soon attracted. In October 1850, 97,531 passengers were carried, while in 1853 they totalled 4.37 million. On 15 November 1851 the *Illustrated London News* described a journey over the 'Camden-Town Railway'. A picture of a different world, it makes strange reading. Leaving Fenchurch Street, the train ran through the crowded industrial East End. But at Stepney (1.75 miles), 'we began to breathe more freely, for we left behind the region of smoke and gigantic chimneys' and were passing 'through the fields to Bow Common'. Soon after Bow station open country was again entered and 'passing onward through the verdant fields we came to the retired village of Homerton'. Then came Hackney, with its watercress beds, and Kingsland. 'In this district large tracts of land belonging to the Lord of the Manor . . . are being laid out for building detached villas of a better class', the visible results of the new railway. At Islington, too, Pentonville Prison, in fields a few years before, was 'nearly surrounded by houses'. Then, 'after passing several beautiful villas we arrived at Camden Town'.

The NL's own lines were virtually completed on 1 January 1852 by the opening of the line from Bow to Poplar, where two branches made connections with the dock lines. After pressure from the NL, a spur from the eastern one at Prestons Road was provided to the Blackwall. But the latter would not allow passenger trains until 1870. By then the steamer connections were no longer a worthwhile prize; the service ceased in 1890 and the connection was severed.

A dock, leased from the Docks Company, was used for the import of coal and other goods. A large goods depot was laid out and leased to the LNW. Poplar Dock became one of the most important Thames-side rail-heads. In 1866 Harrow Lane sidings were laid out at Millwall Junction on the Blackwall. To connect with the dock lines the rise of 1 in 34 of the western branch to the bridge over the Blackwall was avoided when the loop line was opened in 1875 (Figure 17).

Freight traffic, worked by the LNW, began on 1 January 1852. Merchandise to and from the docks was carried, together with some coal transferred from the Midland to the LNW at Rugby. But the principal flow was from Poplar Docks, worked by the shippers, the Northumberland & Durham Coal Company, with its own locomotives, a unique arrangement on a busy suburban line. The NL bought out the Coal Company's rights in 1859 and in 1870 the LNW took over the depots.

The City Corporation, to relieve congestion caused by animals driven to Smithfield Market through narrow streets, opened on 15 June 1855 the Metropolitan Cattle Market off Caledonian Road, leaving Smithfield to deal in carcasses. In anticipation the NL opened a cattle terminal at Maiden Lane. To it the LNW transferred its livestock traffic from Camden in April 1854. The NL laid out exchange sidings at St Pancras Junction, where a temporary connection was provided by the GN in 1850 and a permanent one in 1853. A curve to the Midland was provided in 1867 (Figure 16).

These connections brought local and transfer traffic to the NL. Much was handled by the Company, but two operating features were shared with the London, Chatham & Dover: 'foreign' companies, especially the LNW and the GN, worked their own trains and also owned and staffed their own goods depots. By 1861, 338,817 tons of minerals and 436,385 tons of goods were passing over the NL. In 1871 the figures were 671,173 and 1.12 million tons respectively. Traffic grew steadily until 1900 when the figures stood at 1.2 and 2 million tons respectively and after which they remained fairly stationary.

Passenger traffic was also developing, nurtured by frequent services and low fares. In 1865 second-class fares averaged 0.4d per mile. First and second class only were provided, second-class carriages being used on statutory 'Parliamentary' trains.

In August 1853 a few NL trains were extended from Hampstead Road over the LNW to Willesden and thence to Kew, but congestion was rife on this line with its primitive signalling. Accordingly the LNW promoted the HAMPSTEAD JUNCTION Railway from Camden Town to Old Oak

Junction (Willesden). Opened on 2 January 1860, it was 6 miles long and tunnelled under the Hampstead heights. Absorbed by the LNW in 1867, the NL provided the trains and shared in running the stations.

In 1861, 6.5 million passengers were carried by the NL, but on 16 February the Chairman stressed: '. . . the great disadvantage under which your line labours in consequence of the extremely circuitous route'. It was therefore decided to seek a more direct access to the City. From a triangular junction at Dalston, where there would be a new station at the Southern Junction, a triple line would lead southward to Broad Street. The line would be on a viaduct over a very congested part of the Inner Arc, and some 4,500 persons would be displaced. The NL Act of 1861 therefore included requirements to provide workmen's trains. Rehousing clauses in railway Acts were not introduced until 1874 and were not really enforced until after 1885. As with other lines, the NL's progress towards Central London resulted in even greater congestion and workmen's fares chiefly benefited the better-paid.

The extension was extremely costly. The LNW, interested in a City goods depot as well as passenger access, contributed heavily. To save on the cost of land, Broad Street Goods (closed 27 January 1969) was built on two levels. Passenger traffic began on 1 November 1865 and freight on 18 May 1868. The extension came to be called the 'happy after-thought', for passenger traffic soon doubled, reaching nearly 14 million in 1866. In 1871 quadrupling was completed between Camden Town and Dalston, and it was extended to Broad Street in 1874.

The train service now assumed the form it would retain almost unchanged for nearly fifty years. A fifteen-minute service ran from Broad Street over the Bow line, at first to Fenchurch Street and later diverted to Poplar. Another, also at fifteen-minute intervals, ran to Hampstead Road, calling at all stations, while yet a third service ran semi-fast to Camden, where connection was made with the stopping trains, before continuing over the Hampstead Junction to Willesden. From here trains alternately traversed the North & South Western Junction and the West London. The LNW ran local trains to Watford via Hampstead Road, but the short-lived 'City to

City' express from Wolverhampton (1910–15) was the only long-distance service. The only other major change came with the opening of the Canonbury Spur, which connected Broad Street with the GN. But that was a Cityward thrust by the latter and not a northward one by the NL.

By 1870 the area traversed by the NL's own line had been built over, and by 1890 so had that traversed by the HJ, while there had been much building beyond Willesden. The 14 million passengers of 1866 had become 32.7 million in 1880. Thereafter the rate of increase tapered off, but traffic increased until 1896, when 46.3 million were carried.

The NL had now reached its zenith, its traffic ceased to grow and its arteries hardened. Though an aesthetic joy, its little 4–4–0 tanks and their long rakes of four-wheeled coaches were ill equipped to face the coming electric century. To feature such a train on a poster of 1909 to counter the new Hampstead Tube was somewhat pathetic.

Tramway competition was mentioned at the General Meeting of February 1872, but from 1900 it assumed menacing proportions, particularly with electrification to Hampstead in 1906 and Stamford Hill in 1907. 'To compete with halfpenny tram fares is impossible', lamented the Chairman. Nor was the NL better able to counter the Hampstead Tube and the Metropolitan's newly electrified 'Extension'. At first the decline in receipts was more alarming

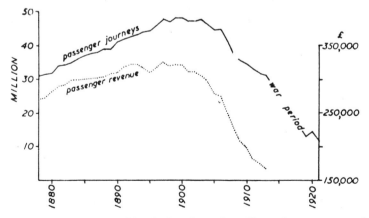

FIG 10 Disaster for the North London: the effect of tramway and Underground competition. (Based on company reports.)

than that in numbers. Between 1900 and 1905 passengers declined by 4 per cent, and revenue by 13.4 per cent, but after 1910 declining numbers became catastrophic. By 1913 numbers were but 44.6 per cent of the 1900 total and by 1921 only 23.3 per cent.

In 1909 a common management with the LNW was introduced and in 1922 the latter took over completely. The NL Board had always been hesitant over electrification, and when it was at last carried out west of Broad Street, it was as part of the LNW's scheme (Chapter VI). Unfortunately, except for a bare announcement that in 1921 there had been a 15 per cent increase in revenue consequent on electrification, absorption into the LNW completely obscured post-electrification trends. The truth, however, is that the North London Line never recovered its former glories. In the inter-war years it soldiered quietly on. There was little investment in stations or signalling. Passenger services were at frequent and regular intervals, and local and through freight traffic was considerable.

Broad Street, gaunt and depressing, stood high above street level. Originally there were seven platforms, but rearrangements in 1876 and 1891 increased the number under the two-arched roof to eight, and a ninth was added outside in 1913. In 1890 the station was extremely busy, with seventy-one arrivals and departures between 09.00 and 10.00 alone. In 1902, 27 million passengers used it, more than twice the Cannon Street total, and, in 1903, 102 trains arrived before 10.30, bringing in 40,000 passengers, second only to the Liverpool Street figure.

THE POST-WAR YEARS

The Richmond service remained the basic activity as others declined. On 14 May 1944 the Poplar service ceased. By 1960 only forty-one trains arrived at Broad Street between 07.00 and 10.00, with about 6,400 passengers, in melancholy contrast with Liverpool Street next door. Of these passengers, 2,500 came from the ex-GN lines in ten trains. Trains over the Canonbury Spur ceased in 1976 with the GN electrification (p. 170), while the Watford service operated only at peak periods after 1962.

Travel on the Richmond trains was redolent of decay, the large stations, with barn-like 'Italian Warehouse' buildings and war damage unrepaired until after 1965, had all been built to handle a traffic far in excess of contemporary numbers, and four were closed altogether. Without marked diurnal peaks, the service was reputedly among London's more profitable ones, but traffic declined after 1955. By early 1985 there were only 6,000 off-peak passenger journeys into and out of Broad Street per week and only 336 arrived daily in the morning peak. In 1963 the service was reduced to twenty-minute intervals and was among the few in London marked for the Beeching Axe. Strenuous opposition by local authorities along the route resulted in a ministerial reprieve, announced on 21 June 1965. A modest modernisation scheme was initiated in 1967.

It remained for the GLC, convinced by the 1974 Rail Study, to persuade British Rail of the potential of the line. The GLC supported the diversion from 15 May 1979 of North Woolwich trains to Camden Road. Meanwhile BR had ineptly proposed cutting back the Broad Street line to Worship Street, 600yd from the entrance to Liverpool Street Underground. Then electrification of the line eastward from Dalston and diversion of the Richmond trains to North Woolwich (p. 205) were authorised, and were inaugurated on 13 May 1985.

Between the now abolished Dalston Western Junction and Stratford, four GLC-financed stations were provided, on former sites at Dalston (Kingsland), Hackney Central and Homerton, and on a new site at Hackney Wick. Rail transport was thus restored to a part of London long deprived of it. The original building at Hackney Central has been sensitively restored for non-railway purposes to recall how remarkable the NL stations were.

This left only the peak Watford trains. Closure of Broad Street was agreed in June 1985 and demolition began in November. A solitary platform remained until the dual-voltage trains were finally diverted into Liverpool Street over the new Graham Road curve on 30 June 1986, the voltage change being made in the new Dalston (Kingsland) station.

In 1956, 81 eastbound freight trains passed daily onto the Hampstead Junction line, 24 of them originating in the Poplar area and some 50 in the ex-Great Eastern area. York

Way (Maiden Lane), London's first freightliner terminal, opened on 15 November 1965, but was closed in May 1968 and the traffic transferred to Willesden. The line experienced the usual decline in freight traffic, all the intermediate depots being closed in the 1960s and the line beyond Victoria Park Junction later abandoned. By 1986 there were some twenty-five westbound freight trains daily through Dalston (Kingsland). This and the need for stock transfer led in 1984 to authorisation of overhead alternating-current electrification from the West Coast Main Line at Primrose Hill to Stratford. By May 1985 the East Coast Main Line and West Coast Main Line had been connected by the conversion of the North London Incline and thence to Primrose Hill.

THE METROPOLITAN

During the 1850s the streets were jammed with slow-moving horse traffic, and a bus journey could be even more protracted than it is today. Schemes were propounded for railways to connect the northern termini and to bring the City within easy reach of northern and western suburbs. These finally reached fruition nurtured by Charles Pearson, a City solicitor and the father of the Metropolitan. On 15 August 1853 the North Metropolitan Railway was incorporated to build a 3.5 mile line from Paddington to Farringdon Street (now Farringdon). The City Corporation and the GW both subscribed, the latter, like all the other railway companies, being interested in access to the City.

By then the whole area was fully built up and the Metropolitan (as it became when reincorporated by Act of 7 August 1854) was necessarily built on the 'cut and cover' principle. Street lines were followed where possible to avoid demolishing property, a cutting being dug and later covered over by brick arches. But even so there was much destruction of slums on the northern edge of the City, the 'ill ventilated cul de sacs and dens of wretchedness in the vicinity of Shoe Lane and Saffron Hill' (T. Hammond, 1853). George Godwin, editor of *The Builder*, estimated in 1864 that 1,000 dwellings housing 12,000 persons were destroyed in making the open cuttings along the Fleet valley near Farringdon. Physical connection was made with the GW at Bishop's Road, adjoining the north side of Paddington. The eastern terminus was in part of the space vacated by the cattle market (p. 83), alongside the rebuilt Smithfield Market. The GW at once leased the latter's basement for a goods station (opened 3 May 1869, closed from 30 July 1962).

The GW had insisted on broad-gauge facilities, but were amenable to mixed-gauge. Construction was slow. The GW became impatient and its meddling led to cooling relations. Eventually the line was officially opened on 10 January 1963, being worked by the GW. In the first three weeks 29,000 passengers were carried, and traffic soon increased. The gas-lit rigid eight-wheelers rumbling beneath the London streets were a tremendous novelty and the fifteen-minute service made it a useful one. William Hardman gave a user's impression in his diary for 26 January 1863:

Yesterday Mary Anne and I made our first trip down the 'Drain'. We walked to Edgeware [sic] Road and took first class tickets for King's Cross (6d each). We experienced no disagreeable odour beyond the smell common to tunnels. The carriages hold ten persons, with divided seats, and are lighted by gas; they are also so lofty that a six footer may stand erect with his hat on.

Relations with the GW soon deteriorated further and the latter gave notice that it would cease working the line after 30 September. But on 1 August it peremptorily advanced the date to 10 August. Instead of capitulating, the Metropolitan obtained rolling stock from the GN. As the discomfited GW withdrew, the GN trains came down the newly completed King's Cross connection to start the next day's service and to maintain it until the Metropolitan's own stock was delivered.

On 1 October the GN began a regular through service to Farringdon, thus obtaining its foothold in the City. So delighted were the commuters on the first trains that they drank the station buffet dry celebrating. On the same day through trains from GW stations also started running.

The success of the Metropolitan was so immediate that the idea of a circular line connecting City and West End rapidly developed and was recommended by a Parliamentary Committee in 1863, when a minor 'Railway Mania' peculiar to London occurred. The first extension was of 0.75 miles to the more convenient Moorgate Street (now Moorgate) station opened on 23 December 1865. With a rail-head some 600yd from the Bank of England, traffic expanded fast. In 1865, 15 million ordinary and 5,498 season tickets were sold, but by 1875 sales had swollen to 43.6 million and 32,941 respectively. In that year the mighty GW issued a total of 36 million ordinary and 13,575 season.

Meanwhile the circular line, invariably known as the Inner Circle, was beginning to take shape. On 29 July 1864 two Acts authorised an extension from Paddington to South Kensington and another from Moorgate Street to Minories. On 1 October 1868 the line from Praed Street Junction (just east of Bishop's Road) was opened to Gloucester Road. An end-on junction with the District was made at South Kensington and this section was opened on 24 December, the day the District itself opened.

On 1 February 1875 trains from Moorgate Street began running into platforms 1 and 2 of the Great Eastern's Liverpool Street station. On 12 July a few yards of track were opened from Liverpool Street Junction into Bishopsgate (now Liverpool Street, on the Circle Line). The spur to the GE was used at irregular intervals until 1904. The last train was an Aylesbury–Yarmouth excursion, reputedly the longest trip ever made by a Metropolitan train.

The reeking soot-laden atmosphere of a steam-worked Underground has faded from memory, and the contemporary prints fail to convey it. Staff reputedly found beards useful as filters. As so often, E. L. Ahrons must be permitted the last word: 'In the old days they [the Metropolitan and the District] provided a sort of health resort for people who suffered from Asthma.'

The station interiors were magnificent, the cuttings being spanned by great glazed arches. The finest of all was perhaps Aldersgate Street (now Barbican) with its 80ft span over four tracks. Its glass disintegrated in the air-raids and the frame was taken down in 1955. Rebuilding has caused other roofs to go one by one, though portions remain at Paddington (formerly Praed Street) and Notting Hill. Rehabilitation at Baker Street has attempted to restore its original condition.

The bare bones of statistics are hard to clothe with flesh, and who, as opposed to how many, used the Metropolitan in mid-Victorian times is obscure. The Act for the Bishopsgate extension contained the usual provision for workmen, but the line was never a great carrier. The Doré prints of troglodytic gnomes condemned by a merciless capitalism to pour off Metropolitan trains on their way to sweated labour is probably incorrect, for, as usual, destruction of slum property merely led to greater congestion near-by. Besides, the line ran for such a short distance through the working-class area that the proletariat still walked. But on the other hand third class accounted for 74.7 per cent of all passengers carried in 1875. Did the crinolines crowding the platforms at Baker Street convey an equally incorrect picture?

THE WIDENED LINES

The connections with the GN at King's Cross consisted of two single-line tunnels, the East Branch, from the GN up side, and the Hotel Curve, to the down side. A west-facing connection from the East Branch was never in regular use and was taken out when the line from the Midland (opened 13 July 1868) was under construction. More importantly, a junction with the LCD was opened at West Street, hard by Farringdon, on 1 January 1866, and a triangular layout was completed on 1 September 1871 by a spur from Aldersgate Street.

Particularly as these connections formed the only north–south route across the City, the heavy passenger and freight traffic would be too much for the double track of the Metropolitan. A second pair of tracks, always known as the Widened Lines, was therefore provided by that company between King's Cross and Moorgate, burrowing under the Inner Circle at Ray Street, just west of Farringdon.

The Widened Lines, sanctioned in 1861, went into use between Farringdon and Barbican on 1 March 1866, being extended to Moorgate on 1 July and westward to King's Cross on 27 January 1868 for goods and 17 February for passengers. It was intended to extend even further west, but only a short tunnel was ever built. This lay unused until 15 March 1926, when a single-line connection was laid through it from the outer rail of the Circle to the eastbound Widened Line. This allowed eastbound Metropolitan trains to reach Moorgate without crossing the inner rail at that station. This practice, the only use by Metropolitan trains of the Widened Lines, ceased on 27 April 1935, the tunnel later being incorporated in the re-sited station of King's Cross (Metropolitan). Goods stations were opened by the GN at Farringdon on 2 November 1874 (closed 16 January 1956) and by the Midland at Whitecross Street (closed 1 March 1936). The Metropolitan opened one at Vine Street off the Circle lines 350yd north of Farringdon on 1 November 1909 (closed 1 July 1936). Wagons were electrically hauled from Finchley Road.

The LCD and the GN began a reciprocal through service on 1 January 1866. This was in addition to the latter's Moorgate service, while the former began running into Moorgate over the Barbican spur on 1 September 1871. The Midland ran trains to Moorgate from 13 July 1868 and through to the LCD from 1 June 1869. In the 1880s there were about 200 trains a day over the Widened Lines into Moorgate and 100 over the LCD link through Snow Hill. The latter ran from stations on the Northern Heights (Chapter VIII) and from Kentish Town to such destinations as Victoria, Herne Hill and Woolwich (via the SE). In 1902 there were 109 northbound trains through Snow Hill and, including those on the Inner Circle, 521 arrivals at Moorgate. A 1903 count revealed 9,887 passengers from GN stations arriving that day before 10.30, 7,018 from Midland stations, 4,816 from SE&C and 20,771 from Metropolitan.

But the great days of the Widened Lines were passing. By 1901 the City & South London Tube was operating through the City, while the new motor-buses and the Kingsway tram-tunnel were soon to speed up road journeys. The GN–SE&C service ceased from 1 October 1907 and its Midland counter-part from 1 July 1908. SE&C trains to Moorgate continued until 1 April 1916, after which the Snow Hill link was severed for regular passenger services and the Barbican spur abandoned.

The Moorgate services of the GN and Midland also suffered, partly from northward extensions of the C&SL, but mainly from the Great Northern & City Tube, which diverted GN passengers at Finsbury Park, and from trams. After World War I they ran in peak hours only. In 1930, 20 trains a day entered Moorgate from the ex-Midland line and 59 from the ex-GN, 19 of the latter coming from High Barnet. All traffic from High Barnet was diverted to the Northern Tube in 1940.

Kentish Town, King's Cross, Moorgate St., 228 Ludgate Hill, Clapham, & Victoria.

METROPOLITAN EXTENSION.—South Eastern and Chatham.

Up. — Week Days—*Continued below.*

Miles	Midland Station,	mn	mn	mn	mrn	mrn	mrn	f	mrn	mrn	mrn	d	mrn	a	mrn	f	mrn	mrn	b c	mrn	mrn	f	mrn	mrn
	Kentish Town.....dep.	...	...	...	3 cl. Workmen's Train.	Workmen's Train.	3 cl. Workmen's Train.	...	Workmen's Train.	....	6 14	7 3	....	7 29	....	7 48	....	8 3	8 20	8 29	....	8 39	....	8 48
—	York Road (G.N.) .. "	...	...	...				...		....	....	7 25	....	7 36	....	....	....	8 14	8 21	8 31	....	8 40	....	8 57
3	King's Cross (Met.).. "	...	...	...				...		....	6 46	7 28	....	7 39	....	....	....	8 17	8 27	8 37	....	8 46	....	9 4
4	Farringdon Street.. "	...	...	...				...		....	6 50	7 32	....	7 43	....	....	....	8 21	8 31	8 41	....	8 50	....	9 8
3¾	Moorgate Street... "	...	...	...				...		....	7 13	....	7 35	....	7 50	8 2	....	8 27	....	8 47	....	8 55	....	9 10
3¾	Aldersgate Street.. "	...	...	...				...		....	7 15	....	7 37	....	7 52	8 4	....	8 29	....	8 49	....	8 57	....	9 12
4½	Snow Hill............	...	...	...				...		....	7 17	7 35	7 39	7 46	7 54	8 6	8 12	8 31	8 34	8 51	....	8 59	9 8	9 15
—	Holborn Viaduct......							615		6e50	....	....	....	....	....	....	....	....	....	....	....	....	....	....
4¾	Ludgate Hill..........	245	315	415	5 0	5 48	6 0	618	6 47	6 56	7 21	7 37	7 43	7 53	7 58	8 11	8 16	8 35	8 39	8 55	9 1	9 5	9 11	9 23
—	St. Paul's.............	....	....	....	....	....	....	....	....	....	....	....	....	....	....	....	....	....	....	....	....	....	....	....
5¼	Borough Road........				5 5	....	6 4	...	....	7 1	7 25	....	7 47	7 58	8 4	....	8 20	....	8 43	9 0	9 6	....	....	9 29
6	Elephant and Castle...	250	319	419	5 7	5 52	6 6	623	6 51	7 3	7 27	....	7 49	8 0	8 6	8 16	8 22	8 41	8 45	9 3	9 9	9 12	9 18	9 32
6¼	Walworth Road........	253	322	422	5 10	5 55	6 9	626	6 54	7 6	7 30	....	7 52	8 3	8 9	....	8 25	8 44	8 48	9 6	9 12	....	9 21	9 35
7¼	Camberwell New Road..	256	325	425	5 13	5 58	6 12	629	6 57	7 9	7 33	....	7 55	8 6	8 12	....	8 28	8 47	8 51	9 9	9 15	....	9 24	9 38
8	Loughboro' Junction...	259	328	428	5 16	6 0	6 14	632	6 59	7 12	7 36	....	7 58	8 9	8 15	8 22	8 30	8 50	8 54	9 12	9 18	9 18	9 27	9 41
8¼	Brixton & S. Stockwell	3 2	...	...	5 19	6 3	6 17	...	7 2	7 15	7 39	....	8 1	8 14	8 19	....	8 33	8 53	8 57	9 15	9 22	....	9 30	9 44
9¼	Clapham & N. Stockwell	3 5	...	...	5 23	6 7	6 20	...	7 5	7 18	7 42	....	8 4	8 17	8 22	....	8 36	8 56	9 0	9 18	9 25	....	9 33	9 47
9¾	Wandsworth Road.....	3 7	...	...	5 26	6 10	6 23	...	7 7	7 20	7 44	....	8 6	8 20	8 24	....	8 38	8 58	9 2	9 20	9 27	....	9 35	9 49
—	Clapham Junc...arr.	...	...	...	....	....	....	...	....	....	....	....	....	....	8 29	....	....	9 5	....	....	....	....	....	9 54
10¾	Battersea Park Road...	310	...	...	5 29	6 13	6 26	...	7 10	7 23	7 47	....	8 9	8 23	....	....	8 41	....	9 5	9 23	9 30	....	9 38	....
11	Grosvenor Road........	314	...	...	5 32	6 18	6 29	...	7 12	7 25	7 49	....	8 11	8 25	....	....	8 43	....	9 7	9 25	9 34	....	9 40	....
11¼	Victoria..........arr.	317	...	...	5 39	6 21	6 34	...	7 17	7 30	7 54	....	8 16	8 30	....	....	8 48	....	9 12	9 30	9 36	....	9 45	....

Up. — Week Days—*Continued below.*

Midland Station,	mrn	mrn	d	mrn	b	mrn	mrn	a	mrn	b	a	mrn	b c	mrn	d	mrn	a	b	aft	aft	a	aft	aft	aft
Kentish Town dep	Except Saturdays.	9 9	....	9 25	9 52	....	9 58	1013	....	1042	1052	11 8	1132	....	....	1149	1149	1219	....	1236	....	1257	....	Sats. only.
York Rd. (G.N.) "		9 16	9 36	....	9 45	9 55	....	1020	1029	....	11 9	1118	....	....	1159	....	1211	1220	....	....	1256	....	....	
King's C. (Met.) "		9 19	9 39	9 32	10 1	9 58	10 7	1023	1032	1053	1112	1121	1139	....	12 2	1159	1214	1226	....	1243	1259	1 5	....	
Farringdon St.. "		9 23	9 43	9 36	10 5	10 2	1011	1027	1036	1057	1116	1125	1143	....	12 6	12 3	1218	1230	....	1247	1 3	1 9	....	
Moorgate St. .. "		9 27	....	9 45	....	10 7	1019	....	1042	....	....	1126	....	1155	....	12 8	....	....	1244	1252	....	1 13	1 24	
Aldersgate St.. "		9 29	....	9 47	....	10 9	1021	....	1044	....	....	1128	....	1157	....	1210	....	....	1246	1254	....	1 15	1 26	
Snow Hill.........		9 32	9 45	9 50	10 7	1011	1023	1029	1046	11 0	1119	1130	1145	1159	12 8	1212	1220	1232	1248	1256	1 5	1 18	1 28	1 36
Holborn Viaduct..		....	....	....	....	....	....	....	....	....	....	....	....	....	....	....	....	....	....	....	....	....	....	....
Ludgate Hill.....	9 33	9 37	9 48	9 55	1011	1016	1027	1033	1051	11 5	1123	1134	1150	12 3	1211	1216	1224	1236	1252	1 1	1 9	1 23	1 32	1 40
St. Paul's........	....	....	....	....	....	....	....	....	....	....	....	....	....	....	....	....	....	....	....	....	....	....	....	....
Borough Road	9 37	9 42	....	9 59	1015	1021	1031	1038	1055	11 9	1128	1139	1154	12 8	....	....	1229	1240	1257	1 6	1 13	1 28	1 36	1 45
Elephant & Castle.	9 39	9 44	....	10 1	1017	1023	1033	1040	1057	1111	1130	1141	1156	1210	....	1222	1231	1242	1259	1 8	1 15	1 30	1 38	1 47
Walworth Road...	9 42	9 47	....	10 4	1020	1026	1036	1043	11 0	1114	1133	1144	1159	1213	....	1225	1234	1245	1 2	1 11	1 18	1 33	1 41	1 50
Camberwell Nw Rd	9 44	9 50	....	10 7	1023	1029	1039	1046	11 3	1117	1136	1147	12 2	1216	....	1228	1237	1248	1 5	1 14	1 21	1 36	1 44	1 53
Loughboro' Junc..	9 47	9 53	....	10 9	1025	1032	1042	1049	11 6	1119	1139	1151	12 5	1219	....	1231	1240	1250	1 8	1 17	1 24	1 39	1 46	1 56
Brixton & S. S.....	9 50	9 56	....	1013	1028	1035	1045	1052	11 9	1121	1143	1153	1210	1222	....	....	1243	1253	1 11	Except Saturdays.	1 27	1 42	1 49	1 59
Clapham & N. S...	9 53	9 59	....	1016	1031	1038	1048	1055	1112	1124	1146	1156	1213	1225	....	....	1246	1256	1 14		1 30	1 45	1 52	2 2
Wandsworth Road	9 55	10 1	....	1018	1033	1040	1050	1057	1114	1126	1149	1158	1215	1227	....	....	1248	1258	1 16		1 32	1 47	1 55	2 4
Clapham Jn. arr.	....	....	....	....	....	1045	....	....	....	....	....	12 3	....	....	....	....	....	....	....		....	1 52	....	2 10
Battersea Park Rd.	9 58	10 4	....	1021	1036	....	1053	11 0	1117	1129	1151	....	1218	1230	....	....	1251	1 1	1 19		1 35	....	1 58	....
Grosvenor Road...	10 1	10 6	....	1023	1038	....	1055	11 2	1119	1131	1153	....	1220	1232	....	....	1253	1 3	1 21		1 37	....	2 0	....
Victoria......arr.	10 5	1011	....	1028	1043	....	11 0	11 7	1124	1136	1158	....	1225	1237	....	....	1258	1 8	1 26		1 42	....	2 5	....

Up. — Week Days—*Continued on page 229.*

Midland Station,	b	aft	a	aft	aft	d	aft	a	aft	aft	aft	a	b	d	aft	aft	aft	aft	b	a	aft	aft	a	aft	aft
Kentish Town dep	1 25	1 38	....	Saturdays only.	1 51	....	....	2 15	2 34	...	Sats. only.	2 53	3 17	....	...	Saturdays.	3 30	3 53	4 21	....	4 32	4 45	4 55	....	....
York Rd. (G.N.) "	....	1 27	1 52		1 59	2 23	....	2 32	....	...		3 9	....	333	...		3 53	4 14	....	4 33	4 39	4 52	5 8	5 12	5 22
King's C. (Met.) "	1 33	1 45	1 55		2 3	2 26	....	2 35	2 41	...		3 12	3 26	336	...		3 56	4 17	4 28	4 36	4 42	4 55	5 11	5 15	5 25
Farringdon St.. "	1 37	1 49	1 59		2 7	2 30	....	2 39	2 45	...		3 16	3 30	340	...		4 0	4 21	4 32	4 40	4 46	4 59	5 15	5 19	5 29
Moorgate St. .. "	....	1 52	....		2 12	....	2 33	....	2 47	3 5		....	....	....	340		4 5	4 26	....	....	4 53	5 4	....	5 26	5 34
Aldersgate St.. "	....	1 54	....		2 14	....	2 35	....	2 49	3 7		....	....	....	342		4 7	4 28	....	....	4 55	5 6	....	5 28	5 36
Snow Hill.........	1 39	1 56	2 2		2 16	2 32	2 37	2 42	2 52	3 9	3 12	3 19	3 34	342	345		4 9	4 30	4 34	4 43	4 57	5 8	5 17	5 30	5 38
Holborn Viaduct..	....	....	....		....	....	....	....	....	....	....	....	....	....	....		....	....	....	....	....	....	....	....	....
Ludgate Hill.....	1 44	2 0	2 7	2 16	2 21	2 35	2 40	2 46	2 56	313	3 17	3 22	3 39	345	350	4 2	4 15	4 34	4 38	4 47	5 1	5 11	5 20	5 34	5 42
St. Paul's........	....	....	....	....	....	....	....	....	....	....	....	....	....	....	....	....	....	....	....	....	....	....	....	....	....
Borough Road	1 49	2 4	2 12	....	2 26	....	....	2 51	3 0	317	3 21	3 26	3 43	...	355	4 6	4 19	....	4 43	4 52	5 6	....	5 25	5 38	....
Elephant & Castle.	1 51	2 6	2 14	2 21	2 28	....	2 44	2 53	3 2	319	3 23	3 28	3 45	...	357	4 8	4 21	....	4 45	4 55	5 8	....	5 27	5 40	5 45
Walworth Road...	1 54	2 9	2 17	2 24	2 31	....	2 47	2 56	3 5	322	3 26	3 31	3 48	...	4 0	411	4 24	....	4 48	4 58	5 11	....	5 30	5 43	5 48
Camberwell Nw Rd	1 57	2 12	2 20	2 27	2 34	....	2 50	2 59	3 8	325	3 29	3 34	3 51	...	4 3	414	4 27	....	4 51	5 1	5 14	....	5 33	5 46	5 51
Loughboro' Junc..	2 0	2 14	2 23	2 30	2 37	....	2 53	3 2	3 11	328	3 31	3 37	3 54	...	4 6	416	4 30	4 43	4 54	5 4	5 17	5 22	5 36	5 49	5 53
Brixton & S. S.....	2 3	2 17	2 28	....	2 40	....	2 56	3 6	3 14	331	3 34	3 40	3 57	...	4 9	...	4 33	4 47	4 57	5 7	5 20	5 25	5 39	5 52	5 56
Clapham & N. S...	2 6	2 20	2 31	....	2 43	....	2 59	3 9	3 17	334	3 37	3 43	4 0	...	412	...	4 36	4 50	5 0	5 10	5 23	5 28	5 42	5 55	5 59
Wandsworth Road	2 8	2 22	2 34	....	2 45	....	3 1	3 11	3 19	336	3 40	3 45	4 2	...	414	...	4 38	4 52	5 2	5 12	5 25	5 30	5 44	5 57	6 1
Clapham Jn. arr.	....	2 27	....	....	....	....	3 6	....	....	341	....	....	....	....	....	....	....	....	....	....	5 30	....	....	6 2	....
Battersea Park Rd.	2 11	....	2 37	....	2 48	....		3 14	3 22	...	3 43	3 48	4 5	...	417	...	4 41	4 54	5 5	5 15	....	5 33	5 47	....	6 4
Grosvenor Road...	2 13	....	2 39	....	2 50	....		3 16	3 26	...	3 47	3 50	4 7	...	419	...	4 43	4 56	5 7	5 17	....	5 35	5 49	....	6 6
Victoria......arr.	2 18	....	2 44	....	2 55	....		3 21	3 29	...	3 50	3 55	4 12	...	424	...	4 48	5 1	5 12	5 22	....	5 40	5 54	....	6 10

a Run through from King's Cross (G.N.) to Victoria; change at Aldersgate Street by other Trains. **b** Through Trains from Kentish Town on Midland Line. **c** Midland Trains, 1 & 3 class. **d** Through Trains from G. N. Line. **e** Except Mondays; starts from Snow Hill on Mondays. **f** Run to the Crystal Palace Line Platform at Loughboro' Junction, and the Main Line Platforms at Borough Road, Elephant and Castle, Walworth Road, and Camberwell New Road.

☞ For **other Trains** between Moorgate Street, Ludgate Hill, &c., and Loughborough Junction, see pages 230, 231, and 234, from Brixton and Clapham to Victoria, see pages 232 to 234. For L. & S. W. Trains from Ludgate Hill to Wandsworth Road, see page 128.

• Passengers from Metropolitan Line change at Aldersgate Street.

The former importance of the Metropolitan Extension of the LCD both as part of the north–south through route over the Widened Lines and for inner-suburban traffic is shown by this extract from *Bradshaw* of June 1904. Before they were killed by competition from Tubes and trams, services were intensive, routes complex and stations closely spaced.

Suspended during World War II for long periods, an even sparser service was restored in 1945. By 1960 there were 16 trains from the GN and 2 from the Midland. The Eastern Region introduced diesel traction in 1959 and the London Midland Region shortly after. The ER trains ceased from 7 November 1976 with the GN electrification (Chapter VIII) and the Hotel and East curves closed. The LMR trains ceased temporarily on 14 May 1979 to allow electrification.

Apart from the brief period for which it operated the Metropolitan, the GW also used the line for through trains, for Paddington was so remote that it would otherwise have been impossible to build up suburban traffic. The last broad-gauge trains ran on 14 March 1869. Eventually the GW's narrow-gauge trains were extended to Liverpool Street. From the 1907 electrification Metropolitan locomotives hauled GW coaches eastward from Bishop's Road. In the 1930s there were five eastbound morning trains and two westbound evening ones. They ran for the last time on 15 September 1939. There is now no physical connection between the Western Region and London Regional Transport at Paddington.

TABLE 7

THE PEAK WITHIN THE PEAK —

PASSENGERS LEAVING SELECTED STATIONS

Station	Census date	Evening peak				Off-peak
		17.01–17.15	17.16–17.30	17.31–17.45	17.46–18.00	18.46–19.00
Liverpool Street	4 Oct '60	7,612	12,960	12,887	10,216	712
Fenchurch Street	4 Oct '60	2,300	2,429	2,666	2,174	549
Baker Street	Nov '59	1,943	1,881	2,953	2,223	474
Moorgate	Nov '59	2,686	2,547	3,350	2,079	340

Moorgate was the largest Metropolitan station, with two Circle platforms and four bays, two electrified, and the two Great Northern & City (now BR) ones below. During a census in November 1959, 15,465 passengers entered the station between 16.30 and 19.00, 3,350 of them between 17.31 and 17.45.

The Widened Lines remained a vital north–south freight

link. The 1951 British Transport Commission Committee on Electrification reported an average of fifty-one southbound trains daily and the Farringdon banker was kept busy assisting trains up to Ludgate Hill. But the constant decline in freight traffic during the 1960s led to eventual closure of the Snow Hill link. The last regular train, a parcels, ran on 23 March 1969; the rails were lifted in 1972.

But the long decline of the route was to be reversed. In 1983 alternating-current electric trains from Luton began running to Moorgate. The GLC, in pursuance of its public-transport improvement policy, funded a feasibility study on the re-opening of the Snow Hill link. The result, together with the success of dual-voltage stock on the GN electrification, convinced even the British Railways Board. In 1986 the 660yd of track were relaid for what would be marketed as the 'Thames Link'. With some trains in 1987, the full service will be running in May 1988, with 6 trains an hour, 2 each from Bedford, Luton and West Hampstead to Gatwick (2), Sanderstead (2), Orpington (1) and Sevenoaks (1). At the time of writing plans are afoot for the restoration of the King's Cross link, possibly on a level to allow Inter-City trains; the complete bypassing and closure of Holborn Viaduct; the emergence of the line *south* of Ludgate Hill; and an Inter-City role for Blackfriars.

THE DISTRICT

The southern part of the Inner Circle, from Minories to South Kensington, was allocated to a new company, incorporated on 29 July 1864. This was the METROPOLITAN DISTRICT Railway, invariably known as the District, to distinguish it from its neighbour. Also built on the 'cut and cover' method, the first section was opened between South Kensington and Westminster Bridge on 24 December 1868. The section thence to Blackfriars went into service on 30 May 1870 and on to Mansion House on 3 July 1871.

All parties assumed that the District would be absorbed by the Metropolitan, and to an impartial observer such a measure would appear a necessity to ensure efficient working of the Inner Circle. It was a curious parallel with the relations between the SE and the East Kent (see Vol 2, Chapter 3), and the only rational explanation of subsequent events was that the two Boards were bent on re-enacting these.

In 1866 the Metropolitan agreed to work the District for 45 per cent of the takings, but the latter regarded this as unsatisfactory and gave a year's notice to terminate the agreement from 1 July 1871. The Metropolitan Directors resigned from the District Board and none other than J. S. Forbes, General Manager of the LCD, was invited to join. In 1872 he became Chairman. The Metropolitan, in the throes of financial crisis, turned to Forbes's inveterate antagonist, Sir Edward Watkin, Chairman of the SE and already known for his dislike of Forbes. A character sketch of these men appears in Vol 2, pp. 42–3.

THE INNER CIRCLE

The bad farce being played out among the Kentish fields was now transferred to the sulphurous catacombs beneath the London streets. But, though respectively controlled by two personal enemies, the two London companies were locked in indissoluble wedlock sealed by the ring of the Inner Circle.

Even before Watkin's advent, the Metropolitan had, until only a week before the District take-over of their own working, refused to countenance the obvious, both companies' trains operating over the other portion of the Circle. The revenue during the early 1870s was disappointing for the District and an amalgamation was sought with the Metropolitan. The latter now resisted the move, urged on by Watkin, waiting as over-confidently for the District to collapse as for the LCD.

Meanwhile the Circle remained uncompleted between Liverpool Street and Mansion House, 1.5 miles. Powers were in existence and public clamour was loud, but the Metropolitan delayed completion by every means possible and the District consistently dragged its feet. Eventually a Metropolitan Inner Circle Completion Railway Company was floated by City interests and incorporated on 7 August 1874. The Metropolitan was compelled to complete to Aldgate, opened on 18 November 1876. But capital for the independent company was not forthcoming, as a result of Watkin's intrigues, the *Railway News* feeling on sufficiently safe ground to accuse him openly.

Plate 17   This muddy rural road is Finchley Road at Golders Green. Land values are rising in anticipation of the arrival of the Tube. (*London Transport Board*)

Plate 18   The same scene in about 1926. Surburban development has been triggered by the Tube extension. (*London Transport Board*)

Plate 19   The first train (19 November 1923) from Hendon Central, on the Edgware line left from now-forgotten rural surroundings. (*London Transport Museum*)

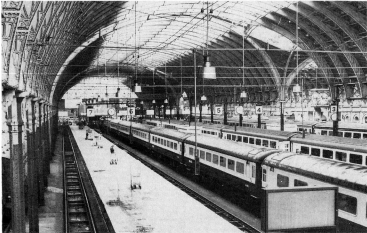

Plate 20 Brunel's original terminus was in the arches of the Bishop's Road overbridge on the far outskirts of London. (*National Railway Museum*)

Plate 21 'A unique work of art', Brunel and Wyatt's roof of the 1854 station survives to echo the exhausts of HSTs. (*Allan C. Mott*)

Plate 22 A turning point in the Paddington story. The last broad-gauge train for Cornwall leaves on 20 May 1892. (*National Railway Museum*)

But even Watkin realised that he must eventually give way and on 11 August 1879 the Royal Assent was given to the Metropolitan & District (City Lines and Extensions) Act. This provided for the taking over jointly of the Completion Company's powers. Parliament, well aware of the nonsensical rivalry of the two companies, laid statutory obligations on them to maintain the Circle service.

The Metropolitan now rushed the completion of its works and opened the line from Aldgate to Tower Hill (closed 1884, reopened on a new site 1967) on 25 September 1882. Watkin delayed work on the joint line by getting the SE to raise difficulties about the passage under Cannon Street station, but these moves failed, and the Metropolitan was forced to sell a half-share in the Aldgate extension to the District and failed to saddle the latter with half the deficit involved through premature opening. The City Lines were opened on 6 October 1884. At last the Inner Circle (13.25 miles) was one in fact as well as in name.

The rivals bickered on, first over the interpretation of the City Lines Act with regard to interest charges, a round won by the Metropolitan. Then in 1885 there was a dispute over through bookings from stations on the City Lines and on the Tilbury (via Fenchurch Street and Mark Lane) to South Kensington in connection with an exhibition. This spread to other bookings and lasted until 1888, the District emerging partially victorious.

The District, without statutory authority, built 11 chains of double line on its own land to allow through running alongside Metropolitan metals from Gloucester Road to High Street Kensington. The motive was to divert its Inner Circle trains over this, the 'Cromwell Curve', to gain extra mileage. But, to use the curve, trains on the inner rail had to cross the outer one twice. The practice was indefensible and lasted only from 1 October to 10 November 1884, but the dispute dragged on until 1903, when the courts ruled that the Cromwell Curve was not part of the Inner Circle and thus that the District could not claim mileage for using it.

TRAIN SERVICES ON THE INNER CIRCLE

The Inner Circle filled a social need, providing inter-terminal

connections, transport from the residential areas of Paddington and Kensington to Central London, and rapid communication between City and West End. Thus most of its traffic
was local. But the great increases which came over the years
were mainly from suburban services coming on to the Circle
from extensions of the two companies. Thus, while there has
always been a basic circular service, these trains have by no
means been the only ones using the Circle.

In 1875, 43.6 million ordinary tickets were sold by the
Metropolitan and 25.9 million by the District. Ten years later
the figures were 67.3 million and 38.9 million respectively,
while in 1895 they were 73.7 million and 40.9 million, with a
further million at the City Lines stations. Between 1875 and
1895 season-ticket journeys over the District increased from
1.5 million to 4.4 million.

By 1903 an average of 28,800 passengers a day were
arriving at Moorgate from Metropolitan stations before 10.30.
At Mansion House the equivalent figures were 17,000 from
stations to the west and 6,000 from those to the east, while 381

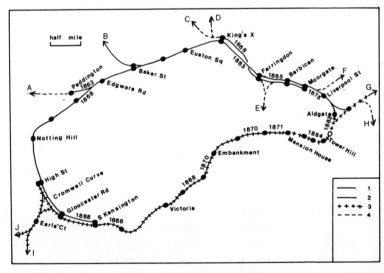

FIG 11 The Inner Circle and its connections: 1 Metropolitan;
2 District; 3 Metropolitan & District Joint (City Lines); 4 main-line
connections; A Hammersmith; B Finchley Road; C Midland;
D Great Northern; E Ludgate Hill; F Great Eastern; G Whitechapel; H East London Line; I Putney Bridge; J Hammersmith.

trains were arriving each day. The Inner Circle was choked with traffic, delays were frequent and extra peak-hour trains on the District impossible. But at the same time it was beginning to suffer competition from tram and bus, while Tube promotion was causing anxiety.

Watkin had retired in 1894 and the breach with the District was slowly healing. But the Forbes influence was stultifying. Because of him the District was reluctant to modernise, and the Metropolitan was unable to pursue an independent course, though they did obtain electrification powers in 1882. By 1900 both were suffering severely from hardening of the arteries. Stock was antediluvian and operating methods had not changed since the 1870s. 'Sewer rats' was the City's name for commuters coming in by Inner Circle and Widened Lines.

But in 1900 the two companies combined to equip the line between Earl's Court and High Street with direct-current traction on the fourth-rail system. An experimental shuttle service was operated for six months, but later the Metropolitan espoused the Ganz of Hungary system of overhead electrification at 3,300V ac.

By then a new figure had appeared, Charles Tyson Yerkes, an American financier. United States money was available for investment in British railways when native capital was short and Yerkes was over to see what fields there were to conquer. Through Sir Robert Perks, a solicitor with District interests, he secured control of that company in 1901. He represented the new century better than Forbes, who was forced to resign his position as Chairman. He died in 1904 and the *Railway Times* wrote an epitaph: 'It is doubtful whether any company, in the long run, benefited materially from his services.'

Yerkes backed fourth-rail direct current, a method already widely used for suburban electrification in the United States. The Metropolitan was unwillingly forced to conform. The first regular service was on the Harrow & Uxbridge Line, but on 1 July 1905 the District inaugurated an electric service between Ealing and Whitechapel, using the southern section of the Circle. By 24 September all the Circle steam trains had been replaced and by 5 November, with the conversion of the Hammersmith & City service, virtually all passenger trains over the Circle were electric.

Electrification brought new life, and took place sufficiently

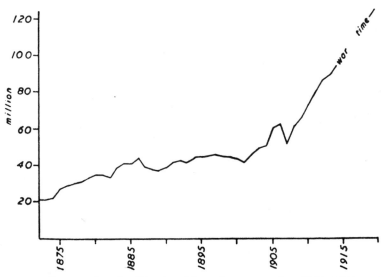

FIG 12 Success for the District. Note the stagnation 1885–1901 and the expansion in the years following 1903–5 electrification. (Based on Board of Trade railway returns. No returns were made during World War I. After 1920 the returns are merged in London Electric Railways.)

early to meet the growing competition. But though traffic figures rose over the critical years between 1905 and 1914 it must be remembered that the period was also one of route extensions and increased building in the outer suburbs. Traffic on the District had tended to stagnate between 1885 and 1901, but from then until 1905, for the reasons just given, passenger journeys (including those of season-ticket holders) climbed from 42.2 million to 51.5 million. In 1908 they reached 61.1 million, an increase of 18.8 per cent occurring over the first three years of electrification.

In 1985 the southern part of the Circle was one of the busiest sections of the LRT system, especially in peak hours. Between 07.00 and 10.00, 30,800 eastbound passengers were conveyed between Sloane Square and Victoria on a typical day. Between 10.00 and 16.00 the number was 26,500. This section has twenty-four trains per hour on each rail, increasing to thirty-six in the peak hour. On the northern section, east of Baker Street peak-period traffic is also heavy, 27,300 eastbound passengers between 07.00 and 10.00. But this falls away off-peak, 16,400 being recorded between 10.00 and 16.00. These are conveyed by a basic service of eight circle and eight Hammersmith trains an hour each way. At peaks this is augmented by services to and from the 'Extension' between Baker Street and the City and thirty-two trains an hour pass King's Cross each way.

THE EAST LONDON LINE

Between 1824 and 1843 Marc Brunel (father of Isambard) built a pedestrian tunnel under the Thames between Wapping and Rotherhithe. A remarkable feat for its time, it was little used and in 1865 the East London Railway was incorporated to take it over as part of a rail route linking the GE with the LBSC and the SE.

This was opened on 7 December 1869 from Wapping to New Cross (LBSC) (now New Cross Gate), where there was a separate station until 1886, the East London trains thereafter using the easternmost platform of the Brighton's station. On 13 March 1871 a spur was opened (closed 1 June 1911) from Rotherhithe to the South London Line at Old Kent Road. On 1 April 1880 spurs were provided to both sides of the SE at its New Cross station. Meanwhile on 10 April 1876 the northern end had been extended from Wapping to Shoreditch, where there was a junction with the GE to allow running into Liverpool Street.

The LBSC worked a service from the start, eventually running between Liverpool Street and Croydon. On 1 April 1880 the SE inaugurated one from Addiscombe to Liverpool Street. From 1876 to 1884 there were some trains between Liverpool Street and Brighton, but these were never popular.

The 1879 City Lines Act authorised a connection from the Inner Circle to the East London. This was to be owned jointly by the Metropolitan and the District and was to start at a triangular junction at Aldgate to a point just south of Whitechapel (East London) station. In 1884 the north curve at Aldgate was vested solely in the Metropolitan. On 6 October 1884 both companies started through services to New Cross and New Cross Gate, the SE withdrawing its trains. In 1886 the GE started running its trains. After electrification of the Circle, the Metropolitan and the District withdrew their trains.

In 1913 fourth-rail electrification of the East London was completed between Shoreditch and the New Cross stations. The Metropolitan now provided all the trains, running through from South Kensington via Baker Street and later from Hammersmith, using stock jointly owned with the GW. Since 1941 the connection at Whitechapel has been unused except for stock transfer. The line now has a self-contained service between New Cross/New Cross Gate and White-chapel, extended to Shoreditch at peaks. In recent years new stock has been provided and some cosmetic work has been done on the Underground stations, which still remain gloomy and primitive.

The line is the second of the four north–south cross-London connections, but its importance has always been limited as the northern junction faced Liverpool Street. By 1960 there were one parcels and three freight trips to New Cross Gate and occasional seaside and football excursions. But it ceased to function as a through route after 17 April 1966.

The line had a complex history of ownership and management but was finally vested in London Transport after nationalisation.

CHAPTER V

The Tubes

The steam-operated urban lines had failed to divert much of the rapidly growing traffic that threatened to choke the Central London streets and which led to the 1905 Royal Commission on Locomotion in London. In 1901 the Greater London railways carried between them 357 million local passengers, while there were 811 million journeys by horse-tram and bus. But the Inner Circle and other lines were working to capacity and some more efficient means of urban transport was needed.

'Cut and cover' had become much too costly. Deep tunnels or 'Tubes' bored without disturbance to buildings and mains services were the only answer. Their success depended on a favourable combination of circumstances: the soft but water-tight London Clay; the invention by J. H. Greathead, a South African engineer, of a 'shield' which made boring a tube through the clay economic; the perfecting of electric traction, the only possible mode; and the availability of capital for works which even in 1900 would cost over £250,000 a mile.

THE CITY & SOUTH LONDON

London's first tube was the Tower Subway beneath the Thames, opened in 1870 and built by Peter Barlow, assisted by Greathead. A small cable-car on 450yd of 2ft 6in track was used at first, but the tunnel soon became a footway. This was closed in 1894 when Tower Bridge was opened. The Tower Subway was followed by numerous schemes, notably for providing Waterloo with better access to the West End. But capital was not forthcoming until Greathead floated the City of London & Southwark Subway Company, which obtained

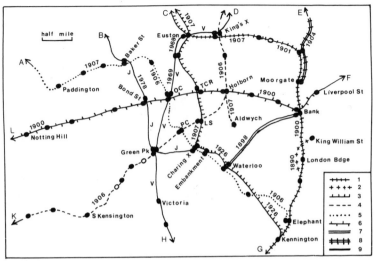

FIG 13 Deep-level Tubes in Central London: 1 City & South London; 2 City & South London (abandoned); 3 Charing Cross, Euston & Hampstead; 4 GN, Piccadilly & Brompton; 5 Baker Street and Waterloo; 6 Central London; 7 Waterloo & City; 8 GN & City; 9 London Transport; OC Oxford Circus; TCR Tottenham Court Road; LS Leicester Square; PC Piccadilly Circus; A Queen's Park; B Finchley Road; C Camden Town; D Finsbury Park; E Finsbury Park; F Stratford; G Morden; H Brixton; K Hammersmith; L Shepherd's Bush; J Jubilee Line; V Victoria Line.

powers in 1884 for a cable-worked tube from King William Street in the City to the Elephant & Castle. Work started on the 1.25 mile line in 1886.

It was soon decided that a 1.75 mile extension to Stockwell was necessary and powers were obtained in 1887. In the following year the Directors announced that electric traction would be used. An 1890 Act authorised a short extension to Clapham Common, a focus of routes from the outer suburbs. By the same Act the Company became the City & South London Railway.

Public service began on 18 December 1890 between King William Street and Stockwell. The gauge was standard, but north of Elephant the tunnel diameter was only 10ft 2in, and it was only 4in wider to the south. There were four intermediate stations and at first a flat fare of 2d was charged. Though this was soon abandoned, one class remained characteristic of the tubes. In contrast first class on the Circle lasted until 1940.

King William Street proving inconvenient, powers were obtained for a northward extension, diverting at Borough, to Angel. This opened to Moorgate on 25 February 1900, the King William Street appendix being closed. The Clapham Common extension went into service on 3 June 1900 and on 17 November 1901 the line to Angel was opened. In 1903 an extension to Euston via King's Cross was authorised and it was opened on 12 May 1907, bringing the route mileage to 7.25.

On the first day in 1890, 10,000 passengers passed the King William Street turnstiles, and by early in the following year 15,000 a day were using the line. In 1901, 13.4 million were carried over 6.9 miles of route, and, in 1911, 26.2 million over the full length. In 1905 the District, with 18 route miles and running powers over as much again, carried 51.5 million. But road competition was keeping c&sl fares low and dividends remained disappointing.

Diminutive locomotive-hauled trains of cars, dubbed 'padded cells', were used until the whole line was rebuilt between 1922 and 1924 to allow standard Tube stock to run through over the new connections with the Hampstead Tube at Camden Town and Kennington. The line now forms an integral part of the Northern Line.

THE CENTRAL LONDON

Shepherd's Bush is a traffic node on the west of Central London similar to Clapham Common in the south. There were a number of projects to connect it by tube with the City along the busy artery of Oxford Street. The Central London was the victor and was incorporated on 5 August 1891 to build a line from Wood Lane, just beyond Shepherd's Bush, to the Bank. In the following year a short extension to Liverpool Street was authorised.

On 30 July 1900 the Shepherd's Bush–Bank section opened, with extensions to Wood Lane on 14 May 1908 and to Liverpool Street on 28 July 1912. Locomotives were first used, but the vibration caused their replacement by multiple units, the universal method of Tube operation ever since. For the first few years a flat fare was charged, and for decades it remained the 'Twopenny Tube' to Londoners. In 1901, the first full year of working, 41.2 million passengers were carried, and 44 million in 1904. It was a more profitable venture than the c&sl.

The initial success of the c&sl initiated a wave of Tube promotion. The Central London's Bill was presented in 1891 and in the following year there were a further six. The one incorporating the Charing Cross, Euston & Hampstead Railway received Royal Assent on 24 August 1893.

Subscriptions for the Hampstead Tube were slow coming in and no progress was made until Yerkes bought the powers in 1900 for £100,000. R. D. Blumenfeld, editor of the *Daily Express*, remarked that Yerkes believed that by 1920 people would travel 20 or more miles to work by electric train and that the horse-bus was doomed. Blumenfeld added: 'Although he is a very shrewd man, I think he is a good deal of a dreamer.'

From now on we are in the familiar world of the holding company and the takeover bid. On 15 July 1901 Yerkes founded the Metropolitan District Electric Traction Company with money from Speyer Brothers, a New York finance house. Through this company the District and the Hampstead Tube were controlled and in 1902 it was reconstituted as the Underground Electric Railways Company of London.

Work on the Hampstead began in September 1903, the tunnels with a bore of 11ft 8¼in, the Tube standard. It opened to public traffic throughout from Strand (now Charing Cross) to Golders Green, together with a branch from Camden Town to Highgate (now Archway), on 23 January 1907. The line emerged into daylight to terminate in the fields bordering the Finchley Road. Most observers were unconvinced of the wisdom of this objective, but a syndicate had already bought up the turnip fields before the announcement of the new line had affected land values. Thus Golders Green was the archetype of the pattern of twentieth-century suburban development: the arrival of an electric railway in hitherto untouched rural Arcady; soaring land values; semi-detached villas; and chain stores.

In 1908, 2.4 million passengers used Golders Green station and the population of Hendon Urban District was 29,000. In 1921, 12.76 million people passed through the station and Hendon now housed 56,000. After that passenger use levelled off (and it was down to 6.5 million in 1986), but consequent on the Tube extensions of 1923–4 the population of Hendon grew to 72,000. The 1961 figure was 151,500. Golders Green is typical of the tube extension stations in that its forecourt became a terminus of local bus routes, but full integration of bus and rail was in the distant future.

On 6 April 1914 the short extension from Strand (now Charing Cross) to Charing Cross (now Embankment) was opened to increase interchange facilities with the District and Bakerloo Lines. In 1959 exchange traffic amounted to 30.9 million out of a total usage of 49 million. On 20 April 1924 the connection with the c&sl at Camden Town went into use with its complex, non-conflicting junctions. On 13 September 1926 a southward extension from Charing Cross through Waterloo linked with the c&sl at Kennington, and on the same day the 5 mile line from Clapham Common to Morden opened.

The two Tube lines were now completely integrated, though the c&sl Company survived until 1932, and they became the Morden–Edgware Line, acquiring the present designation of Northern Line in 1937.

THE BAKERLOO

One of the origins of the Bakerloo was the wish of Westminster businessmen to enjoy the last hour's cricket at Lord's without leaving their offices unduly early. There was, besides, an urgent need for north–south connections across the West End. To meet this the Baker Street & Waterloo was incorporated on 28 March 1893 to build a 3 mile line. Waterloo would at last be in direct contact with the West End, but the lsw did not back the project as it did the Waterloo & City. As yet the West End was not an important commuter goal. At Baker Street there would be interchange with the Metropolitan's 'Extension', offering passengers on that line more direct access to the West End.

Money was short and work began only in 1898. On 6 August 1900 powers were obtained for extensions to Paddington and to the Elephant, 1 mile in each case. But in January 1901 the London & Globe Finance Corporation, which had largely financed the scheme, failed. The works lay derelict until Yerkes bought the interests for £360,000 in 1902.

On 10 March 1906 the section between Baker Street and Kennington Road (now Lambeth North) was officially opened and the short Elephant extension came into use on 5 August. At first traffic was disappointing, only 20,000–30,000 passengers a day, but it eventually picked up.

In contrast with the Northern Line there have been no further southward extensions, though local authorities have urged one to Camberwell and Lewisham. In 1960 the matter was referred to the Transport Users' Consultative Committee, who reported adversely on the grounds of declining population and adequate bus and BR services. This latter would not have been endorsed by local residents.

The northern end was extended to Marylebone on 17 March 1907 and to Edgware Road on 15 June. Paddington was not reached until 1 December 1913, by which time the Tubes and the Inner Circle served all main-line termini except Holborn Viaduct and Fenchurch Street and, save in Clerkenwell, no part of Central London was more than 400yd from an Underground station.

G. H. F. Nichols of the *Evening News* coined the line's title and it has been the 'Bakerloo' ever since. G. A. Sekon, who disliked the American invasion of London's transport, inveighed vainly against the word in the *Railway Magazine*: '. . . some latitude is allowable perhaps to halfpenny papers . . . [but] to adopt its gutter title is not what we would expect from a railway company'. One wonders what he would have said about 'BedPan' (p. 160).

THE PICCADILLY

The Brompton & Piccadilly Circus Railway was incorporated on 6 August 1897 for a 2.75 mile line from Piccadilly to Earl's Court. At the same time the District, for which some humorist in the advertising department had coined the title the 'Daylight Route', its sulphurous murk becoming ever more congested, obtained powers for a deep-level electric line between Earl's Court and Mansion House. In 1899 the smaller company was empowered to make connection, but nothing further developed.

The Great Northern & Strand Railway was incorporated on 1 August 1899 to construct a tube from Wood Green (now Alexandra Park) station via Finsbury Park to a terminus under the Strand at King's College. The GN's benevolent interest stopped short of financial aid. Like the LSW, it was more concerned with the greater prize of the City.

In 1901 both tube companies came under the control of the Yerkes group, which sought powers to connect them physically and to abandon the section beyond Finsbury Park. On 8 August 1902 they merged and by Act of 18 November became the Great Northern, Piccadilly & Brompton legally and the Piccadilly for everyday use. The same Act authorised transfer of the District's deep-level powers west of South Kensington. The Piccadilly opened throughout from Finsbury Park to Hammersmith at a formal ceremony on 15 December 1906. Junction tunnels were built at South Kensington, but electrification of the District rendered them redundant.

The merging of the original scheme left a curious vestigial appendix in the last 0.25 mile of the GN & Strand between Holborn and Aldwych (Strand to 1915). Opened on 30 November 1907, it has always been worked by a shuttle service of a single two-car train. Used in World War II as an air-raid shelter, it reopened on 1 July 1946 for peak hours only. Since then users have declined from about 1 million annually to 400,000 in 1986.

THE GREAT NORTHERN & CITY

The GN&C originated in yet another effort by the Great Northern to develop suburban traffic north of Finsbury Park while reducing congestion to the south (Chapter VIII). It was in effect a Cityward thrust by the GN in the same way as the Waterloo & City was by the LSW.

The company was incorporated on 28 June 1892 to build from a junction on the Canonbury Curve (Chapter VIII) to Moorgate. Through running was envisaged (a scheme realised eighty-four years later), the tunnels being 16ft in diameter. The interested parties fell out over through running. Quarrels were resolved but the junction was not proceeded with. Instead the GN built a terminus under its Finsbury Park station, leasing it to the GN&C.

The line was opened on 14 February 1904, and 306,992 passengers were carried in the first fortnight, a figure regarded as satisfactory. Lack of through running was always regretted but traffic increased after 31 December 1904, when the GN introduced 'three-route' seasons from suburban stations available to Moorgate via the GN&C or the Widened Lines or to Broad Street.

Anxious to strengthen its position, the Metropolitan took over the line from 1 July 1913. Large-size stock was used until 13 May 1939, when standard tube stock took over. From 4 October 1964 services were cut back at Drayton Park, the tracks beyond being taken over by the Victoria Line, greatly reducing the line's utility. On 28 February 1975 the worst accident ever experienced on London Transport lines occurred when a train ran into Moorgate at high speed and piled up into the short dead-end tunnel beyond. The line then closed to allow conversion for use by BR, which had taken it over. New connections were built from Drayton Park, where the change-over from third-rail direct current to overhead alternating current takes place, up to Finsbury Park. On 8 November 1976 the GN&C was at last linked into the main-line system.

THE VICTORIA AND JUBILEE LINES

The Victoria line originated in the grandiose planning schemes for London during and immediately after World War II. The British Transport Commission was asked by the Minister of Transport to examine the rail proposals, and a London Plan Working Party was set up in 1948. It suggested the building of 49.25 miles of tube (the total then in operation was 66.75) as a first priority. These were in five 'routes' and 'Route C' became the Victoria Line.

This was planned to run from Walthamstow to Victoria via King's Cross. Its purposes were to put north-east London on the one hand and Victoria on the other in closer touch with the West End; to supplement the overcrowded Central Line; and above all to divert more traffic from the streets. In 1955 London Transport obtained sanction, but claimed that the expected traffic would not cover the interest payable; that the line was a social necessity; and that the Government should guarantee the interest charges. This the Government was reluctant to do, its policy being to count the economic cost and not the social benefits of public transport. But on 20 August 1962 it provided financial support and work soon started.

The Victoria Line opened from Walthamstow to Highbury on 1 September 1968, to Warren Street on 3 November and on to Victoria on 7 March 1969. With 75 per cent grant-aid under the 1968 Transport Act the Victoria Line was pushed on to Brixton, opening on 23 July 1971.

Traffic built up fast and the Victoria Line became the busiest LT line. In 1985 an average of 20,400 northbound passengers were conveyed during the busiest hour between Victoria and Green Park. Off-peak loads are also heavy; the 29,400 passengers between 10.00 and 16.00 were exceeded only by the 31,100 between Holborn and Chancery Lane on the Central.

The principal feature is the high degree of automation. The Victoria Line trains are driverless and in the charge of an 'attendant'. Only one of its sixteen stations has no interchange facilities with other LT and BR lines, while there is cross-platform exchange at five stations, including Oxford Circus (with the Bakerloo), Highbury (with BR) and Finsbury Park (with the Piccadilly).

The JUBILEE LINE, opened officially on 30 April 1978 between Baker Street and Charing Cross, also had its origins in the 1948 London Plan Working Party. It eventually crystallised as the Fleet Line, to traverse the West End, Fleet Street and the City to Fenchurch Street, the latter still without tube interchange. Beyond, it was to provide infrastructure for a dockland revival and was to end in Lewisham using the Thames Tunnel. The high cost east of Fenchurch Street led to alternative schemes. Work started in 1971, but ended at Charing Cross and powers to extend to Fenchurch Street were allowed to lapse on 31 December 1982.

UNDERGROUND

Up to 1914, with the exception of Golders Green and of Kensington to Hammersmith, the Tubes' basic function was urban rather than suburban. Each line maintained a 'rapid transit' shuttle service beneath city streets for short-distance passengers. Extensions between 1920 and 1960 converted them into suburban railways with characteristic vast commuter peaks which, superimposed on existing urban traffic, brought new operating problems. The original Central Line ran for 6.5 miles beneath crowded streets from Shepherd's Bush to the Bank. It is now possible to board a tube train at Ongar, a small Essex market-town, and travel 38 miles by Central Line to the western outpost of Greater London, West Ruislip.

Yerkes died on 4 December 1905, and Edgar Speyer of Speyer Brothers succeeded him as Chairman of Underground Electric. But there was a surprise appointment as deputy and general manager (and also Chairman of the District) of Sir George Gibb, general manager of the mighty North Eastern. It was proof that the Yerkes group was more than a collection of bankrupt local lines.

There was also a new star in the ascendant, perhaps the greatest of all the personalities connected with London railways, Albert Stanley, Lord Ashfield, the real creator of London Transport. Stanley was born Albert Knattries at Derby in 1874 of parents en route from Central Europe to the USA. He returned to England in 1907 as Albert Stanley to become general manager of the District after a successful career in tramways. On Gibb's retirement in 1910 he took over his offices.

In July 1907 Gibb had established the London Passenger Traffic Conference to coordinate fares and services outside as well as within the Yerkes Group. Stanley introduced the famous UndergrounD logo (the combined rectangle and hollow circle), used by all members of the Conference and still that of London Regional Transport.

On 1 July 1910 the Piccadilly, financially the most successful, became legally the London Electric Railway and absorbed the Hampstead and Bakerloo companies. The change had no significance for the travelling public. For them it was the UndergrounD group that mattered, for it coordinated fares, provided through bookings and built the magnificent interchanges at locations such as Piccadilly, Oxford Circus and Leicester Square.

Through the Common Fund Act of 1915 UndergrounD controlled London Electric Railways, the District, the Central London, the c&slr, most of the private tramway companies and the London General Omnibus Company, though all retained their legal identity. Headquarters were at 55 Broadway, which eventually became the office block over St James's Park station on the Circle. UndergrounD, under the successful direction of Stanley, demonstrated the practical advantages of a planning monopoly in city transport. It was thus the germ of that brainchild of Herbert Morrison, implemented by the 1929–31 socialist administration, the London Passenger Transport Board.

THE LONDON PASSENGER TRANSPORT BOARD

The LPTB was created by the 1933 Act and was an example of the device of exercising monopoly through a public corporation. A Board, chaired by Lord Ashfield, was appointed to control all road and underground rail services within an area of 1,986 square miles with a population of 9.5 million. In all the Board took over 5 railway companies (including the Metropolitan), 14 municipal tramways (including the extensive LCC system) and three private ones, and 61 bus companies (including the large Tilling Group). The Board's nominal capital was £109.8 million, mostly held in fixed-interest, non-voting stock. In 1934 it owned 174 route miles of railways, on which 315.8 million passenger journeys

TABLE 8

TRAFFIC AT SOME PRINCIPAL TUBE STATIONS
(Figures in millions)

	1959			1986
	Originating and terminating	*Exchange*	*Total*	*Originating and terminating*
Bank & Monument*	22.7	14.7	37.4	24.8
Charing Cross†	18.2	30.9	49.1	13.5
Leicester Square	16.8	15.6	32.4	21.4
Oxford Circus	27.1	13.2	40.3	51.1
Piccadilly	30.6	11.0	41.6	26.4

* Excluding Waterloo & City traffic.
† Now Embankment.

originated. In that year there were 525 million local journeys on main-line railways within the London Transport Area.

This latter was much larger than Greater London as we have defined it. The scope of the constituent companies was also wider than the carriage of passengers. So we find that the Board in its early days was a freight carrier – 3 million tons and 56,000 head of cattle in 1934. In places its activities were distinctly rural. Steam-hauled trains waiting while their guards opened unattended level-crossings contrasted oddly with the electrified automation of the tubes.

All passenger bookings between places within the Area were pooled and divided in the proportions fixed on 11 June 1935 by the London Passenger Transport Arbitration Tribunal. The LPTB received 62 per cent (for its road services were included in the pool) and the Southern 25.6. Even the extensive London & North Eastern suburban services brought their owners but 6 per cent. The London, Midland & Scottish, then owners of the Tilbury line, got 5.1 per cent, and the GW only 1.3.

The LPTB's main task was to weld the diverse constituents into a unified system. A secondary task was to raise capital for extensions into the suburbs, particularly those in the north-east. But in addition numerous Central London stations were rebuilt and all experienced considerable traffic increases. The appointment of Frank Pick as Vice-Chairman of the LPTB in 1933 resulted in the emergence of a distinctive house style which embraced new stations and posters and which put London Transport in the forefront of corporate image building. Time has weakened his work, without replacing it with anything nearly as creative.

LONDON TRANSPORT IN THE POST-WAR ERA

Under the terms of the 1947 Transport Act the property and functions of the LPTB were vested in the British Transport Commission and administered by the London Transport Executive. Lord Ashfield continued as first Chairman of the latter until his death in 1952. By 1959 rail journeys had risen to 669 million, a 116 per cent increase over 1934.

The British Transport Commission was dissolved under the 1962 Transport Act, and on 1 January 1963 an independent

TABLE 9
GROWTH OF TRAFFIC AT REPRESENTATIVE TUBE STATIONS

	Millions of tickets issued, 1959	Percentage increase, 1938–59	Percentage increase, 1931–8
Chancery Lane	2·7	−12	18
Green Park	3·0	40	41
Holborn*	5·0	−17	12
Hyde Park Corner†	1·6	13	33
Knightsbridge‡	3·3	25	24
Leicester Square	6·8	21	13
Marble Arch	4·4	36	48
Warren Street	1·8	−3	33
TOTALS	28·6	10	23

*Includes British Museum traffic in 1931.
†Includes Down Street traffic in 1931.
‡Brompton Road traffic in 1931.

London Transport Board took over from the Executive. But the 1960s saw a recognition of the need for overall transport planning and the 1968 Transport Act and 1973 Local Government Act saw public transport brought, along with roads, under the control of the new Metropolitan Counties. The counterpart for London was the London (Transport) Act 1969, which brought London Transport under GLC control, except for the 'green' (Country Services) buses and Green Line coaches, which were taken over by the National Bus Company. But BR services remained firmly outside the GLC's control. In 1974 the Labour Party captured the GLC, their campaign having included the abandonment of proposed 'motorway boxes'. They pursued a policy of favouring public transport especially rail, and the results are mentioned a number of times in this book.

In the 1979 General Election a Conservative Government was returned which vigorously pursued a policy of obtaining greater cost-effectiveness in the extensive support given to local authorities, and unfortunately transport planning became a victim of the internecine war which resulted in the abolition of the GLC in 1985. Once again there was to be no overall transport planning.

Under the 1984 Act, London Regional Transport was set up, under the direct control of the Secretary of State for

Transport. It was a policy-making body, day-to-day operation being carried out by two wholly owned companies, London Buses Ltd and London Underground Ltd. The former was forced to compete against outside competitors for routes put out to tender by LRT, but not even the Secretary of State could devise a similar system for rail. He did, however, set up the London Passenger Transport Group, which for the first time implemented coordination with BR instead of adding to the stock of frequently expressed but pious platitudes about it.

The consequences for policy of this institutional reorganisation have been considerable; these are dealt with more fully in Chapter XI, where there is an overview of recent developments.

CHAPTER VI

Main Lines and Middlesex

THE GREAT WESTERN RAILWAY

In 1835 London ended abruptly at Marble Arch. On the clay plain to the north-west were large farms and a few small villages. In contrast, among the orchards and market-gardens of the Thames gravels a line of towns and high-class suburbs stretched out along the Bath Road to Hounslow.

Through this area ran the Great Western Railway, incorporated on 31 August 1835 to connect Bristol with London. The Act envisaged the new line joining the London & Birmingham at Kensal Green and a common approach to Euston. The decision to employ a gauge of 7ft 0¼in rendered this impracticable, but the L&B had also proved difficult. Instead a site was selected near Paddington village. The line was opened to Maidenhead on 4 June 1838 and eventually through to Bristol on 30 June 1841. There were but few houses near the terminal yards, but in the 1850s the area became built over with large terrace houses interspersed with Gothic-style churches.

The small villages of Acton and Ealing were the only ones near the line. West Drayton, 13.25 miles, was the first station. Ealing and Hanwell were opened in December 1838 amidst fields, while Hayes was reputedly the most backward part of Middlesex, where 'dirt, ignorance and darkness reign supreme' (*Hayes Past and Present*, E. Hunt, 1861). But new settlements soon began to grow round the stations as they opened. Ealing had an 1841 population of 8,407. Growth was slow until 1871, when the figure was 18,189. But in 1863 the service to the City by Metropolitan had begun and the town was more convenient for commuters. In 1901 the inhabitants numbered 47,510.

But, though season tickets had been introduced in 1851, the GW made no consistent effort to develop suburban traffic. An Ealing policeman told the LCC's 1892 inquiry into workmen's services that he had to call numerous artisans at 03.30 so they could walk the 4 miles to Shepherd's Bush, the nearest station issuing workmen's tickets.

Most of the area served by the GW main lines only became extensively built up after 1910, and then mainly because of underground and tram extensions. Ealing's population grew fivefold between 1901 and 1951. Hayes and Harlington grew from under 5,000 in 1911 to 67,912 in 1961.

Local employment opportunities were numerous and job ratios have been high since the 1930s. In 1952 there were 593 industrial firms in Acton, employing 38,400 workers, and in Hayes 148, employing 26,800. By 1980 London Airport accounted for nearly 50,000 jobs. In 1952 ratios were 182 in Acton and 121 in Hayes. Numbers working in Central London are small, some 15 per cent of Acton's working population and only 7 per cent of Southall's. It follows that even at peak periods station-to-station traffic tends to be heavier than that to and from Paddington.

Though freight traffic has declined since 1960 to virtual vanishing point, in earlier years it was heavy. In 1952 at the three adjacent stations of Southall, Hayes and West Drayton 89,500 tons of merchandise were forwarded and 318,000 tons received. Four hundred thousand tons of coal were dealt with.

In 1871 the line was widened between Paddington and Westbourne Park and stations opened there and at Royal Oak. In 1878 a fly-under for the Hammersmith & City trains went into service west of Royal Oak. At least four lines were provided to Southall by 1 October 1877 and on to Slough by 25 November 1878, the new lines being narrow gauge only.

PADDINGTON

The site of the original terminus was west of the Bishop's Bridge, which later became that of the now closed goods station. In 1839 there were fourteen daily departures. The departure side of the present Paddington opened on 16 January 1854 and the arrival side on 29 May. There were three departure platforms and three arrival, the groups being separated by five sidings. By 1855 there were still only twenty daily departures, of which nine called at the four intermediate stations to West Drayton.

The first narrow-gauge train left for the Birmingham line (via Oxford) on 1 October 1861. T. H. Wright (locomotive superintendent, Neath) said: 'Some of the Broad Gauge bigots wondered whether the train would reach its destination.' It did, only three minutes late, carrying with it the death sentence of the broad gauge.

On 10 January 1863 Bishop's Road station was opened on the north side. It was used by the Metropolitan trains, the Hammersmith & City trains after 1864 and a few of the GW's infrequent suburban trains, including of course the through ones to the City.

In June 1878 an additional arrival platform (No 9) came into use. The central carriage sidings were replaced by more platforms in 1884 and 1893. Broad-gauge services began to decline after 1870. Thus in 1878 there were 48 departures (18 for beyond Maidenhead), of which 7 were broad gauge, all the broad-gauge ones being for Bristol and beyond. There was also a solitary return trip from Windsor, said to have been retained in deference to Daniel Gooch, who lived there. But the broad gauge was long a-dying in the West and in June 1884 there were still six passenger and two freight departures, while 'Ocean Specials' from Plymouth and broccoli and potato trains from Cornwall were also broad gauge. But Friday 20 May 1892 was the sad day ending Brunel's large vision. The last departure was the 17.00 for Plymouth, hauled by 4–2–2 *Bulkeley*, which returned with the last up train, the 'Mail', arriving early next morning.

By 1903, 39 suburban (only 9 before 10.30) and 64 main-line trains were arriving daily at Paddington and Bishop's Road, with 9.2 million passengers using the stations. In 1909 work began on platforms 10, 11 and 12 under a new roof span; they were completed in 1916. In 1933 Bishop's Road was incorporated and colour-light signalling installed. In 1967–8 the approaches were rearranged and re-signalled, the LRT lines becoming completely segregated and using only the northern island of the former Bishop's Road. The other island is used for BR suburban services, bringing the number of main-line platforms to fourteen.

In 1960, 104 trains left daily for destinations beyond Reading and 76 for there or nearer. They carried some 32,000 passengers, an average of 117 per train. By 1985 departures were 80 and 54 respectively. While through services via High Wycombe, Moreton-in-Marsh and Kemble have virtually disappeared, those to Bristol and South Wales have increased. The number of departing passengers had fallen to about 25,000.

The years since 1960 have seen DMUs take over the suburban services, while High Speed Trains (HSTs) were introduced from 1976 on the Bristol and South Wales runs, later extended to the West of England and in 1984 to Cheltenham and Worcester. Since 1980 linking of end-to-end services has produced some curious workings via Birmingham; to Manchester (Piccadilly) and to Hull for example. Suburban traffic is comparatively light. In 1985 the basic service was of only three departures per hour.

Suburban traffic has always been light, though it has greatly increased in recent years. In 1960 there were only 7,000 arrivals in the peak period. In 1985 there were 12,600, an increase of 16.1 per cent over 1981. The large majority of the commuters come from beyond Slough, which is the edge of Greater London, and many came from beyond Reading in locomotive-hauled trains from Banbury, Didcot and Newbury.

Paddington's glory is its great triple-arched roof, the result of a partnership between M. Digby Wyatt, the architect, and I. K. Brunel. In the words of Christian Barman, it is 'a unique work of art remarkable for many qualities'. The original frontage, in Eastbourne Terrace and therefore seldom seen, is large but dreary, while the frontage onto Praed Street is that of the 1930s hotel. Mid-Victorian Paddington is immortalised in W. P. Frith's painting, 'The Railway Station', of 1862. But though broad-gauge trains, crinolines and top hats have gone, the roof remains unchanged to echo the roar of diesel engines.

The 'persona' of Paddington is still unique among the London termini. Waterloo is brash and parvenu, but Paddington is an aristocrat and by no means a decayed one. From Paddington, commuters ride in comfort to Thames-side villas, businessmen travel to Bristol and South Wales, and holiday traffic to the South West is still important. But it is to the cathedral cities of the grassy western shires that one really feels the trains are bound, carrying archdeacons, colonels' widows and 'backwoods peers' returning thankfully from brief visits to the Lords.

THE GREAT WESTERN & GREAT CENTRAL JOINT LINE

Fierce competition with the LNW for the Birmingham traffic led the GW to shorten its lengthy route through Oxford. The Great Central wanted alternative access to London, since the Metropolitan's line was congested and the company obdurate (Chapter VIII). They made common cause, and in 1897 obtained powers for a line from Old Oak Common through the Chilterns to High Wycombe and beyond. As far as Northolt Junction, where the line from Marylebone would join, it would be owned by the GW, but north-westward by the GW&GC Joint Committee, incorporated by Act of 1 August 1899.

In 1903 the new line was used for a service out to Park Royal during the Royal Agricultural Society's Show. In the following year a regular service of auto-trains was started between Westbourne Park and Greenford, but through GW freight traffic did not start until 4 April and passenger on 1 July 1910.

In 1905 Old Oak, 3.5 miles from Marble Arch, was on the edge of London and beyond the line traversed '23 miles of verdant tranquillity', being used almost solely for long-distance traffic, though intermediate stations were patronised by picnic parties. In that year the Royal Agricultural Society abandoned its new showground at Park Royal, and on it the Ministry of Munitions erected factories during World War I. Between the Wars a large industrial estate grew up. In 1952 B. A. Bates found there were 302 plants, including Guinness's brewery, employing 32,680 workers, making it 'the most important industrial area of London'. In that year Park Royal goods depot handled 246,000 tons of merchandise and 100,000 tons of coal. In 1968 it became a Freightliner terminal and freight traffic is still handled.

Brentham Garden City Estate dates from 1911, but in no other area a comparable distance from London was development so slow. In the hamlet of West End (Northolt) only three houses were built between 1837 and 1935. The building boom dated only from the middle 1930s and it was not until the late 1950s that the area out to West Ruislip had become built over.

The GW provided a number of halts additional to the stations at Greenford and West Ruislip, serving them by infrequent auto-trains right up to 1947. As part of the 1935 scheme to improve transport in London (Chapter IX), the GW was to build an extra pair of tracks from North Acton Junction, on the Ealing & Shepherd's Bush line, to Denham, for the exclusive use of Central Line Tube trains. After a delay caused by World War II these were opened to Greenford on 30 June 1947 and on to West Ruislip (8 miles from North Acton) on 21 November 1948. Nothing was done about extending to Denham. The growing outer-suburban traffic from as far as Banbury was concentrated on Marylebone, from which there is a basic hourly DMU service for High Wycombe and beyond.

Meanwhile the line has lost any main-line functions. In 1960 there were twelve down fast trains from Paddington for Birmingham and beyond, of which one, the 17.10, still carried a slip portion for Bicester. There were also five semi-fasts from Marylebone for the Great Central route. But in 1966 the GC line north of Ashendon Junction was closed. The Birmingham trains enjoyed increased custom during the West Coast Main Line electrification, but the service ceased when that was completed in 1966. Only a solitary round trip from Birmingham uses it to reach Paddington. The once important through freight traffic has also virtually disappeared.

BRANCHES FROM THE GREAT WESTERN

The HAMMERSMITH & CITY, 2.5 miles, was opened by the GW on 13 June 1864 as a double line of mixed gauge from Green Lane Junction (the site of Westbourne Park) to the growing high-class suburb of Hammersmith. Skirting the newly built-up area, the only intermediate stations were Notting Hill (now Ladbroke Grove) and Shepherd's Bush. A good service to the City popularised the district, and Latimer Road (1868) and Goldhawk Road (1914) were opened to serve neighbourhoods which had been built up by 1890. On 1 July 1864 a spur opened from Latimer Road Junction to the West

London line at Uxbridge Road Junction.

Improved relations with the Metropolitan led to the line being vested jointly in the two companies from 15 July 1867. Thereafter the Metropolitan provided the basic service, broad gauge being removed beyond Latimer Road Junction in August 1868 and to the West London in March 1869. The H&C then became virtually a branch of the Inner Circle, though the GW ran some through trains, notably a Paddington–Brighton service in 1906–7. On 5 November 1906 electric working began, jointly owned stock being used. The district served has experienced very mixed fortunes and some of London's worst slums can be seen from the train windows.

The EALING & SHEPHERD'S BUSH Railway, 4 miles, was authorised in 1905. The scheme envisaged a branch from the main line at Ealing Broadway to Shepherd's Bush, where there would be a suburban terminus providing interchange with the Central London. There would also be connections with the Northolt line at North Acton Junction and with the West London just north of Wood Lane.

Probably following the decision to enlarge Paddington, the terminal project was abandoned and the line cut back to Wood Lane, the Central London obtaining powers in 1911 for a short extension to make an end-on junction. The E&SB opened for goods on 16 April 1917. Tube trains were projected over it on 3 August 1920, traversing an area that was then open country but is now fully built up, largely with factories.

The line started from virtually a separate, two-road station adjoining the GW's Ealing Broadway and was quadruple from North Acton Junction to White City, the northern pair not being electrified. These were used by freight trains and also for milk to Wood Lane. They closed on 9 March 1964, the section to the west being closed to freight as early as 19 June 1938. In 1947 Wood Lane was superseded by the new White City station.

The GREENFORD LOOP was authorised in 1897 as a 1.5 mile double line with a triangular junction at each end from West Ealing on the main line and Greenford on the Northolt. In 1903 it was used by a roundabout service for the Royal Show, regular services began on 1 May 1904, and it became a useful link for through freight and the occasional passenger special. The exiguous local traffic was maintained by auto-trains (diesel railcars since 1958) from Ealing Broadway, cut back at Greenford with electrification. Lying behind the marshy Brent valley, the district was late developing, but after 1925 housing estates and factories grew up in Perivale. Traffic at the three intermediate halts has grown enormously and contrasts with the still rural operating methods.

The BRENTFORD branch, 4 miles long, was built from Southall to Brentford Dock to give the broad gauge a water outlet on the Thames. The Great Western & Brentford Company was incorporated on 14 August 1855, leased to the GW in 1859 and vested in it on 1 January 1872. The branch was opened for goods on 18 July 1859, and passenger traffic began on 1 May 1860 but was never important. It was more convenient to reach London by LSW, while trams and buses captured the local traffic. The infrequent auto-trains were withdrawn on 4 May 1942.

The line was of importance, however, for goods transferred to and from water and in later years in connection with local factories, but this declined after 1960. In 1860, 58,000 tons of goods and minerals were carried. In 1956, 180,054 tons of merchandise and 20,572 tons of minerals were dealt with at Brentford Dock (closed 31 December 1964). In that year Brentford Town, serving factories along the Great West Road, handled 38,355 tons of goods and 193,510 tons of minerals. The branch was saved by the 1977 establishment of a town-refuse depot where containerised rubbish is railed to fill gravel workings near Didcot. Originally the branch was single, but in October 1861 a narrow-gauge track was laid. The broad-gauge track was narrowed in 1876 and the line was worked as an orthodox double one. Now single as far as Firestone Box (Brentford Town), it has been lifted beyond.

The UXBRIDGE branch was authorised on 16 July 1846 when the Great Western & Uxbridge was incorporated. Opened from West Drayton on 8 December 1856 as a single line 2.6 miles long, it was narrowed in 1871 and doubled in 1880.

Also from West Drayton is the branch to STAINES WEST, a single line opened to Colnbrook on 9 August 1884 and on to Staines on 2 November 1885, where the manager's house of a former grain mill was taken over for the station offices. The branch was distinctly rural; passengers from Yoeveney had to signal the driver to stop. When closed to passengers on 29 March 1965 it was operated by a single diesel car. But industry was increasing and in 1958 Colnbrook, though it had only 15,000 passengers, handled 30,000 tons of merchandise. The branch remains open to serve several private sidings.

THE LONDON & NORTH WESTERN RAILWAY

The first section of the London & Birmingham Railway was opened from Euston Square to Boxmoor on 20 July 1837, the full service to Birmingham beginning on 17 September 1838. On 16 July 1846 the LNW was formed by amalgamation, including the L&B.

Paradoxically the 'Premier Line', along with the GW, had the least direct influence upon the capital's growth. The company was only interested in its vast long-distance traffic. Its interest in its associates such as the North London, the West London and the North & South Western Junction was in the opportunities for through traffic.

EUSTON

Euston Square had been laid out in about 1815 on land belonging to the Fitzroy family, a branch of the ducal house of Grafton with a seat at Euston Hall, Suffolk. On Drummond Street, parallel with Euston Road, the London & Birmingham erected the famous 'propylaeum', the Age of Elegance applied to the transport revolution, but this portico gave access to mean train sheds. Sir John Summerson, the architectural critic, commented, 'As an approach to the modest little station building . . . [the portico] was manifestly absurd', but it was an attempt to make a great station a worthy ornament of the city it served.

The buildings behind the portico were begun in 1846. Included was the Great Hall, a magnificent waiting-room designed by P. C. Hardwick (son of Philip, designer of the portico) and famous for the breadth of unsupported ceiling and the stairway up to the noble Shareholders' Room. But behind lay a dark warren of offices.

Thenceforward Euston grew chaotically. In 1861 there was still only one arrival platform, though there were five for departures. The original turnplates for marshalling the tiny four-wheeled coaches were still in place and G. P. Neele, one of the LNW's greatest officers, wrote: '. . . the clatter incidental on a train coming in and going out over these tables was amazing'. In 1892 four more departure platforms were provided. They had a separate entrance and were styled the West station. Confusion resulted from cabs arriving at the wrong entrance and trying to get to the right one, leading a director to complain: '. . . you have turned Euston into a Waterloo'. Eventually the separate entrance was closed.

The Euston of 1962 had fifteen platforms, some rarely used. Nos 1 and 2 (1871–3) together with No 3 (the 1837 arrival) were for main-line arrivals. Nos 4 and 5 (the 'wooden platform' of 1891) were electrified. No 6 (the 1837 departure platform) was used for both arrivals and departures. No 7 (always the 'Kensington' as it was once used for a service thereto) and No 8 were too short save for an occasional Tring local and parcels loading. Nos 9 and 10 dated from 1840, the former known as the 'York', as trains were despatched from it to the Hudson Empire via Rugby. These two were chiefly, and No 11 solely, used for parcels. Nos 12–15 were the main-line departure platforms and the original West station.

This was the station which passed with the Steam Age. The destruction of the portico was regretted, but passengers and railwaymen could only welcome the convenience of its successor. Proposed in 1938, work started on it in 1963 and the new station was formally opened by the Queen on 14 October 1968. From 3 January 1966 all trains were electrically hauled. There are fifteen passenger platforms, Nos 9 and 10 being additionally equipped for direct-current trains. There are also four long and two short parcels platforms. The main feature is the great concourse. With its associated passenger facilities, it has the functional utility and architectural impersonality that render it indistinguishable from any modern airport anywhere in the world. The 15 acres of flat roof and unimpressive frontage in overcrowded London are an appalling indictment of contemporary planning. The LCC refused commercial development over the station on the grounds that extra traffic would be generated on the streets (despite the excellent Underground and main-line-rail access), while allowing free rein for new office blocks to flood the streets further along the Euston Road.

Judged on statistics of train and passenger numbers, until 1966 Euston had always been one of the quietest London termini, but it has been well known for the important, if few, expresses dealt with. There was always an impression of intense activity; travellers encumbered with children and baggage, and the mountains of mails and parcels all took up more space than do long-distance commuters.

In 1841 there were 13 departures daily, only the 15.00 for Aylesbury via Leighton Buzzard terminating short of Rugby. By 1878 there were 38 departures and even by 1903 arrivals totalled only 78, of which 36 were considered suburban. In 1960 there were 54 long-distance arrivals and 27 outer-suburban ones from stations as far out as Bletchley. The direct-current electric service to Watford had a basic frequency of twenty minutes but there were no departures for Northampton between 08.45 and 11.45. Commuters arriving during the morning peak numbered only some 5,000.

But after electrification passenger traffic expanded rapidly, over 40 per cent in the first year. In 1967 immediately after electrification there were 65 basic daily main-line departures. By 1985 there were 80 main-line, 64 alternating-current outer-suburban and 55 direct-current locals. In the census that year 14,036 passengers were recorded as arriving between 07.00 and 09.59. A total of 66,000 passengers passed through daily.

THE MAIN LINE FROM EUSTON

Natural obstacles were heavier than on the GW. From the Euston platform-ends the line rises for a mile in a deep cutting up the 1 in 77 Camden Bank. Cable haulage was used until 1844. For many years after, trains were piloted. If the assisting engine was going no further than the summit it would be slipped and would draw ahead, the driver waving to a trusted pointsman, who would switch the pilot into a siding and reverse the points for the train. From 1 January 1869 less spectacular assistance in the rear was provided until steam gave way to diesel.

At Camden the London & Birmingham laid out its main yards, though did not implement its plan to provide the passenger terminal at this remote spot. The locomotive depot closed when steam was superseded and rail access to the goods depot was severed after transfer of sundries to National Carriers under the 1968 Transport Act.

The complex layout of burrowing junctions at the approach to Primrose Hill Tunnel (1,220yd), piercing the Hampstead Ridge, dates from 1922. G. F. A. Wilmot pointed to the 'elbow bends' by which this and subsequent lines avoided the 400ft high Northern Heights, thus reducing grades and tunnelling.

Beyond, the line traverses the clay plain, making for the Hatch End gap in the South Herts Plateau before crossing the Chilterns by the Gade and Bulbourn valleys and the Tring Gap. Deep cuttings are needed through the gaps. Harrow (1831 population 3,861) was the only place of consequence short of the market-town of Watford (5,293 in 1831) and was given the only intermediate station. Until 1844 a suburban service was non-existent and it was very sparse after that. G. P. Neele found out the hard way: 'On one occasion, travelling from Euston by a train I fully expected to call at Kilburn [his home], I found myself landed at Harrow about 5.0 p.m; there was no train due back until 7.0 p.m.'

In the 1850s the LNW, in a rare bid for suburban traffic, offered free seasons for up to fifteen years to commuters buying property near Harrow, but the train service remained unattractive and not until the late 1860s, when there was a good service to the City from Willesden Junction, was there a significant growth in near-by Harlesden.

On 1 July 1858 a 'third line' (up goods) was completed between Watford and Primrose Hill. By 1875 there was also a 'fourth line' and all four tracks were being used by passenger trains. The extra tracks were gauntleted through Primrose Hill Tunnel until a new bore came into use on 1 June 1879. It was then possible to inaugurate an hourly service to Watford and in 1885 workmen's tickets were introduced at stations out to Willesden.

By 1900 suburban traffic was growing in spite of the LNW, and in the following year Tube extensions were authorised from Golders Green to Watford. This forced the LNW into action. It started work on the 'New Lines' to develop suburban traffic beyond Willesden. These opened between Kensal Green Tunnel and Harrow (where a new station was provided) on 15 June 1912, and on 10 February 1913 to

Plate 23   The tiny roadside station opened on Acton Lane in 1841 or 1842 was the fore-
runner of Willesden Junction. (*National Railway Museum*)
Plate 24   Willesden Junction in about 1880. This is the station opened in 1866 and
rebuilt in 1894. (*L&GRP*)

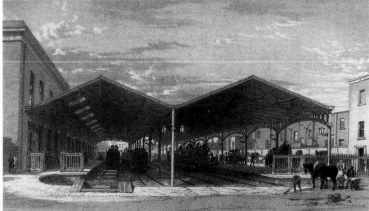

Plate 25 The propylaeum of Euston station, flanked by two hotel blocks, formed a dignified entrance to the new terminus. The Age of Elegance and the Age of Steam had met to adorn London. (*National Railway Museum*)

Plate 26 But the train shed beyond was rudimentary and mean. (*National Railway Museum*)

Plate 27 A photograph from the 1950s of Euston's No 5 platform (left), facing the original departure platform shown in the middle picture. (*G. M. Kichenside*)

Watford Junction. The original intention was to bring them from South Hampstead in a deep-level Tube to a terminus below Euston, but in 1911 it was arranged for Bakerloo trains to be projected over the electrified New Lines. On 13 January 1915 the BAKERLOO was extended from Paddington to Kilburn Park and on 11 February to link up with the LNW at Queen's Park. The Tube trains ran to Willesden from 10 May 1915 and to Watford from 16 April 1917.

Operation of the LNW's electric trains had to await the completion of the third Primrose Hill bore and the layout beyond, the full service to Euston and Broad Street being inaugurated on 10 July 1922. Until 1961 the basic Watford service remained about eight trains an hour, but the off-peak Broad Street trains were withdrawn in 1962 and from 1965 the LT trains terminated at Queen's Park apart from a few through ones to Harrow at peaks. By 1980 there were only three trains an hour, from Euston, reflecting the general decline in BR off-peak middle-suburban frequencies.

WILLESDEN JUNCTION

In 1841 or 1842 a tiny roadside station was opened on Acton Lane (where Harlesden opened on 15 June 1912), enjoying a service of two trains each way. Neele said passengers believed it was provided for the sole benefit of Capt. Huish, who lived near-by. Certainly it was remote from the small village of Willesden. On 1 September 1866 it was replaced by Willesden Junction, 400yd west of where the West London and the North & South Western Junction diverged and where the Hampstead Junction threw two connections across the main line to join them. Low-level platforms were provided as well as high-level ones on both connections.

The two sets of high-level platforms were quite separate and from each was a thirty-minute service to the City. Passengers were given no indication from which platform the next train would leave. This and the labyrinth of entrances and passages caused the station to be known as 'Bewildering Junction' or the 'Wilderness'. On 12 August 1894 a rebuilt station opened with a single group of high-level platforms, reduced by the LMS to a single island.

The station on the New Lines opened on 15 June 1912, with

a stairway up to the Richmond-line platform. The main-line station was a depressing place with seven platforms and two bays, in 1961 served by only twenty-eight outer-suburban trains. These ceased to call after 3 December 1962 and the station was demolished in preparation for electrification. The still extensive marshalling yard has been the terminal, since September 1965, of electrically hauled main-line freight trains. On the site of the steam sheds is the freightliner terminal, operational from 29 August 1967 and greatly enlarged in 1969.

SUBURBAN GROWTH

Thus LNW policy and Middlesex clay inhibited London's north-western spread. Neele wrote of the mid 1860s: '. . . [south of the Thames] a residential element had very largely grown up at almost all stations, but along the North Western system there was hardly any growth'. Kilburn and Kensal Green grew between 1860 and 1900 as depressing extensions of Paddington. Queen's Park was laid out at the end of that period as an experiment in better-quality working-class housing. There was some building at Harlesden and in 1875 Stonebridge Park was 'a cluster of sixty or eighty smart new villas for City Men'.

But the expansion of Willesden and Wembley was initiated mainly by the Metropolitan and the trams. The population of Willesden grew from 3,879 in 1861 to 15,869 in 1871 and by 1901 it housed 114,582. The LCC reported: 'The North Western and Great Western touch Willesden Junction and probably no part of London is so poorly provided with workmen's trains.'

Further out there was little development until after the direct-current electrification. But after 1920 it became spectacular. Factories sprang up in Willesden and Wembley (especially on the site of the 1924 Exhibition) and all along the New Lines villas multiplied and new stations opened. Carpenders Park, opened in 1914 as a wooden halt to serve a golf-course, dealt with 200,000 passengers in 1937. In 1957, at the newly rebuilt station sandwiched between an LCC estate and a speculative estate, 1.3 million ordinary tickets and 32,011 seasons were sold.

On 25 June 1886 the HARROW & STANMORE (absorbed in 1899) was incorporated to build a single-track branch, 2 miles long. Opened on 18 December 1890, its construction resulted in 'a very considerable growth of residential buildings around the terminus' (Neele). During the 1930s the area was built over and Belmont was opened on 15 September 1932, but Stanmore was more conveniently served by the new Metropolitan branch (p. 152) and the little cottage-style terminus closed on 15 September 1952 (6 July 1964 to freight). The service terminated at Belmont until closure on 5 October 1964.

On 3 July 1860 the WATFORD & RICKMANSWORTH received powers for 4.5 miles of single line from Watford Junction to the market-town of Rickmansworth with its silk mill and watercress beds. Opened on 1 October 1962, it was vested in the LNW in 1881.

At Bushey station the New Lines were diverted away from the main line to make a triangular connection with the branch at Croxley Green Junction, whence the line was doubled to Watford Junction, and High Street was rebuilt as an island platform. The Junction was enlarged and now has five terminal platforms, four through main-line ones and a separate one for the St Albans trains. Originally the latter had two through platforms and a bay. The Act of 26 July 1907 authorising the New Lines also sanctioned a 1.25 mile single line from Croxley Green Junction to CROXLEY GREEN, opened on 15 June 1912.

Electric trains began running to Croxley Green on 30 October 1922 and to Rickmansworth on 26 September 1927. Passenger services to the latter were withdrawn on 3 March 1952. Consent to closure of Croxley Green was refused and an exiguous peak-hour service plies from Watford Junction. There is a proposal to link the LT Watford branch to it and divert trains from their remote terminus.

THE WEST LONDON AND WEST LONDON EXTENSION

The Birmingham, Bristol & Thames Junction was incorporated in 1836 to connect the London & Birmingham and the GW with the navigable Thames. In 1844 it became the

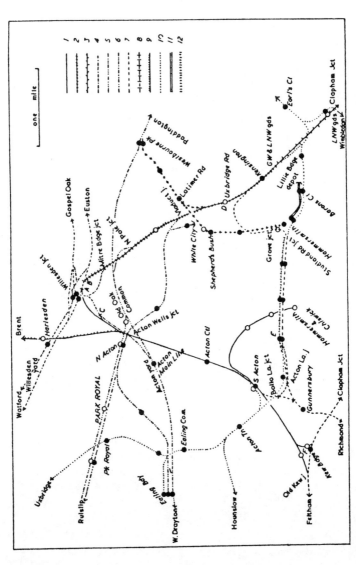

FIG 14 The railways of West London: 1 North & South Western Junction Railway; 2 West London Railway; 3 West London Extension Railway; 4 LNWR; 5 GWR; 6 GWR – Ealing & Shepherd's Bush; 7 and 8 LSWR; 9 Midland; 10 District; 11 Piccadilly; 12 Central London; A North & South Western Junction; B West London Junction; C North & South Western Old Oak Junction; D GWR and LNWR goods depots; E Turnham Green station; F Midland

West London and, after much delay, on 27 May 1844 it opened a 2.5 mile single line of mixed gauge and rudimentary stations from West London Junction on the LNW at Willesden, across the GW on the level at Wormwood Scrubs, and on to the basin of the short Kensington Canal. The district was then one of market-gardens, and the line was so much lampooned in *Punch* as leading from nowhere to nowhere that it became 'Mr Punch's Railway'.

A lavish passenger service was started – with no connections. Its withdrawal on 30 November was no surprise. Not only was traffic sparse – it was alleged that a winkle-seller was the only passenger on the first train – but also the GW was obstructive. The West London's Minutes of 25 October 1844 tell a sorry story. The 17.55 from Kensington was delayed so long at the GW crossing that it did not reach West London Junction until 19.00, and the solitary passenger had missed the last train to Harrow. He was brought back to Kensington 'very much disappointed and dissatisfied' and hired a post-chaise to take him to Harrow at the Company's expense.

In 1860 the GW crossing was replaced by a bridge, but the line remained little used until 1863 when the West London Extension was opened on 2 March, allowing Mr Punch's Railway to reach somewhere at last. Jointly owned by the LNW and GW (one third each) and the London & South Western and LBSC (one sixth each), the West London Extension was authorised in 1859 as a double-track line of mixed gauge linking the WL with Clapham Junction. The two northern lines leased and doubled the WL.

At various times connections were laid in with the Ealing & Shepherd's Bush (closed 9 March 1964), the Hammersmith & City (closed to passengers 20 October 1940 and goods 1 March 1954), the GW from North Pole Junction and the Hampstead Junction at Willesden. The LSW branch (closed 21 October 1940) from Richmond came in at the north end of Kensington station, and the District at the south end, and at the southern end of the line there were connections with the LSW, the Brighton and the Chatham.

This multiplicity of connections allowed development of transfer freight traffic between the northern and southern lines, while the northern lines also opened depots south of the river, as well as along the West London and the Extension. In spite of equivalent possibilities for through passenger traffic, this did not begin until 1904 and never reached large proportions. Most spectacular was the rise and decay of suburban traffic.

KENSINGTON had but one platform until 1869, when it was rebuilt in LNW style with two long platforms, each with a bay at each end, and was served by loops off the through roads with scissor connections in the middle. Though in Russell Road, it was named Addison Road.

From 1 April 1863 the GW operated a service between Southall and Victoria until 22 March 1915, broad-gauge trains being replaced in 1866. On 1 July 1864 a broad-gauge service from the Hammersmith & City was put on. On 1 August 1872 this became part of the narrow-gauge, thirty-minute MIDDLE CIRCLE between Moorgate and Mansion House. In September 1867 the LNW inaugurated a thirty-minute service between Broad Street and Kensington (later Victoria LBSC), diverting it to Mansion House on 1 February 1872 to become the OUTER CIRCLE. This was augmented by trains from Euston or Willesden to various destinations south of the river. A LSW service was established from Richmond to Waterloo and to Clapham Junction on 1 January 1869.

Thus during the 1860s Addison Road became the key point in West London suburban services, and was soon surrounded by large houses spreading over the fields from Kensington and Chelsea. From them emerged frock-coated businessmen to board trains of four-wheeled coaches hauled by diminutive tank engines to the City over routes inconceivable today. Addison Road epitomised the Age of Steam, gaslight and horse-cabs, and its glory died with them. Underground and buses offered direct routes to the West End and City and local north–south passengers deserted rail for road.

Even so, 4.1 million passengers used the station in 1903 and it shared in the first period of electrification. On 5 November 1906 electric trains took over the Middle Circle (curtailed at Earl's Court on 1 July 1900 and at Addison Road on 1 February 1905). The Outer Circle was also turned back at Earl's Court from 1 January 1909 because of congestion eastward. This was replaced in 1912 by a Willesden–Earl's Court shuttle, operated by District electric trains from 1 July

1914, replaced on 22 November by LNW ones.

Between the Wars a steam service was still provided by the Southern between Clapham Junction and Addison Road, supplemented by a few LMS ones from Willesden to Clapham Junction. By 1938 the passenger-user figure for Addison Road had shrunk to 1.3 million, and this included Olympia exhibition traffic. War hastened the demise of the now uneconomic services. The advertised steam services ceased on 20 October 1940 and the electric ones, LMS from Willesden and LT, now from Edgware Road, via Westbourne Park, on 3 and 20 October respectively.

On 19 December 1946 Addison Road became Kensington Olympia. It reopened on exhibition days for an LT shuttle service from Earl's Court. In 1986 this became a regular service from the bay platform at High Street Kensington. A peak-hour service, at first unadvertised, was maintained to Clapham Junction; in 1968 there were two departures and in 1986 six.

In 1904 services from the North to the Kent and Sussex resorts were inaugurated, but daily services ceased in 1939. Advertised holiday trains were reinstated for a short period after World War II. On 24 May 1966 a Motorail terminal was opened with four platforms, and by this time the station had only one operational through platform. In 1968 there were up to seventy-nine services weekly. But after the 1982 summer season the terminal was closed and the services were diverted. In 1979 a through service from Manchester to Gatwick via Reading was inaugurated over the West London. On 12 May 1986 the Inter-City City Sector, spurred on by the M25 and aware of the numerous near-by hotels, increased the through trains to six southbound and seven northbound. Northern terminals include Manchester, Liverpool, Birmingham and Reading. The Southern ones are Dover, Brighton and Newhaven. Trains to and from the last two also call at Gatwick. All trains call at Kensington. Unfortunately an additional stop has to be made at West London Junction for the diesel/electric change-over. Numerous excursion and charter trains have always traversed the West London.

At one time Kensington dealt with a large parcels and milk traffic, but this has ceased. All the goods depots along the route have been closed, but it remains important for through freight. In 1986 some twenty-eight daily trains were booked to pass through Kensington, with more running on certain days.

THE NORTH & SOUTH WESTERN JUNCTION AND ITS ASSOCIATED LINES

In 1851 the North & South Western Junction was authorised to link its eponymous railways by 3.75 miles of double line from Willesden (N&SW Junction) to Old Kew Junction on the Hounslow Loop. Neele says that it was promoted by Southampton interests and neglected by the main lines. T. C. Mills, goods manager at Camden, preferred to cart goods across London. Eventually Archibald Scott of the LSW realised its potential and arranged with his company to work the freight traffic.

This began on 15 February 1853 and local passenger services, always a North London concern, on 1 August. At first traffic was light as the area was completely rural. In 1858 trains were extended to Twickenham and in 1863 to Kingston. To avoid reversals, curves were opened on 1 February, one eastward facing to New Kew Junction, the other bypassing Barnes station. On the former a station (Kew Bridge from 1868) was built; it later became a tram and bus centre.

The route on from Kew Bridge was so indirect that the LSW obtained powers in 1864 for a 3 mile line from South Acton Junction (the site of the present station) to Richmond (New), a terminus adjoining the LSW's Old Station. It was opened on

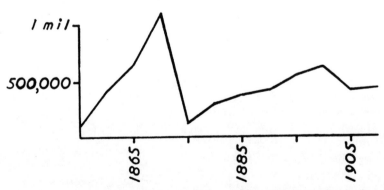

FIG 15 Passenger traffic on the NSWJ. The peak in 1870 is probably due to the opening of the line to Richmond and the subsequent decline resulting from competition from other routes thereto.

1 January 1869, after which NL trains ran alternately to Richmond over the new line and to Kew Bridge. The Barnes curve was abandoned.

On the same day the LSW opened a 3.25 mile branch from the Acton–Richmond line at Gunnersbury through Hammersmith (Grove Road) to Addison Road. At Hammersmith two connections were provided, with the Hammersmith & City at Grove Junction (1 June 1870) and with the District at Studland Road Junction (1 June 1877).

At the northern end of the NSWJ were three links, the main one, with the Hampstead Junction (Chapter IV), being opened in 1860. Then, on 1 October 1868, the DUDDING HILL LOOP was opened to goods trains between Acton Wells Junction (0.75 miles south of Willesden) and the Midland at Welsh Harp (where there was a station from 2 May 1870 to 1 July 1903). A triangle here was completed by a spur to Cricklewood (opened 2 May 1870 as Child's Hill). This 3.75 mile link was promoted by the Midland & South Western Junction (not to be confused with the better-known Wiltshire company), incorporated in 1864 and absorbed by the Midland in 1874. Always an important freight link, it has also been used by passenger specials. At Acton Wells the GW opened a spur from its main line on 1 January 1877. Mainly for freight, it also hosted a Southall–Willesden passenger service between 1888 and 1912, and irregularly thereafter.

The value of the NSWJ and the closely associated Acton–Richmond line was greatly enhanced by these connections. Over the years suburban trains of six companies worked into Richmond. Since the town was apparently adequately served by the Windsor Line to Waterloo, some explanation of its attraction is necessary. In the 1860s it was the first place of consequence beyond Kensington and Chelsea, so was one of the few possible objectives. It was one of the chief riverside towns and was already becoming a high-class dormitory suburb, from which prosperous commuters were finding the journey to the City via Waterloo tedious. Finally Richmond and Kew were great centres for Londoners' day outings.

In 1912 the erstwhile Outer Circle was diverted down the NSWJ, doubling the original NL thirty-minute service. For its part the LSW inaugurated an hourly service from Richmond to Addison Road, trains continuing alternately to Ludgate Hill and to Waterloo via the West London Extension, which ceased after 3 June 1916. GW and Metropolitan trains arrived at Richmond via Grove Junction but, as this connection was never electrified, the Metropolitan service ceased at the end of 1906, when the H&C was converted, the GW steam service ending on 31 December 1910.

The Midland operated unsuccessfully and intermittently over the NSWJ between 1875 and 1902, after which Harlesden and Dudding Hill, the stations on the Dudding Hill Loop, were permanently closed to passengers. A SUPER OUTER CIRCLE (1878–80) ran from St Pancras to Earl's Court via the LSW's Acton curve, which had completed the triangle north of Gunnersbury in 1878.

On 1 August 1905 the District service to Richmond went over to electric traction, and on 1 October 1916 the LNW followed suit with the Broad Street–Kew Bridge/Richmond service. On 12 September 1940 all the Kew Bridge trains were withdrawn. Richmond now has a basic service of three London Midland Region and four LRT trains per hour. Gunnersbury, now the basement of an office block, had the roof of its island platform blown off by a freak tornado on 8 December 1954. 'Storm destroys underground station' was the somewhat misleading headline.

Riverside location and Georgian architecture give Richmond and Kew charm and inflated property values. North of the river, houses are smaller and Acton is heavily industrialised, the whole area served being built up between 1890 and 1914. The NSWJ, though leased to the operators, kept its legal identity until 1923. Unlike the West London, the NSWJ still retains its suburban traffic and, unlike it, it has never been important for through passenger trains, but it has long been vital in London's freight routes. In 1956, 80 westbound goods trains were scheduled daily through Acton Wells Junction and 45 passed on to the Southern. The flow remains heavy. In 1986 there were 45 daily westbound goods trains through Acton Wells with more on certain days.

A single line to HAMMERSMITH & CHISWICK from Acton Gate House Junction (at Acton Lane) was the NSWJ's only branch. Used for goods since 1 May 1857, it had an erratic and primitive passenger service from 8 April 1858 to 1 January 1917 and was abandoned from 3 May 1965.

CHAPTER VII

Clay, Houses and Electric Traction in Middlesex

THE DISTRICT AND THE PICCADILLY IN WEST LONDON

In 1960 suburbia stretched continuously along the 8.5 miles of line between North Ealing and Ickenham where forty years earlier scarcely a house would have been visible from the train window. This social change was largely brought about by electric railways, built into open country by enterprising promoters. 'Gaily into Ruislip Gardens runs the red electric train'; thus Sir John Betjeman opened his poem 'Middlesex', a satirical look at the commuting way of life. While it is true that Middlesex clay formerly inhibited building, it is also true that the GW and LNW had done little to encourage suburban traffic.

The District reached the area by slow stages. Its 1864 Act of Incorporation sanctioned an 'X' layout at Earl's Court with arms to the Inner Circle at South Kensington (via Gloucester Road) and at High Street; to Addison Road; and to a station alongside West Brompton on the WL. On 12 April 1869 a West Brompton–Gloucester Road service was inaugurated; it was extended to Blackfriars on 1 August 1870 and to Mansion House on 3 July 1871. An engineer's report of 7 September 1869 stated that the other links were ready, but the one to Addison Road was unused until the Outer Circle started in 1872.

Because the company lacked money and credit, but 'cast their eyes enviously upon the fair and rich traffic district of the South Western suburban system' (Sir Sam Fay) and also on GW preserves, westward extensions were made through nominally independent companies.

On 9 September 1874 the HAMMERSMITH EXTEN-SION opened the mile of line from Earl's Court to Hammersmith Broadway. Further extensions were abandoned when the LSW granted running powers to Richmond, the HAMMERSMITH JUNCTION company opening the connection to Studland Road Junction on 1 June 1877. A District branch was then opened on 1 July 1879 from Turnham Green on the LSW to EALING BROADWAY. The GW persuaded the District to drop its attempt on Uxbridge by consenting to a connection at Ealing and the inauguration of a Mansion House–Windsor service, which lasted only from 1 March 1883 to September 1885, after which Ealing remained the terminus. The West Brompton branch was extended to PUTNEY BRIDGE on 1 March 1880, trains eventually reaching Wimbledon on 3 June 1889.

By 1880 Hammersmith had become the edge of the built-up area, but good District services and, after 1900, electric tramway extensions advanced London's frontier to beyond the NSWJ by 1914. Electric traction began between Earl's Court and Ealing on 1 July 1905, Earl's Court and Putney Bridge on 23 July (on to Wimbledon on 27 August) and Earl's Court and Richmond on 1 August. To deal with the increasing traffic the LSW quadrupled its line between Studland Road Junction and Turnham Green, giving the District sole use of the southern pair of tracks. After the LSW's service ceased in 1916 the northern pair lay derelict.

The HOUNSLOW & METROPOLITAN Company, promoted by local landowners bent on increasing property values, was incorporated on 26 August 1880 to build a branch from the District's Ealing line at Mill Hill Park (Acton Town from 1910) to Hounslow Barracks (Hounslow West from 1925). When opened on 1 May 1883 it deviated from the authorised route at Osterley to terminate at Hounslow Town. A single line from Lampton Junction (Osterley) to Hounslow West opened on 21 July 1884, the section to Heston Hounslow (Hounslow Central from 1925) being doubled in 1910. But the remaining 62 chains on to Barracks remained single until 1926, 300 trains a day using it in 1913. The spur to the Town was closed on 1 April 1886, but was reopened, together with a spur to complete the triangle, upon electrification. The Town station was finally closed on 2 May 1909 with the opening of Hounslow East. From 1933 Piccadilly trains took over working the Hounslow lines, District trains running only to Ealing.

The development of London Airport led to proposals to extend beyond Hounslow West. Eventually it was decided to approve this route rather than a spur from the Windsor Line near Feltham. On 19 July 1975 it was opened to Hatton Cross, serving the maintenance area, and on 16 December on to Heathrow Central. A single-line circular extension brought the line to Terminal 4 on 1 April 1986.

The EALING & SOUTH HARROW Railway was incorporated on 25 August 1894 to build a 5 mile line from Hanger Lane Junction, just short of Ealing Broadway. It was part of the District's second drive on Uxbridge. There were also hopes it might be used by the still-born London & South Wales as its approach to London. Ready in 1901, Yerkes used it as test track for electric trains, providing a service between Acton Town and Park Royal for the Royal Show of 23–7 June 1903. The next day a full service was put on through to South Harrow.

On 13 June 1905 an electric service was inaugurated between Hounslow Barracks and South Acton via Acton Town. It used a double-line spur between the two last named, hitherto unused for public traffic. The junction with the NSWJ was removed in 1915 and the spur singled in 1932. On 1 July 1905 the electric trains were diverted to Earl's Court, leaving the South Acton service to degenerate into a one-car shuttle train over the spur which ceased on 28 February 1959.

In 1932 four tracks came into use all the way from where the Piccadilly emerged at the surface just east of Baron's Court to Northfields, incorporating the parallel District and Piccadilly tracks to Hammersmith, and the existing four tracks between Studland Road and Turnham Green which were leased from the Southern. The remainder of the LSW branch east of Studland Road was abandoned. Piccadilly trains use the inside pair of tracks, running non-stop from Hammersmith to Acton Town, the District trains, on the outer pair, calling at all stations.

In 1914 continuous building extended to Chiswick Park, but while Hounslow and Ealing were both expanding, the lines thither and to South Harrow ran through open and almost deserted country. Between 1925 and 1939 the whole area became closely built up, while pockets of industry also sprang up. Traffic growth meant rebuilding all the stations.

The 'little halt' at Northfields now has two long island platforms. Among the smaller stations, Sudbury Town, its traffic swollen from 60,000 to 1.25 million passengers a year (1.6 million in 1985), was rebuilt in 1931 in the adventurous style of Charles Holden, which became the model for later LT stations.

THE METROPOLITAN 'EXTENSION'

The stages by which the Metropolitan just missed trunk-line status were piecemeal. On 13 April 1868 a single track, mostly in tunnel, was opened from the Inner Circle at Baker Street to Swiss Cottage by the METROPOLITAN & ST JOHN'S WOOD (incorporated on 29 July 1864, worked like all the other subsidiaries by the Metropolitan, and absorbed in 1882). There was no through running from the City between 1869 and 1907. Anything like a full service had been impossible since 1892, when alterations left only a single road from the 'Extension' to the Circle (Outer Rail), but such a service began on 4 November 1912, when the present layout came into use. In 1929 Chiltern Court, a large block of flats, was completed, an early example of the use of 'air rights' over a station.

By 1903 Baker Street had 929 steam trains arriving daily from east and west along the Circle and from the 'Extension', while 13.2 million passengers were passing the barriers annually. Thirty years later the daily number of trains had risen to 1,438, now all electric. In 1959 a census revealed 14,550 people entering the station between 16.30 and 19.00 daily, the large exchange traffic being additional. In 1985, 17.6 million passengers passed the barriers.

A double-track extension, emerging fully into the open at Finchley Road, was sanctioned on 5 August 1873 from Swiss Cottage to the River Brent, and was opened on 30 June 1879 to West Hampstead and on to Walm Lane (now Willesden Green) on 24 November. Doubling out to Swiss Cottage was not completed until 1882. Suburban development was little more than the large villas of St John's Wood. West End Lane, on which West Hampstead station stands, had for years been a favourite country drive of Queen Victoria. The KINGS-BURY & HARROW, jointly owned by the Metropolitan and the St John's Wood companies, was authorised on 16 July 1874 to build on further. The 5.5 miles opened on 2 August 1880 with but one intermediate station. There are now five. Harrow-on-the-Hill station (now of course completely rebuilt) was in 'Queen Anne' style and established the tradition of good architecture maintained by the Metropolitan and London Transport. Thirty-six trains arrived daily. By 1961 there were 185 down trains from Baker Street.

The project included a connection back at Finchley Road with the adjacent Midland. From 1 October 1880 exchange of freight traffic began, for the Metropolitan was opening goods depots along the Extension served by its own trains. Used until 1948, it was removed in 1953.

Under Watkin's leadership the pace of extension accelerated, though the ultimate objective was kept a close secret. The HARROW & RICKMANSWORTH company, incorporated on 7 August 1874, opened its line to Pinner on 25 May 1885 and to Rickmansworth on 1 September 1887. 'What could be the object of carrying the line through a district consisting only of farms and fields?' asked a contributor to a local newspaper. But construction was hastened forward into the Chiltern fastnesses, the small town of Chesham being reached on 8 July 1889. From a junction at Chalfont Road (now Chalfont & Latimer) the line pushed on through Amersham and by the Wendover Gap through the crest of the Chilterns to reach Aylesbury on 1 September 1892. This left Chesham on a single-track branch.

Still the Metropolitan forged on. On 1 July 1891 it took over the AYLESBURY & BUCKINGHAM, hitherto worked by the GW. The line had been opened on 23 September 1868 from Aylesbury to the LNW's Bletchley and Oxford branch. Verney Junction was so isolated that it was named after the local landowner. In 1897 a through service from Baker Street began over the 50.5 miles.

The motive behind this thrust became public in 1893 when the Manchester, Sheffield & Lincolnshire, also under Watkin's chairmanship, obtained sanction for its long-coveted London Extension and became the Great Central. It was to build southward to Quainton Road on the Verney line and enjoy running powers thence to Harrow South Junction. From there to Canfield Place, behind Finchley Road station, the

Metropolitan would provide an extra pair of tracks to be rented to the GC for its exclusive use.

Watkin had envisaged fusion of the two companies, but ill-health had forced his retirement in 1894 and union with the impoverished GC held no attraction for the now flourishing suburban railway. For Willesden had almost doubled its population in ten years, while Wembley and Harrow, for so long ill-served by the LNW, were growing fast. Even rural Neasden had 150 season-ticket holders by 1888. In addition relations were soured by the personal animosity of J. Bell, Watkin's successor, towards Pollitt, the GC general manager.

'METROLAND'

The Metropolitan now concentrated on developing the countryside of Middlesex and south Buckinghamshire. Edwards and Pigram suggested that the Metropolitan catered for the new stratified society: lower middle classes with an income secure enough to obtain an easy mortgage; managerial classes in outer estates; and country gentry travelling a few days a week. In 1904 'for the convenience of hunting gentlemen' a train left Baker Street at 09.05, hunters to be boxed at Finchley Road by 09.00. Suburban settlement was encouraged not only by electrification, frequent services and reasonable fares, but by lavish advertising and by land speculation and building. These last activities were handled by the Surplus Lands Committee, whose work was transferred in 1919, to comply with legal requirements, to the Metropolitan Railway Country Estates Ltd. Its first estate was laid out at Cecil Park, Pinner, and by 1939, 4,600 houses had been built on 'Met' estates.

Eventually from Wembley far into the Chilterns became 'Metroland', but there are really three Metrolands: the small terrace and semi-detached houses of the 1920s out to Wembley; the larger semis and detacheds of the 1930s to Northwood; and the large and costly properties of Moor Row and out into the Chilterns. Wembley, a hamlet in Harrow Parish until 1894, numbered 10,277 in 1881, 31,217 in 1911 and 124,843 in 1961. The old town of Harrow, spreading over the plain around the Hill, mushroomed from 49,020 in 1921 to 96,756 in 1931 and 219,494 in 1951. Local job opportunities

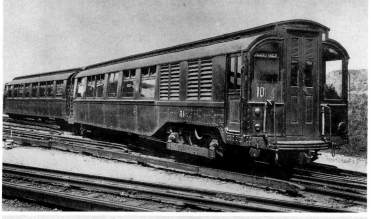

Plate 28 The Inner Circle in steam days. A train on the 'Outer Rail' approaches Aldgate station in about 1902. (*London Transport Museum*)

Plate 29 Motor car and trailer of the Charing Cross, Euston & Hampstead Tube. (*London Transport Board*)

Plate 30 An early District electric train at an unidentified spot, perhaps on the Ealing & South Harrow. Note the American influence upon the rolling stock under Zerkes's regime, and also the invasion of building upon rural Middlesex after District incursions. (*L&GRP*)

FAR-FLUNG METROLAND

Plate 31 Baker Street, gateway to Metroland. On the right an electric locomotive prepares to take an Aylesbury train as far as Rickmansworth. (*L&GRP*)

Plate 32 Quainton Road, distant outpost of the urban Metropolitan Railway, presents a striking contrast to Baker Street. The branch to Verney Junction is seen diverging to the right. (*L&GRP*)

Plate 33 A Metropolitan freight train in rural Buckinghamshire in 1903: an illustration of the company's desire to achieve main-line status. (*L&GRP*)

TABLE 10

TRAINS ON THE METROPOLITAN 'EXTENSION' LINE
(Mondays to Fridays)

	Miles from Baker Street	1901	1913	1961	1986
Leaving Baker Street	0	123	295	449*	445†
Terminating at:					
Willesden Green	3.75	31	62	–	19‡
Neasden	5.0	46	91	6	4
Wembley Park	6.5	–	–	43	87
Stanmore	9.75	–	–	155	132
Harrow	9.5	21	49	27	9
Uxbridge	16.5	–	42	107	83
Pinner	12.5	–	27	–	–
Rickmansworth	17.5	13	–	2	6
Watford	17.5	–	–	63	72
Chesham	25.75	3	14	2	2
Amersham	23.75	–	–	19	31
Aylesbury	38.25	3	10	25#	–
Verney Junction	50.5	6	–	–	–

* 251 Metropolitan and 198 Bakerloo trains.
† 217 Metropolitan and 228 Jubilee trains.
‡ Includes one terminating at West Hampstead.
# The LT service was cut back to Amersham after 9 September 1961.

are limited and a high proportion of the working population travels to Central London, except where, as at Rickmansworth, there are pockets of industry.

The 1930s perhaps epitomise the Metropolitan. From the floodtide of houses sweeping across rural Middlesex and from the Chiltern towns it carried breadwinners daily to the City, wives to the West End weekly and families to the occasional dinner and show. In the other direction hikers crowded weekend trains out to the Chilterns.

DEVELOPMENTS OF THE EXTENSION

On 1 March 1906 the Harrow–Canfield Place tracks were leased to the GC, and on 2 April all Metropolitan property north of Harrow was leased to a Metropolitan & Great Central Joint Committee. Thereafter increasing traffic matched by constant improvements converted an orthodox steam line into a specialised 'rapid-transit' system.

On 1 January 1905 electric working by multiple units began

between Baker Street, Harrow and Uxbridge. Electric loco-motives were provided to haul through trains, steam taking over at Willesden Green until 1 November 1906, Wembley Park until 19 July 1908, and Harrow thereafter. On 5 January 1925 electric traction was extended to Rickmansworth, where the fastest locomotive changes in the world were carried out. On 12 September 1960 locomotive haulage was abolished and multiple units began running to Amersham, all LT services to Aylesbury being withdrawn. The Chesham branch was also electrified.

In 1932 the Metropolitan carried 4 million tons of merchandise and minerals, but from 1 November 1937 the LNE took over the goods workings and provided power for the trains north of Rickmansworth. Two Pullman cars were introduced on 1 June 1910, even running out to Verney Junction. They were withdrawn on 7 October 1939.

Quadrupling of the Metropolitan tracks between Finchley Road and Wembley Park was completed in stages between 30 November 1913 and 31 May 1915. The section on to Harrow went into service on 10 January 1932 but, beyond, all continued to share one pair of lines, electric and steam trains; suburban, express and freight; LT and LNE. The 1935 Plan (Chapter IX) provided for further quadrupling but this was not completed to Watford South Junction until 18 June 1962.

South of Finchley Road there were only two tracks. To eliminate this bottle-neck, made worse by three intermediate stations, the Metropolitan planned a tube from Kilburn to the Circle Line at Edgware Road, rebuilding the latter in 1926 as a start. Then, as part of the 1935 Plan, a tube was built to bring the Bakerloo from Baker Street to join the Extension at a rebuilt Finchley Road. This opened on 20 November 1939 with two intermediate stations.

Finchley Road had been rebuilt in 1913, but as it had no exchange functions and only a single island platform between the 'slow lines', it was therefore again rebuilt to allow cross-platform interchange. The tracks were rearranged so that the Bakerloo trains could use the central pair and could call at all stations to Wembley Park. To the north they diverged on a new burrowing junction for Stanmore, their place being taken on the main line by Metropolitan stopping trains. The Stanmore trains were diverted to the Jubilee line when it opened on 1 May 1979. In 1903, fifteen trains left Baker Street between 18.00 and 19.00. During the same period in 1962, forty-three trains left Finchley Road, where all trains called for cross-platform interchange, carrying some 20,000 passengers. There has been little change since in the numbers of peak-hour trains, though off-peak Metropolitan frequencies had by 1986 fallen to 4 per hour to Uxbridge, 4 to Watford and 1 to Amersham.

UXBRIDGE

What was to become the Extension's busiest branch was promoted by the HARROW & UXBRIDGE, incorporated on 6 August 1897 to extend the District's South Harrow Line (Chapter IV) and originally a subsidiary of that company. But District resources proved unequal to raising the capital, and accordingly the local promoters persuaded the Metropolitan to work the line. This was authorised on 9 August, together with a link from Rayners Lane to the Extension at Harrow North Junction. The District was consoled with running powers from South Harrow.

The branch was finally opened on 4 July 1904, worked by a steam shuttle service until electric trains began running through from Baker Street on 1 January 1905. Disputes delayed through running of District trains until 1 March 1910.

It was an area of oaks in the hedgerows and fields of hay grown for London stables. Ruislip (3,556 in 1901) was the only intermediate station and the service of forty-eight Metropolitan and fifteen District trains each way in 1910 was lavish. Ickenham, with a 1921 population of 433, was the only other place. Its halt opened on 25 September 1905 with such short platforms that trains had to draw up twice. While surrounding estates were being built, commuters walked in wellingtons along the muddy roads to the stations. Rayners Lane, dating from 26 May 1906, for years served 'Two or three . . . houses, a sewage farm and a rifle range' (A. A. Jackson). Ruislip Manor Halt, opened on 5 August 1912, had a field path for access and trains stopped only on request.

The halts formed the nuclei of the new communities. Parades of shops were built at the entrances and fields disappeared beneath red brick-and-tile semi-detacheds and tiny gardens. The Robinson Estate was laid out at Rayners Lane between 1929 and 1952, and Metropolitan Railway Country Estates laid out Harrow Garden Village there after 1928. The number of residents served by the line grew from 48,000 in 1931 to 95,000 in 1938. Between 1931 and 1951 the population of Ruislip/Northwood Urban District rose by 326 per cent, the largest increase in Greater London.

Bookings at Ruislip Manor rose from 17,000 in 1931 to 1.3 million in 1939 (1.5 million in 1986) and those at Rayners Lane from 22,000 in 1930 to 4 million in 1937 (3.2 million in 1986). London Transport rebuilt the halts to Charles Holden's designs as worthy centres of the new suburbs.

Uxbridge has a different and longer history, being one of several towns which grew up where important roads, in this case the Oxford Road, crossed the broad, marshy Colne valley. With a large market, its prosperity also depended on the coaching trade. In 1831, with 3,043 souls, it was one of the more important Middlesex towns. The townsfolk bitterly opposed the GW Bill, but there is no evidence that, once it became law, they refused the line passage through the town. In any case there was rejoicing when the branch from West Drayton to Vine Street close to the town centre put the town on the railway map. Some through trains ran to Paddington, but passengers were few, especially to Central London, and the service was withdrawn from 10 September 1962. Freight traffic ceased on 13 July 1964.

Powers were obtained on 28 June 1861 by the UXBRIDGE & RICKMANSWORTH to extend up the Colne to the LNW at Rickmansworth, but they remained unused. Instead, on 2 August 1898 the GW received sanction to link it with the GW&GC near Denham. In the event the line only reached a terminus at High Street, which robbed it of any real utility. A sparse auto-train service from Denham was provided between 1 May 1907 and 31 August 1939. High Street was closed to general goods traffic on 25 September 1939, but handled coal until 2 April 1962.

Neither branch had much effect on Uxbridge, which stagnated picturesquely, its coaching trade dead and its flour mills dying, and the population figure for 1901 was almost the same as it had been seventy years before. The significant year was 1904, which saw the coming of both the Metropolitan and the electric trams. In the short run, the latter had more effect, cars running through to Shepherd's Bush and finally ending Uxbridge's isolation. During the decade 1901–11 the population grew threefold to 10,374. By 1931 it reached 31,887 and, by 1961, 63,762. There is much local industry and the proportion of the working population travelling to Central London is much smaller than from other stations on the line.

The Metropolitan's terminus was in Belmont Road. It had a simple red-brick building on one platform, but the other was shelterless and to it District and Piccadilly trains were exiled. It became hopelessly inadequate and on 4 December 1938 was replaced by a spacious station in the High Street. The bus station adjoins to provide a model traffic centre, its architecture worthy of its central site. In the post-war period Piccadilly trains took over from District and off-peak they now terminate at Rayners Lane.

THE GREAT CENTRAL

On 26 July 1898 GC coal trains began to come south past Quainton Road. But after a row with Bell, who on 30 July personally stopped the passage of one onto the Metropolitan, regular running did not begin again until 15 March 1899, the day passenger traffic commenced at Marylebone, a date linked with the completion of quadrupling works north of Canfield Place. Merchandise traffic began on 11 April. Marylebone was approached from Canfield Place by 2 miles of double track mostly in a covered way.

The GC's advent found favour with a public obsessed with the perceived monopoly enjoyed by established companies and the *Railway Magazine* lyrically hailed the newcomer. It trumpeted 'eminently satisfactory' on learning that the first three trains out of Marylebone carried fifty-five passengers between them. But other journals were more sceptical.

Nor did long-distance traffic ever develop satisfactorily. In November 1903, 13 northbound passenger, 1 parcels and 12 freight trains passed Quainton Road daily, and this did not greatly vary over the next fifty years. In 1902 Sir Sam Fay was recruited as general manager. His characteristically vigorous policy included the building up of outer suburban services, for the Company could ill afford to neglect any source of revenue.

Fay set an example by living at Gerrards Cross.

On the Aylesbury line, the agreement with the Metropolitan precluded stops short of Harrow. Outside peak hours, services were irregular, and even in 1961 there were only seven such (against a virtually hourly service from Baker Street). Though the Neasden–Northolt line was built through open country, lavish station accommodation was provided. But housing development brought little traffic to the four stations, for it was abstracted by the parallel Ealing & South Harrow. In recent years the number of trains calling (eight down trains at Sudbury Hill in 1985) has probably been the smallest in London apart from Clapham and Wandsworth Road. Beyond West Ruislip, however, traffic is heavy. A town-rubbish forwarding depot was established at Northolt Junction in 1981; the receiving one was at Calvert (for the old clay-pits).

DECLINE, FALL AND RISE AT MARYLEBONE

The red, Tudoresque façade at Marylebone, strangely provincial and more becoming to, say, a Hereford, together with the pretentious hotel building, vacated by the Railways Board in 1986 before once more becoming an hotel, conceal the four platforms of the little-used terminus. The spacious concourse was provided to serve four more platforms never built. For most of the day it is so quiet that actors in television series are frequently being filmed arriving from all sorts of impossible places.

In 1903 there were only 14 daily arrivals. By 1958 these had increased to 61, but 53 were suburban services non-existent in 1903. The five down Manchester trains were by then carrying an average of seventy-nine passengers apiece. In 1959 all services other than one or two overnight ones were cut back at Nottingham. From 18 June 1962 all suburban services were operated by diesel multiple units and service frequencies were boosted. On 5 September 1966 regular passenger services north of Aylesbury ceased. A 1961 census day saw 6,069 passengers leaving on forty-nine trains, nearly half of them on the ten trains departing during the busiest hour.

Marylebone has been used to relieve other termini for excursions and holiday overnight trains, while during the

Euston rebuilding trains were diverted at Bletchley to Aylesbury. Freight traffic at Marylebone ceased in 1952, the goods shed becoming a parcels depot until 28 March 1966, when the traffic was diverted to Euston. The coal depot closed in 1967 and the 28 acre goods yard was sold to the GLC for housing. Neasden marshalling yard and locomotive sheds were also closed.

Since the 1962 dieselisation the suburban services have been starved of investment, in stark contrast to the other northern lines, and Aylesbury has had a worse service than any other town of comparable size and equivalent distance. The only surprise was that closure notices were not posted until 1984. High Wycombe trains could be diverted to Paddington, while all passengers on the Aylesbury line could be accommodated by a shuttle to Amersham and Baker Street trains thence. The consequent furore by commuters who preferred the elderly DMUS indicated that LT trains were regarded as unsuitable for outer-suburban conditions.

A number of local authorities took BR to court to compel it to allow discussion of the costs involved. The judgement was favourable to BR, but the delay allowed full mobilisation of the opposition. Meanwhile a rather impracticable scheme to convert Marylebone to a coach station approached through the narrow tunnels by a dedicated road was rejected by National Travel (there would have been a 6in clearance between coaches passing at high speed). In 1986 withdrawal of closure proposals was announced, the ostensible reason given being the increase of LRT traffic, but investment and development were promised for what was now being marketed as the 'Chiltern Line'. Since 1984 Christmas shopping excursions have been run to Milton Keynes via Aylesbury from the High Wycombe line and this may presage a regular service beyond Aylesbury.

In 1986 Marylebone became the only London terminus to see regular steam working. Very popular luxury and high-cost excursions were run.

METROPOLITAN AND GREAT CENTRAL BRANCHES

With the opening of the GC extension to Quainton Road the line to VERNEY JUNCTION sank to branch status. From 6

July 1936 Metropolitan trains ceased to run beyond Aylesbury, the LNE also withdrawing its local service. Through parcels and freight trains ran until 6 September 1947, when they were all diverted over the Calvert Spur.

The line to BRILL was the oddest ever to come within the LT fold. Built privately by the Duke of Buckingham and opened in part during 1871, it was taken over by the Oxford & Aylesbury Tramroad Company in 1894. As part of an abortive attack on the West Midlands, the Metropolitan took over on 1 December 1899. Thenceforward an aged but spotless 4–4–0T and a rigid eight-wheeled coach with an occasional wagon attached maintained a service until the LPTB closed this working museum from 1 December 1935. In its last year the line carried a daily average of fifty-eight passengers and 34 tons of goods.

The electrified CHESHAM branch (3 miles), winding down the side of its Chiltern valley, remains single track. It is worked off-peak by a shuttle service, through trains to Baker Street and beyond being provided at peak periods.

On 2 November 1925 the Metropolitan and the LNE opened a joint 2.5 mile branch from a triangular junction south of Rickmansworth to WATFORD. LNE steam trains ran in equal numbers to the Metropolitan ones until the folly of this dawned on them and in May 1926 the Metropolitan took over entirely. A shuttle service from Rickmansworth lasted from 1925 to 1934. The Watford terminus, in traditional domestic style, is in a quiet residential street far from the town centre. Yet it has four off-peak departures for London hourly against two from Rickmansworth.

The newest branch is from Wembley Park to STANMORE, promoted by the Metropolitan and opened on 10 December 1932. Though the district was still rural, 144 trains a day were provided. As a result, within five years it had been largely built over. From 20 November 1939 all trains were Bakerloo (now Jubilee).

In 1924 the LNE opened WEMBLEY STADIUM station for the Empire Exhibition. It had a platform on a single track that made a complete loop from the Northolt line. Until closure in 1968 a frequent roundabout service was run from Marylebone for Cup Finals and on other occasions.

CHAPTER VIII

The Midland and the Great Northern

THE COMING OF THE MIDLAND

Both the Midland and the Great Northern were major carriers of coal and freight and had an important express passenger business. But their policy towards suburban traffic diverged and consequently the pattern of suburban growth differed between, say, Hendon and Hornsey, or Boreham Wood and Barnet.

Prior to 1857 all the Midland's London traffic passed through Rugby, but in that year the Company reached Hitchin on the GN. On 1 February it began to work passenger trains into King's Cross. Its service was sparse, there being but seven departures a day from King's Cross in 1864, but with the limitation on line capacity imposed by primitive signalling and braking, congestion on the GN was severe. Naturally if anyone had to suffer it was the tenant Midland, so, in 1862, 1,000 Midland passenger trains and 2,400 freight trains suffered severe delay. The LNW was also prone to place embargoes on Midland traffic on the grounds of congestion.

Independent access to London became a necessity. As a first step, though enjoying full rights at King's Cross Goods, on 2 January 1865 the Midland opened St Pancras Goods on a branch from the GN–NL curve (p. 83), giving it access from both the GN and the LNW. On 22 June 1863 a line had been sanctioned from Bedford to St Pancras passenger terminus on Euston Road.

As with the other lines entering London from the north, the main natural obstacles were the Chilterns, the South Herts Plateau and the Hampstead Heights. These were crossed by using the Luton Gap, by Elstree Tunnel and through the long Haverstock Hill Tunnel (1,833yd), approached by similar

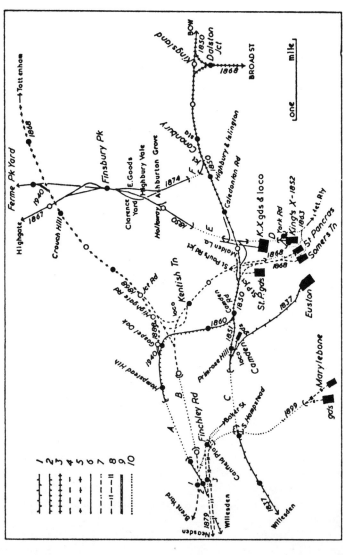

FIG 16 The approaches to the northern termini: 1 LNWR; 2 Hampstead Junction Railway; 3 NL; 4 Midland; 5 Tottenham & Hampstead Junction Railway; 6 GNR; 7 Metropolitan; 8 GC; 9 war-time spurs; 10 lines in tunnel. Tunnels: A Hampstead; B Haverstock Hill; C Primrose Hill; D Gas Works; E Copenhagen; F Canonbury.

elbow bends to the parallel one at Primrose Hill. On the south side of the Brent valley, which was crossed on a nineteen-arch viaduct, land was purchased to lay out a marshalling yard. After passing through the small cathedral city of St Albans, no other place of consequence was passed before Kentish Town.

There has been confusion as to the opening dates of the St Pancras extension, but the ground has been cleared by Geoffrey Webb, who is of the opinion that through merchandise (not mineral) began on 9 September 1867. On 13 July 1868 a local ('suburban' would be a misnomer) service began between Bedford and Moorgate, using the 'St Pancras branch' which diverges at St Paul's Road Junction and leads down to the Widened Lines. St Pancras itself was opened on 1 October.

ST PANCRAS

By 1865 London had expanded northward to Kentish Town and the last 1.5 miles were through a built-up area. There was the usual outcry about loss of amenity when it was found that six of the 400 trees in Camden Square would be destroyed. But the 3,000 houses razed in Agar Town and Somers Town were no loss, as they were among the most horrifying London slums and 'bounded by mountains of refuse from Metropolitan dustbins' in an area inappropriately named La Belle Isle. Fortunately the Norman Church of Old St Pancras escaped, though Churchyard sidings commemorated a near miss.

The Regent's Canal proved an obstacle to the Midland and its neighbours. The LNW crossed over it and descended Camden Incline; the GN dipped under in Gas Works Tunnel, with a steep grade beyond; only the Midland, after bridging it, continued on the level, so the terminus was raised on arches 12–17ft above Euston Road. The street level was given over to storage of Burton beer, an important traffic for the Midland. To economise on space the arches were built with spans of 24ft 9in, a multiple of beer-barrel dimensions.

Gilbert Scott's immense Gothic façade dominates Euston Road. The building was once a hotel, but is now let as offices, though happily there is a firm proposal to restore hotel functions. Reflecting the solid but romantic opulence of the mid-Victorian period, it was rated as 'one of the chief architectural ornaments of the metropolis'. After a period in which it was regarded with aesthetic horror, contemporary taste has restored it to its former position.

The station behind is equally bold in conception. The seven platforms, all except No 1 accessible to electric trains, are covered by a 25,000 sq ft glazed roof with a single span 240ft wide and 100ft high. F. S. Williams wrote in 1877: '. . . in result we have an arch, not only of extraordinary lightness and beauty, but of equally extraordinary strength'. It was the work of W. H. Barlow. The Scott booking-hall has been well restored.

In 1874, 18 Midland and 6 Great Eastern (Chapter IX) trains left St Pancras on weekdays and at St Paul's Road Junction were joined by 59 trains from Moorgate and 14 more working through from the London, Chatham & Dover. By 1903 there were 38 suburban and 28 main-line arrivals at St Pancras, the latter being considerably less than Euston's 42 and the 41 at King's Cross. But the ordinary-passenger 'user' figure that year was 2.5 million compared with the 2.6 million at Euston. So train occupancy was greater, doubtless because of third-class comfort on the Midland. In addition there were a calculated 7.3 million season-ticket journeys compared with the 1.9 million at Euston. Census day in 1961 recorded seventy-seven trains leaving with 16,636 passengers. Between 16.00 and 19.00 there were fourteen departures with 5,561 passengers. This represents a peak-period concentration of only 35 per cent, vividly underlining the then relative unimportance of suburban traffic.

At the height of the closure mania there were plans to divert long-distance trains to Euston, to provide a service from Leicester to Moorgate, and to close St Pancras. In 1969 these were officially shelved, partly because the latter had become a listed building, and partly because of increasing traffic boosted by the eclipse of Marylebone.

Investment has been stop-go; the improved services by new DMUs in the early 1960s were allowed to stagnate until suburban electrification and the introduction of HSTs in 1983 for long-distance. In 1985 on Mondays to Fridays there were 27 HST departures, 3 locomotive-hauled and 37 electric. In that year too the Edinburgh and Aberdeen Travelling Post

Offices were transferred from King's Cross as Derby had become an intermodal mail centre. But for passengers, while St Pancras was once a gateway to Scotland, Ireland and the West Riding, trains no longer go further than Sheffield, other than three evening trains (1986 timetable), one to Barnsley and two to Leeds. In 1986 some 22,000 passengers passed through daily.

THE MAIN LINE

Somers Town goods station, the site of which is now being occupied by the new British Library, adjoined St Pancras and was developed as a potato market. In the 1960s it was worked as a single depot with St Pancras Goods, dealing with outward traffic while the inward was concentrated on the latter. Together they formed a then typical large London goods station, of a type now completely disappeared. About 85,000 consignments a week were dealt with, collected and delivered by 330 lorries. In 1960, twelve 'fitted' and two 'non-fitted' trains arrived daily, mainly from midnight onward from such centres as Glasgow, Leeds, Sheffield, Burton and Bedford. The whole complex was closed for freight on 5 June 1967 and for coal on 23 April 1968.

The passenger locomotive depot was at Kentish Town, as were the original carriage sidings. The latter were later transferred to Cricklewood, also developed as the electric depot, 5 miles out. Land values precluded a site further in. Cricklewood is also the terminal (opened in 1977) of containerised town rubbish for despatch to Stewartby (Bedfordshire) for filling in the clay-pits of the brickworks. Just to the north, Brent marshalling yard was one of the largest in London. During the 1950s an average of 25,000 wagons passed through weekly. Today it is scarcely used. Hendon was the terminal of the 'Condor' container service to Glasgow, precursor of the Freightliners and running between 16 March 1959 and 20 October 1967. The main line was quadrupled to Elstree by 1895 and later throughout our area. Up it there used to trundle an endless succession of coal trains, now vanished. Even in 1956 there were fifty up freight trains daily through Elstree, compared with about fifteen in 1985.

On 29 July 1862 the Tottenham & Hampstead Junction was incorporated to build 4.5 miles of double track from the GE's Cambridge line at Tottenham North Junction to Gospel Oak station on the Hampstead Junction. The Midland and the GE each contributed a third of the capital. The 4.25 miles from Tottenham to Highgate Road (closed 1 October 1915) opened on 21 July 1868 with a GE service from Fenchurch Street via Stratford. This lasted only until 31 January 1870, for it was impossibly circuitous and only at Holloway was there much building.

Shortly after, the triangular layout was completed at the Tottenham end, and on 3 January 1870 the Midland had finished a spur from Kentish Town to Highgate Road, completing the triangle from Carlton Road Junction to the palindromic Junction Road Junction on 2 April 1883. On 1 October a service was inaugurated between Moorgate and Crouch Hill via Kentish Town, extended on 1 May 1871 to a new station at South Tottenham, built in open country. Later, in 1894, Midland trains were projected over the Tottenham & Forest Gate to Barking (Chapter IX).

A meagre GE service started in 1885 between Chingford and Highgate Road and this was extended to Gospel Oak on 4 June 1888. Normal traffic was light, but on bank holidays the families of artisans and clerks, who largely inhabited the area, poured out to Hampstead Heath and Epping Forest. Regular service ceased in September 1926, but bank-holiday trains ran until 1939. No physical connection was provided at Gospel Oak until 23 January 1916, and then only for freight. It was removed on 3 September 1922.

On 1 July 1902 the T&HJ passed into the joint ownership of the Midland and the GE. Today the boundary between the London Midland and Eastern Regions is just west of Crouch Hill. The main passenger flows over this important link have been: (1) the Midland suburban service to be described; (2) the much sparser GE suburban trains; (3) Midland trains, regular and excursion, to Southend, operated between 1895 and 1961; (4) up to six GE trains daily each way between St Pancras and Cambridge (1870–1923) (considering St Pancras to be more convenient than Liverpool Street for the West End, the GE acquired running powers in return for allowing Midland goods trains to work into the docks; race specials ran to Newmarket by this route and even royalty patronised it); (5) the Tilbury boat-trains, St Pancras being preferred for its facilities for passengers encumbered with baggage to Fenchurch Street until 1963, when electric trains from the latter were used until the traffic vanished.

In the years after 1939 the main function of the T&HJ was as a link in the freight 'belt line'. This was made possible by the permanent restoration of the Gospel Oak connection on 11 March 1940. In 1953, thirty-six westbound freights passed through Upper Holloway daily. They originated from the London, Tilbury & Southend (via the Tottenham & Forest Gate), from the docks and Temple Mills (via Tottenham South Junction), and from Ferme Park. Destinations were equally diverse, including Brent, Wellingborough, St Pancras Goods, Acton (Western Region), Feltham and Hither Green.

Mention must be made of the spur up to the GN main line at Harringay. Partially built in 1870 and used during World War I, it was fully restored on 8 January 1940 and used by freight trains to Ferme Park until 28 April 1968. After 1983 it was used by HSTs in Midland service to reach Bounds Green depot. Another spur was provided in 1879 from South Tottenham to Seven Sisters. That to Tottenham North Junction closed in 1961.

SUBURBAN SERVICES AND SUBURBAN GROWTH

The Midland's half-yearly report of 19 February 1869 said of the new London extension: 'It is proper to mention there is every possibility of a large passenger traffic in the suburbs of London.' At first this traffic was encouraged and eventually there were six stations on the 4 miles from St Pancras to West Hampstead and nine on the Tottenham & Hampstead Junction.

In 1874, of the 59 down trains leaving Farringdon Street, 24 were for the T&HJ and 35 for the main line, 10 terminating at Finchley Road, 5 at Haverstock Hill and 20 going to Hendon and beyond. Largely because of this very adequate service, the whole of the district traversed by the T&HJ became built up between 1870 and the opening of St Ann's Road station on 2

October 1882 (closed 9 August 1942). By 1900 suburbia also reached out to Cricklewood and there had been some development around Hendon and Mill Hill stations.

Much traffic was lost to trams and buses after 1905, but though the Midland suffered as severely as other lines, it had other than suburban fish to fry and made no attempt even to reduce the losses. The T&HJ service was greatly reduced and five of its stations closed. On the main line the service was reduced to a pale shadow and Camden Road (1 January 1916), Haverstock Hill (1 January 1916) and Finchley Road (11 July 1927) were closed.

The LMS also made no attempt to develop traffic from the Middle Zone and, uniquely for London, the service down the main line remained unimproved throughout the 1920–40 period. Between West Hampstead and Elstree, 8 miles beyond, there were only three intermediate stations. The enormous development of Hendon came about as a result of tube extensions, and while Mill Hill Broadway grew up at the station, the residents preferred the bus to the tube at Hendon Central.

The trend was not reversed until an interval service of DMUS was inaugurated on 11 January 1960 on both the main and T&HJ lines. At Elstree forty-five trains now called instead of thirty. Speeds were considerably increased and competitive fares were introduced. In March 1961, 88,723 passenger journeys were made from St Albans, a 27 per cent increase over March 1959.

But the service eventually stagnated, until 15 July 1983 when the full electric service to Bedford (53 route miles) was inaugurated. Needless to say the irresistible but infelicitous portmanteau 'BedPan' was eagerly embraced by the media and rejected by BR, who market the service under the uninspired 'Midland City'. The basic service is half-hourly to all stations from Moorgate to Luton and half-hourly semi-fast from St Pancras to Bedford. The consequence has been an upsurge in traffic and outer-suburban development, which daily fills the large station carparks at Radlett and beyond. The signal centre at West Hampstead controls the 62 route miles out to Irchester.

The hourly T&HJ diesel service was increased to half-hourly on 1 June 1981. In connection with electrification it was

COMMUTER FASHIONS AT LIVERPOOL STREET I

Plate 34   In the 1880s segregation of classes by train as well as by carriage was still rigid. The 1255 for Enfield (on Saturday 25 October 1884) exclusively carried workmen. (*GE Magazine*)

Plate 35   But a homeward-bound workman, who happened to be later, would have felt ill at ease among the bowler- and top-hatted clerks waiting for the 1355 that day. (*GE Magazine*)

COMMUTER FASHIONS AT LIVERPOOL STREET II

Plate 36 Bowlers had given way to boaters on the 'Jazz' Service of 1920, while the War had broken down the male exclusiveness of the City. (*Railway Gazette*)

Plate 37 Passengers on the new electric trains from Chingford and Enfield in 1961 arrived in undiminished numbers. But on this one at least women appear to be in the majority among the hatless commuters. (*Author*)

diverted from Kentish Town to Gospel Oak, though connections were less convenient. The spur from Highgate Road to Kentish Town was taken up.

THE GREAT NORTHERN RAILWAY

The Great Northern was also a major carrier of coal, merchandise and long-distance passengers. But in addition it allowed suburban traffic to develop to such an extent that, like the Sorcerer's Apprentice, the Company found it had created a rising tide that threatened to swamp the difficult approach to King's Cross. The 'suburban opportunity' became the 'suburban incubus' and the period 1875 to 1978 was spent by the GN and its successors in spasmodic attempts to remove it.

Under powers obtained on 26 June 1846 after a bitter struggle (Vol 5, *The Eastern Counties*), the GN built its main line from Doncaster to London. The Hitchin Gap was used to cross the Chiltern scarp and southward to Wood Green the full width of the South Herts Plateau was traversed, involving seven tunnels and the impressive Digswell Viaduct. The final obstacle was the spur of high ground outside King's Cross. It was this that made widening costly and did most to turn the 'opportunity' into the 'incubus'.

A goods depot was provided on Maiden Lane (now York Way) and here a temporary passenger terminus opened on 7 August 1850. Goods traffic began on 12 December and coal early the next year, the delay being caused by disputes with the South Yorkshire Railway and lack of interest on the part of the coal-owners. The GN was the first railway to bring coal to London in quantity. The struggle with sea-borne coal was intense and a rate war brought prices down from 30s to 17s.

In 1851 the Great Exhibition brought a flood of excursionists, the first mass movement on pleasure bent. Since there was no telegraph, Maiden Lane had no knowledge of special trains until they arrived. The return was equally chaotic. On one occasion 3,000 would-be passengers arrived to find that the trains would accommodate 1,000. A party of Yorkshiremen invaded a Lincoln train declaring it must take them home. Edmund Denison, the Chairman, was restrained from attempting to dislodge them single-handed, while cattle trucks were brought up, presumably for the Lincoln passengers.

The short extension to King's Cross was ready in 1852, and the first train to leave was the 07.00 Parliamentary for York on 14 October. The station had an arrival platform (the present No 1) and a departure one (No 8) separated by fourteen tracks, the whole covered by a great twin-arched roof, each with a 71ft span. The offices were all ranged along the departure platform.

A separate and severely plain hotel, still in use, was provided in 1854. Lewis Cubitt's façade, a mere screen, is even plainer. It stands modestly behind and below St Pancras. Cubitt said it was 'to depend for its effect on the largeness of some of its features, its fitness for its purpose and its characteristic expression of that purpose'. Modern taste applies the architect's yardstick both inside and out and finds that King's Cross measures up. Denison commented on its low cost, but the shareholders protested at 'the extravagance in erecting so splendid a station'. Their view would have appeared to have prevailed at most other GN stations.

In 1872 St Pancras Road was diverted away from the front of King's Cross to its present junction with Euston Road. The vacant space became cluttered with miscellaneous hutments dubbed the 'African Village'. They were mercifully swept away to complete the 1973 concourse, when at last the terminus became convenient for passengers and staff.

In 1855 there were 19 departures, 4 of them expresses. By 1862 there were 30, 10 expresses, 13 local and 7 Midland. On 1 October 1863 the 'Suburban and City' service was inaugurated to Farringdon Street (p. 89), and from 1 January 1866 through goods and passenger trains began to the London, Chatham & Dover. On the East branch, a platform corresponding to the later York Road station was in existence in 1866, but down trains coming up from the Metropolitan had to set back into the departure platform.

During 1862 a platform with a 'stepped' face was provided on the arrival side and numbered 2, 3 and 4. On 30 September 1868 the Midland used King's Cross for the last time, but the relief was only temporary. With the opening of suburban branches, numbers of trains grew. By August 1873 departures had swollen to 89; 20 were long distance, but there were 60 suburban trains from the Widened Lines and 9 from King's Cross. Accordingly a 'local' station was opened in 1875 with a separate booking-office in Cheney Road, now an area of crumbling shambles. On the site of the present platforms 9 and 10, it had three platforms and only two roads, a third being added in 1895.

Not until 1 February 1878 was there a platform on the 'Hotel curve'. But it was on a 1 in 60 gradient (within the tunnel itself the grade was 1 in 48). Until dieselisation came, on 23 March 1959, at peak periods the steam trains would emerge from the smoke-choked 'rat-hole' every few minutes, engines at full throttle. Then, with a load increased by some couple of hundred commuters, the big tank locos would have the task of getting the packed eight-coach trains into motion on the heavy grade before plunging into Gas Works Tunnel.

By January 1893 there were 539 daily movements into and out of the station. There were 43 main-line and 31 local departures from the terminal platforms, while 98 passenger and 77 goods trains blasted up the Hotel Curve. This led Sir William Acworth, the railway economist, to quote 'a competent critic' as saying: '. . . the King's Cross porters despatch human beings and the Finsbury Park people collect tickets faster than on any line I know'.

However, on 18 December 1893 a new island platform came into use, one side for arrivals and the other for departures. In 1903, 15.4 million passengers were dealt with, making it the busiest northern terminus. This was the result of the heavy suburban traffic, 54 per cent of the journeys being made by season-ticket holders.

In 1922 the rigid division into arrival and departure sides was broken down by running up suburban trains into the suburban platforms. On 15 December 1924 this part of the station was enlarged by two further platforms within the Hotel Curve. In September 1926 two more departure platforms (now Nos 6 and 7) were provided. They were very narrow and in 1938 were widened by taking out the No 9 road. Thus for a long time the present No 8 was numbered 10. The 'stepped' platform was also straightened into one long face.

Suburban traffic declined after 1903 and in 1952 less than half the number of trains arrived before 10.30 as had done so fifty years previously. Growing commuter traffic from Potters

Bar and beyond only partially compensated for losses of Middle and Inner Zone traffic diverted to Tube extensions. In 1960 daily 'user' averaged 30,000 in winter, 18,000 suburban and 12,000 main line. But in summer the latter figure swelled to 25,000 a day and to 50,000 on Saturdays.

Since 1950 the tendency on the long-distance services has been to provide more frequent and lighter trains with fixed formations. This was reinforced by the introduction of HSTs which by 1982 had a virtual monopoly. The only locomotive-hauled trains were night sleepers and extras. Between 1978 and 1987 (when electrification was extended to Peterborough) all outer-suburban services were converted to electric traction. These developments have resulted in increasing long-distance and outer-suburban traffic. The average daily number of passengers dealt with in 1986 was 37,000.

MAIN-LINE DEVELOPMENTS: KING'S CROSS TO FINSBURY PARK

Even in 1864 congestion of the double-track approach to King's Cross had become serious. James Allport, general manager of the Midland, complained: 'The Midland can never tell with anything like certainty at what time their trains will reach King's Cross.'

The terminus lay at the foot of 1.5 miles inclined at 1 in 107, the line passing through Copenhagen and Maiden Lane (or Gas Works) Tunnels. Between the two the line to the goods station and engine sheds branched off at Belle Isle.

In 1866 a second Copenhagen Tunnel was sanctioned, as was, in 1872, the spur from Finsbury Park to the North London at Canonbury (Chapter IV). This allowed freight trains, which hitherto had passed over Maiden Lane spur to the North London (for the docks and Royal Mint Street depot, outside Fenchurch Street), to avoid Copenhagen Tunnel altogether. Unfortunately Royal Mint Street was somewhat remote, though less so than King's Cross, a serious matter as cartage costs were high as a result of a rise in horse prices in the 1870s. So the GN leased a site at Farringdon Street and opened a depot there on 2 November 1874 (closed 15 January 1956). Trains would have to traverse the tunnels and the situation was as before.

Therefore in 1874 powers were sought for a second Gas

Works Tunnel. Things were now quite out of hand. In that year commuters were two and a half times as numerous as seven years before. Suburban trains were taking half an hour over the 1.5 miles from Holloway to the Metropolitan. Indignation meetings were held and a deputation was sent to wait on the GN. Thoroughly alarmed, the latter sought relief in the form of running powers for suburban trains into Broad Street via the Canonbury Spur. The LNW prevented the North London from granting these and in desperation the GN invited the NL to run trains from Broad Street out to its suburban stations.

GN goods trains began running over the Canonbury spur on 14 December 1874, followed on 18 January 1875 by the NL trains. These operated until the inauguration of the GN electrification in 1977, although after July 1945 they were operated by LNE and Eastern Region crews and on a much reduced scale. Instead of the seventy-three up trains of 1906, the twelve of 1960 brought in just over 2,500 commuters.

Goods trains began using the new Copenhagen Tunnel in August 1877 and soon after a flyover was provided at Holloway for the goods-depot branch. The duplicate Gas Works Tunnel went into service on 4 March 1878. The two tracks in this were both up, those in the original tunnel becoming down. Segregation of Metropolitan traffic on the outer roads was now possible south of Belle Isle.

Traffic increases soon nullified these improvements. The Chairman, Lord Colville, reported in January 1882 that 'towns were springing up within two or three miles of King's Cross as fast as people could build them'. In the two years to 1881 season-ticket holders increased by 25 per cent to 14,420. Goods traffic over the Widened Lines had reached massive proportions. Finally, two serious accidents fuelled justifiable public alarm over the signalling system. On 10 December 1881 four trains piled up in the darkness of Canonbury Tunnel and on 25 January 1882 a collision occurred in dense fog at Hornsey.

There was no option but to seek powers for third double-line tunnels. On 10 February 1882 Lord Colville said: '. . . the matter can be delayed no longer. We are now carrying traffic which produces £3,400,000 on the same rails near London as twenty years ago when there was traffic producing £1,300,000 only; besides we are influenced by the enormous suburban traffic . . .' The new Copenhagen Tunnel came into use in June 1886 and Gas Works in June 1892. Since then signalling improvements, the diversion of suburban traffic and the eventual ending of through freight have kept the situation well under control, so much so that the long-awaited 1977 simplification of the layout in the 'throat', has reduced the tracks to four and allowed abandonment of the second Copenhagen and Gas Works Tunnels. The goods flyover was rebuilt for passenger trains. At the same time the platforms beyond No 10 were also abandoned, except one for motorail purposes.

In 1960 there were some twenty-four daily departures from King's Cross Goods, compared with five in 1986. The freightliner terminal was opened in 1966 and this and aggregate and cement terminals are the remaining activities. Holloway station, just north of Copenhagen Tunnel, opened as a 'ticket station' in 1854 and closed on 1 October 1915. Here on the up side were the cattle docks serving the Metropolitan Cattle Market.

MAIN-LINE DEVELOPMENTS: FINSBURY PARK TO WELWYN GARDEN CITY

The original stations were Hornsey, Colney Hatch (New Southgate), Barnet (New Barnet), Potters Bar and Hatfield. On 1 July 1861 a wayside station was opened on the Seven Sisters Road, 2.75 miles from King's Cross. Hornsey Wood with its tea-gardens was near-by, but little other traffic was expected at its two wooden platforms. By 1867, however, it had become the junction for the Edgware branch. Traffic was increasing and the directors recommended a footbridge and 'waiting shed', but in the following year the proprietors were protesting at expenditure on platform canopies.

In 1869 Hornsey Wood became Finsbury Park, adopted as the name of the station. On 14 December 1874 rebuilding with four platforms was completed. By 1912, 550 trains a day were calling at the four island platforms served by six lines. Finsbury Park had become the key point of the suburban system. Passengers from the northern suburbs interchanged between trains bound for King's Cross, Moorgate or Broad

Street, or took the tube to the City or West End. Suburban trains were also terminated to relieve pressure on the lines down to King's Cross. To speed this exchange each local line was served by two platforms, the knowledgeable using trains as bridges between the platforms. An extra down island and outside road were added in 1911.

The post-war years saw decline: no more trains to the Northern Heights, passengers deserting the outdated Main and Hertford line services, and the Moorgate and Broad Street services skeletal. In 1961, 218 trains called, less than half the 1912 figure. But electrification reversed the trend, though platforms have been reduced to three islands served by five tracks with extra up and down goods/empty carriage roads.

In 1866 land had been bought south of Finsbury Park and eventually some 40 acres of sidings and depots were laid out. Clarence Yard (1874–1960) dealt with the down traffic and East Goods the up (1877–1960). Off the Canonbury Line were Highbury Vale (1876–1971) and Ashburton Grove (1884–1960), mainly for marshalling local trains. At Ferme Park (Hornsey) up and down marshalling yards were opened in 1888. They ceased to function as such in 1973, the down yard is now carriage sidings and the up the electric depot. There are more carriage sidings at Waterworks; and at Bounds Green (Alexandra Palace) is the HST depot.

Six tracks were available to Alexandra Palace (formerly Wood Green) from 1892. Quadrupling to New Barnet was sanctioned by the 1882 GN Act, but financial stringency prevented completion until June 1892. This included two tunnels, but there were three tunnels in the 2.5 miles from Greenwood Box (New Barnet) to Potters Bar and this bottleneck remained until widening was completed on 3 May 1959.

As a measure of later freight activity, there were fifty-six northbound trains daily through Alexandra Palace in 1957. Among the up services were express meat and fish trains from Aberdeen, Hull and Grimsby, vegetable trains from Peterborough and coal trains from Doncaster. In stark contrast, the 1985 timetables show only six northbound freightliners and six other trains.

In 1852 King's Cross was on the edge of London and Maiden Lane led out to Copenhagen Fields, a resort of holidaymakers. The *Illustrated London News*, describing the journey of the official train at the GN's opening, said that on emerging from Copenhagen Tunnel the train 'went skimming along a region of cornfields. This sudden transition from the busy haunts of life to quiet rural scenery, undisturbed even by the presence of a villa, is what chiefly strikes one . . .'

But the reporter sent by the same journal to cover the opening of the Alexandra Palace in 1873 found that it was not until Finsbury Park had been passed that 'bricks and mortar began to give way to fields and hedges'. Throughout the 1860s there had been much building in Holloway and along the Seven Sisters Road. This was respectable enough, but noisome slums had deflowered Copenhagen Fields.

In those early days North Middlesex and South Herts were a land 'of indifferent farming and a thinly peopled country-side'. The *Railway Times*, reporting evidence to the Committee considering the London & York Bill in 1845, talks of 'Passing over the first ten miles [from London] only, along which there was absolutely no population except a few farmers, country gentlemen and rusticating merchant princes . . .'

In 1866 passengers awaiting the 08.45 at Hornsey watched a hare being chased across neighbouring fields. But in the 1870s rows of small terrace houses spread across Hornsey and Wood Green, a process completed in the next decade so that they became Lord Colville's 'towns'. Of yellow stock bricks and slate roofed, they are as characteristic of that age as the Metroland houses are of a later one. Every front downstairs window had its small bay, and in most an aspidistra could be seen through lace curtains. In 1931 an LCC survey found 248 in every 1,000 of the occupied population of Hornsey to be clerks.

Hornsey grew from 19,387 inhabitants in 1871 to 61,097 in 1891, but the main period of growth in districts north of Wood Green was slightly later. At first the demand was for larger houses, and Thorne says of Friern Barnet that it was a scattered suburban area, many of the houses being residences of wealthy citizens, but at that date East Barnet had but 992 souls, though nearby Southgate was rapidly growing.

The higher ground was chiefly sought after for those large villas. So, when the rate of building accelerated after 1890, rows of small houses were built along the line. The GN policy of frequent services and reasonable season-ticket rates created a salient of continuous building that reached out to New Barnet by 1914. This is an equivalent distance from the centre to Harrow and to Sidcup, both of which were then far beyond the edge of Greater London. In this the GN showed the inconsistency of its policy. By 1870 suburban development had become an 'incubus', but it was continuously encouraged.

Even today there is open country between stations beyond, but Potters Bar grew enormously between 1930 and 1960. The opening of Brookman's Park in 1926 and Welham Green in 1986 gives clues about building dates. Both Hatfield and Welwyn Garden City became New Towns after World War II, leading to their main period of growth.

ENFIELD AND HERTFORD

Alexandra Palace (formerly Wood Green) station on the main line was opened in 1859 and on 4 April 1871 a 4 mile branch was opened to Enfield, an old-established and flourishing town, but already served by the Great Eastern (Chapter IX). The intervening country was almost deserted, its cold clay soils unpopular for agriculture and building. In 1875 Thorne described Palmer's Green as 'a little gallery of houses along the Enfield Road', and, because of landowners' reluctance to sell, not a single house went up in the area between 1876 and 1888. Bowes Park (station opened 1880) and the Bycullah Estate (Enfield) grew up after 1880, but the main building period did not come until trams were introduced along the parallel Green Lanes in 1907–9.

The GN's desire to bypass the Greenwood–Potters Bar and Welwyn North bottle-necks led to the branch acquiring strategic importance when incorporated into the HERT-FORD LOOP, a move eventually preferred to the original scheme of extending the High Barnet branch. The Loop was opened from just beyond Grange Park station to Cuffley on 4 April 1910, and a single track through Hertford to rejoin the main line at Langley Junction (Stevenage) was ready on 4

March 1918, the second track coming into use in 1920 (Vol 5, Chapter V). A new high-level station was provided at Enfield Chase, the old terminus remaining a goods depot until 1974.

Because of limited accommodation at Enfield Chase, peak-hour trains were reversed at Gordon Hill, though there was a basic half-hourly service to Hertford North. In addition the Loop was much used as an alternative route. In 1957, eleven down and thirteen up through freight trains were booked over it. Through passenger trains are still diverted in emergencies. The author experienced this four times between 1982 and 1986.

THE GREAT NORTHERN ELECTRIC

The 1955 Modernisation Plan envisaged suburban electrification as incidental to conversion of the East Coast Main Line, as happened on the West Coast Main Line, but the main scheme was shelved soon after, and though from time to time an imminent start to suburban electrification was announced, no definite date transpired. Dieselisation was introduced in 1959 with an improved thirty-minute service to Hatfield and to Hertford.

But thereafter services stagnated, as did investment, semaphore signalling persisting until modernisation was completed in 1977. On 18 August 1971 the press announced government grants towards electrification, which was considered eligible for an infrastructure grant under the 1968 Transport Act. On 8 November 1976 Stage 1 (36.25 route miles) was inaugurated with a twenty-minute service between Moorgate and Welwyn Garden City and another between the former and Hertford North. Stage 2 (33.75 route miles) went into service on 6 February 1978 with three semi-fast trains an hour from King's Cross to Royston (in 1985 one was cut back at Letchworth), and in the following year one train an hour was projected beyond Hertford North to Letchworth. Promotion was vigorous under the title of 'Great Northern Electrics'.

In 1984, approval was given for the electrification of the East Coast Main Line to Edinburgh, work starting from Hitchin in January 1985. On 3 November 1986 the first electric train in public service on the line left Huntingdon for

King's Cross, the full outer-suburban service to Peterborough being inaugurated on 11 May 1987 with a basic hourly service augmented at peaks. Electric expresses would not be running for a further two years.

The Welwyn and Hertford services in their earlier years acquired a reputation for unreliability caused by technical and labour-relations difficulties. This prevented the service making a full impact. The outer service, connecting growing New and established towns, fared better, and since the 1980 deregulation, the lack of success for parallel commuter coaches compared with those of north Kent tells its own story.

THE NORTHERN HEIGHTS

To the north of London the scenery is hilly and diversified. The uplands of the South Herts Plateau are about 350ft high, diversified by deep valleys. From the plateau two prongs of high ground reach out south-westward, the Hampstead ridge and, behind it and much more cut up by valleys, that on which Chipping Barnet and Edgware stand. These are known as the 'Northern Heights'.

Because they are crowned with gravel, making water supply and drainage easy, the Northern Heights had more and larger villages than grew up on the clay plain to the west. During the eighteenth century Highgate and Hampstead had become favoured suburbs for the wealthy and artistic, and by 1860 such people were beginning to 'discover' the small town of Chipping Barnet and the surrounding villages.

But the LNW passed miles to the south and west of the high ground and the GN skirted it to the east. A number of schemes were floated to provide much-needed communication with this isolated district. Finally on 3 June 1862 the Edgeware (*sic*), Highgate & London was incorporated to build a single line from Seven Sisters (Finsbury Park) to Edgware, 8.75 miles. The company was sponsored by the GN and absorbed by it on 15 July 1867. What such a line meant to individuals may be judged from evidence given to the Parliamentary Committee by W. Hammond, vestry clerk of Finchley. Living in Whetstone he had business interests in the City. He travelled in by bus or coach, taking 90 to 105 minutes to the Bank at a cost of £30 a year. First-class annual rail seasons were to be £10 or £12 and the journey time was to be 50 minutes.

The line opened on 22 August 1867. Nothing but fields existed between Finsbury Park and Highgate, while, beyond, only Finchley (population 4,937 in 1861) and Edgware (705 in 1861) were of any importance at all. Mill Hill was tiny and remote from its station (now Mill Hill East).

On 13 May 1864 a short branch was authorised from Park Junction, 0.5 miles beyond Highgate, to Muswell Hill. The ridge here is capped with glacial clay and gravel and there were no villages. The objective was the proposed Alexandra Palace. The 0.75 mile extension to the walls of the Palace was the concern of the Muswell Hill Railway.

The branch was ready for the opening of the Palace on 24 May 1873. The day was fine and the ensuing rush was, according to Grinling, still talked of in the King's Cross booking-office twenty-five years later. On the first sixteen days 99,000 people travelled over the line. But on 9 June the Palace was burnt out and the branch was closed until the Palace reopened on 1 May 1875. The Muswell Hill Railway, one of the shortest in England, was not taken over by the GN until 1911. Its vicissitudes were manifold and it closed seven times between 1875 and 1898.

The 4 mile branch from the optimistically named Finchley & Hendon (later Finchley Church End and now Finchley Central) to High Barnet, authorised on 16 July 1866, opened on 1 April 1872.

Both branches were built as double-track and the original line was doubled to Finchley Central by January 1870. The section beyond remained single and became the branch after the opening of the High Barnet line, partly because the Midland was a more direct route from the Mill Hill area.

Until 1914 the service was extraordinarily good by the standards of the time. In 1872 there were 23 weekday departures from High Barnet, 15 from Edgware (terminating at Finchley) and 6 more from Finchley. By 1904, 51 up trains were leaving High Barnet, but 20 of the 23 Edgware departures still terminated at Finchley. There were 46 departures from Muswell Hill, 29 originating at Alexandra Palace. There were additional trains from East Finchley and Highgate and over 100 up trains called at stations on the

London side of Park Junction.

The climb up to the Northern Heights was severe. King's Cross Metropolitan to Finsbury Park was bad enough, but thence to Park Junction the 2.5 miles were continuously inclined at either 1 in 75 or 1 in 60, up which the diminutive tank engines would blast their slow way dragging long peak-hour trains of crowded four-wheelers.

They were crowded because a good service, low fares and healthy pleasant surroundings all encouraged suburban development. Stroud Green station opened in 1881 to serve the new streets covering the slopes of the Highgate ridge. Muswell Hill grew up between 1890 and 1910. After 1904 Hampstead Garden Suburb came into being between East Finchley and Golders Green stations. Beyond, houses were springing up round the stations out to Barnet. But the Edgware branch still penetrated a rural backwater. Barnet had grown from 3,375 inhabitants in 1871 to 11,335 in 1911, but in that year Edgware's population was still under a thousand.

After 1920 building extended out along the Great North Road to join Barnet with London, and Finchley with Hendon. But a salient of country separated Finchley/Whetstone from New Mill Hill/Edgware, and Old Mill Hill, Totteridge and Arkley remained curiously rural even in 1960. From 1914, however, train services fossilised. From 1915 the off-peak services to Moorgate and Broad Street ceased. The Gresley 'Quad-art' (quadruple-articulated sets) stock provided after 1925 was austere enough, but disgracefully the LMS was running sets of four-wheelers out from Broad Street, perhaps to make Moorgate passengers thankful for small LNE mercies. It was no way to counter tram and later trolley-bus competition along the Great North Road out to Barnet.

The steam service, now notoriously unreliable in winter, was saturated and the LNE lacked the capital for the radical improvement needed. The 1935 Plan (p. 192) therefore provided for the whole Northern Heights service to be transferred to London Transport. The Northern Tube was to be extended from Archway to surface at East Finchley. Tube trains would then run out to High Barnet and, over a doubled branch, to Edgware. The Northern City Tube (GN&C) was to be extended from Drayton Park to a new island platform on the east side of Finsbury Park, the Tube trains running on to

Alexandra Palace. Highgate would become a two-level exchange point between the two services, and the short Park Junction–East Finchley section would go out of regular use.

Northern Line trains began running to East Finchley on 3 July 1939 and to High Barnet on 14 April 1940. Steam trains continued to run to East Finchley until 2 March 1941, but the Edgware service was suspended from 11 September 1939 to facilitate doubling. Then, on 18 May 1941, tube trains were extended over the single line to Mill Hill East, principally to serve the barracks. All further work ceased because of World War II.

After 1945 London Transport had second thoughts. Costs had risen more than fares were likely to; the Green Belt would be rigidly protected, while war damage in the City had markedly reduced the commuter flow thither. Work was not resumed, and in February 1954 London Transport announced abandonment.

Meanwhile steam trains still chugged up to Alexandra Palace, but in the periodic post-war crises of staff and coal shortages it was the Palace services which were reduced or suspended first. Patrons thus got into the habit of bussing to Finsbury Park to catch the Tube. By 1954 two-coach trains, making some dozen trips from Finsbury Park, carried an average load of forty-five passengers. They ceased to run on 5 July 1954, though goods trains ran to Muswell Hill until 14 June 1956.

The 57 steam trains from High Barnet were replaced by 212 electric ones. Originating journeys from the eight stations increased from 3.5 million in 1934 to 12 million in 1947. By 1959 this had fallen to 11.6 million and by 1986 to some 10 million. G. F. A. Wilmot, in his excellent *The Railway in Finchley*, shows that this declining trend obscured an increase in peak loadings. In 1950 trains leaving Finchley Central for High Barnet between 17.30 and 18.00 carried an average of 1,690 passengers between them. Ten years later the figure had increased by 36 per cent. It has been in the off-peak periods that loadings have suffered most, which has led to lower revenue to set against nil cost savings.

A large proportion of the working population travels to Central London. For them the electric service is more frequent and, apart from periods of difficulty and consequent discontent, more reliable than in steam days, though since all trains stop at all stations schedules are little quicker. Whether crowded tube trains represent an advance in human dignity is another matter, especially compared with BR stock on the GN Electrics. The line does show some of the difficulties and limitations in extending tube-type services into the outer suburbs.

THE PICCADILLY EXTENSION

From the suburbs, old and new, along the main line to Potters Bar and the Hertford Loop to Gordon Hill, the percentage of the employed population travelling to Central London has been among the highest in Greater London. In 1951 the figures were 37 per cent from Hornsey, 35 per cent from Southgate and 30 per cent from Wood Green. The area has always been a problem one and thus was of special concern to the North and North East London Traffic Enquiry of 1925. The report stated:

> As far as concerns the suburban services of the L.N.E.R., it was generally admitted that if regard be had to their statutory obligation and to the limitations of a steam railway, there was little fault to be had in the manner in which the Company operated their local lines. But in not electrifying their suburban system they have exhibited a want of consideration for the needs of suburban traffic which the travelling public . . . feel they are entitled to expect from an important company possessing a monopoly of railway facilities north of Finsbury Park.

Those whose memories of the LNE embrace only Gresley Pacific locomotives and streamlined expresses will not realise how bad its suburban services were, starved of investment during the inter-war years. Its faults were compounded by its bitter rearguard action resisting public pressure and opposing Tube extension. Commuters voted with their feet, leaving the Underground at Finsbury Park not to join the LNE, but to partake in the unedifying nightly scramble for trams and buses across streams of northbound vehicles.

The LNE eventually bowed to pressure and on 4 June 1930 powers were obtained to extend the Piccadilly, which was financed under the Development (Loan, Guarantee & Grants) Act of 1929. The 7.66 mile extension, mostly on the surface beyond Bounds Green, was opened in stages, to Arnos Grove on 19 September 1932, to Enfield West (now Oakwood) on 13 March and to Cockfosters on 31 July.

To Bounds Green the line served a built-up area, relieving road traffic (30,000 a day were coming in to Finsbury Park by tram and bus) and cutting deeply into LNE traffic. Bounds Green is 400yd from Bowes Park, and Arnos Grove is 0.5 miles from New Southgate. Northward was the open farmland of Enfield Chase. This part of the line was speculative, but the builder was quick to follow. 'Old Southgate' was a village, but there were none to be served by Arnos Grove, Oakwood and even Cockfosters. But in less than five years all became large suburbs, centred on the stations. Southgate became a borough only in 1933, but by 1961 had a population of 72,051.

THE TUBE TO EDGWARE

Though powers to extend the Hampstead Tube from Golders Green to Edgware had existed for twenty years, work did not start until 1922. On 19 November 1923 the 1.75 miles to Hendon Central were opened, followed by the 3 miles on to Edgware on 18 August 1924.

The extension gave rise to a tremendous housing boom in Hendon during the 1920s and at Edgware during the next decade, for the area had hitherto been retarded by the poor services offered by the GN and the Midland. The 'London Electric Doric' stations became the foci of shopping streets interspersed with drinking palaces in 'Brewers' Tudor'. Hendon Central and Edgware also became the termini of numerous bus routes radiating out through the avenues of semi-detached villas.

At Edgware the country-style GN terminus survived unaltered, dealing with goods and parcels after closure to passengers in 1939. The near-by LT terminus was built as a through station. Under the 1935 Plan it was proposed to extend the line through virgin country to Bushey Heath. A connection would also have allowed Tube trains from Finchley over the former GN branch to enter the LT station. Work began but was interrupted by World War II and eventually abandoned. The car sheds, erected near Elstree, became the Aldenham bus overhaul works, finally closed in 1986.

CROSS-LONDON LINK

Plate 38 The Ray Street flyunder. A train on the Widened Lines approaches Farring-don Street on the lower level. The Inner Circle is above. (*London Transport Board*)

Plate 39 An LCD train at Harringay GN station in about 1900, using Snowhill and the Widened Lines.

Plate 40 A 1987 view of the restored Snowhill connection at Farringdon. Note the third-rail and overhead electrification systems. Farringdon is the changeover station. (*Allan C. Mott*)

Plate 41 A 1987 view of the tunnel exit from the Hotel Curve into King's Cross Surb-urban Station. (*Allan C. Mott*)

Plate 42   Early days on the Eastern Counties Railway: an animated scene at Shoreditch terminus in about 1850. (*National Railway Museum*)

Plate 43   The Thames Tunnel. A train leaves the under-river section of the East
London line and enters Wapping station. (*London Transport Board*)

Plate 44   The same scene today. (*Allan C. Mott*)

After steam suburban services on the Northern Heights ceased, freight trains (mainly for coal) continued to run to Cranley Gardens (closed 18 May 1957), to High Barnet (closed 1 October 1962) and to Edgware (closed 1 June 1964). In all, nine depots and Mill Hill gasworks were served. In 1956 nine trains ran daily, eight from Highbury Vale and one from King's Cross Goods. The line from Finsbury Park up to Park Junction was retained until 1970 for LT stock transfer. Access to the car sheds at the latter is maintained by a short section of line from East Finchley.

CHAPTER IX

Suburban Traffic Extraordinary:
The Great Eastern

In 1840 the north-eastern suburbs of London were more extensive and more industrialised than those of any other sector. Sixty years later this was still true. It was also true that they had become the most homogeneous, now being almost exclusively peopled by unskilled workmen, artisans and lower-paid clerks. All this was largely the result of policies continuously pursued by the Great Eastern Railway after its formation in 1862.

By 1920 the GE had built up a steam suburban system unrivalled anywhere in intensity and capacity, but steam was already outmoded for such a task. Thus the period up to 1935 saw this system, incapable of radical improvement short of electrification, fighting a losing battle with overwhelming traffic increases from expanding suburbs.

After 1935 came a struggle to electrify, a task which certainly could be said not to have been successfully completed until 1960 and probably not until 1987. Conversion took two forms: the Southern's system of handling only suburban traffic by electricity; and the Northern Heights pattern of projecting tube trains over former steam branch lines.

The story of the GE is told in Volume 5. Its nucleus was the Eastern Counties line, authorised on 4 July 1836 to build a 5ft gauge railway from London to Norwich. The first section was opened from Devonshire Street, 0.75 miles east of Bethnal Green, to Romford on 20 June 1839. Though Brentwood was reached on 1 July 1840, financial stringency delayed opening to Colchester until 1843 and to Norwich until six years later. On 1 July 1840 an extension was opened to the permanent terminus at Shoreditch (Bishopsgate from 1846) which was in the closely built-up eastern suburbs.

On 4 July 1836 the Northern & Eastern Company was incorporated to build a line from Islington to Cambridge, which was to be the first stage in a trunk-line to York. But the N&E was even more impecunious than the Eastern Counties and was forced to seek authority to divert the London end to join the EC at Stratford. From Stratford to Broxbourne opened on 15 September 1840, to Harlow in the following year and to Cambridge in 1845. As always, the EC was meanly intransigent. Only declining fortunes forced them to allow in the N&E trains at all. Their tolls were so high that the N&E had to charge higher fares than those on competing coaches and buses. The situation was resolved by leasing the N&E to the EC from 1 January 1844. In September and October both lines were converted to standard gauge.

On 2 April 1849 the Blackwall Railway, anxious to increase traffic into Fenchurch Street, opened a link from Stepney to the EC at Bow Junction, 1 mile west of Stratford. Typically the EC was reluctant to grasp this opportunity to reach a terminus more conveniently sited than Bishopsgate, and no physical connection was made until 1854.

EC services were infrequent and fares high; it is small wonder that suburban traffic failed to develop. But by 1864 the newly constituted Great Eastern had initiated a change of policy. There were now 29 departures for the Broxbourne line, 14 of them for Enfield (branching off at Angel Road). Down the Romford line there were 16 trains, 12 calling at all stations. But the inconveniently sited Bishopsgate was now becoming inadequate, while the Fenchurch Street (used since 1854) tolls were a constant burden.

On 17 December 1862 the general manager and the engineer recommended a Cityward extension on grounds which included the possibility of further developing suburban traffic: 'The importance of this Company's suburban traffic will be felt when the fact is known that within 18 miles of London the passenger traffic considerably exceeds £100,000 per annum.'

The recommendation was accepted and on 31 December 1863 the Board announced the formation of the Great Eastern Metropolitan Station & Railways Company to extend the line to Liverpool Street. The new terminus was opened for suburban traffic on 2 February 1874. A total of 1,071 people, considerably fewer than for the Broad Street extension, were displaced, but the Act obliged the GE to provide workmen's trains. However, the Company developed these services far beyond the statutory minimum, with major consequences for the growth and social composition of the north-eastern suburbs.

Bishopsgate became a goods depot (rebuilt 1881, burnt out 5 December 1964 and abandoned) to supplement the original Brick Lane depot (later Spitalfields, closed 6 November 1967). The two depots played a large part in provisioning London from the farmlands of East Anglia. In a December week of 1847, 27,000 sacks of grain and flour were received at Brick Lane, and, in 1906, 100,000 tons of potatoes were received at Bishopsgate, while 1,000 tons of green peas were dealt with on 7 July.

THE LEA VALLEY AND HACKNEY DOWNS GROUP OF LINES

From Stratford the N&E ran up the Lea valley, but the settlements were on the high ground to the west. The stations were thus inconvenient, while Tottenham (Hale), serving a town of 8,584 inhabitants in 1841, was the only one of any importance. Until access to Maiden Lane (NL) became possible, it was used to unload cattle.

To reach more of these settlements a single-line branch, authorised in 1846, was opened on 1 March 1849 from Angel Road through Lower Edmonton to Enfield. In 1841 both these were important, with populations numbering 9,027 and 9,367 respectively. Edmonton had become a residential suburb for wealthy Londoners, and industry was unobtrusively represented by glass and soap works. Charles Lamb had written of Enfield: 'I had thought in a green old age to have retired to Ponders End – emblematic name, how beautiful.' But industrialisation of the Lea valley had already begun with the establishment of the Royal Ordnance Factory at Enfield Lock.

On 23 June 1864 the GE obtained powers for a branch from the Lea Valley Line, through Walthamstow (population 7,137 in 1861) to High Beech in Epping Forest, already a popular resort. Then on 29 July another line was authorised from Bethnal Green, on the main line out to Stratford, northward to Hackney Downs. There it would split, one branch continuing along the high ground west of the Lea to join the Angel Road–Enfield line; the other swinging eastward across the Lea to join the proposed High Beech line, with a north-facing spur from Clapton Junction to Copper Mill Junction on the Lea Valley Line.

The original High Beech scheme was replaced by an Act of 20 June 1870, which sanctioned the present route, which had already opened from Lea Bridge to Shern Hall Street (Walthamstow) as a single line on 26 April. The Chingford extension was opened on 17 November 1873, when Shern Hall Street was replaced by Wood Street. In the early 1870s trains would wait in Hoe Street station (now Walthamstow Central) for any intending passenger seen running across the sur-rounding fields. Chingford, a small village of 1,137 souls in 1871, was the gateway to Epping Forest, and excursion traffic reached prodigious levels. On Whit Monday 1920 over 100,000 passengers arrived. But thereafter numbers declined as rising living standards made longer trips to the seaside and deeper country more common. The Chingford branch was doubled by September 1878 and opened to the present, larger terminus a mile to the north. The old station served as the goods yard until 4 October 1965.

TABLE 11

THE HACKNEY DOWNS GROUP OF LINES –

DEPARTURES FROM LIVERPOOL STREET BETWEEN
17.00 AND 17.59

	1874	1884	1920*	1958	1962	1970	1986
White Hart Lane	2	–	–	–	–	–	–
Palace Gates	–	2	3	–	–	–	–
Enfield	2	3	10	4	6	6	4
Wood Street	2	1	6	–	–	–	–
Chingford	1	2	6	8	9	9	4
Cheshunt and beyond†	–	1	4	7	12	12	14
TOTALS	7	9	29	19	27	27	22

* 'Jazz Service'.
† Including trains via Lea Bridge and Southbury Loop.

The first part of the Hackney Downs route, from Bethnal Green to Stoke Newington, opened on 27 May 1872. On 22

June the line on to Copper Mill Junction opened, followed by the link to the Chingford line on 1 August. Over the years more and more trains were diverted from the Stratford–Copper Mill section, which lost its last passenger trains in 1985.

On 22 July 1872 the line from Stoke Newington to Lower Edmonton Junction was ready, the present high-level station being provided just short of the junction. The Hackney Downs trains began running over the newly doubled line to Enfield Town. At the latter the old station was demolished to make way for a new one. It was a seventeenth-century house, later a school attended by the poet Keats. Part of the façade can be seen in the Victoria & Albert Museum. A third platform was provided in 1902. Until 11 September 1939 a few trains ran from Lower Edmonton Low Level to Angel Road, the line remaining open until the goods depot closed on 7 December 1964.

The Enfield line crossed the Tottenham & Hampstead Junction at Seven Sisters (not to be confused with the station which became Finsbury Park). Here a spur to South Tottenham opened on 1 January 1880. There was also a 2 mile branch opened to Green Lanes (later Noel Park) on 1 January 1878 and on to Palace Gates on 7 October. Palace Gates, near the GN's Wood Green (now Alexandra Palace), was a rather optimistic name, as indeed was the latter's recent renaming. But there was a plan to extend across the GN to an end-on junction with the Muswell Hill Railway (p. 172). In 1929 the LNE laid in a connection with the Hertford Loop, and in 1944 this was fully signalled and regularly used by freight trains and excursions to Southend.

The last section was completed on 1 October 1891 with the opening of the Churchbury Loop from Bury Street Junction on the Enfield line to Cheshunt on the Lea Valley. The district was undeveloped and the inconvenient shuttle service could not compete with the electric trams which ran out to Waltham Cross from 1904. Regular service ceased on 1 October 1909, though trains for munitions workers operated between 1 March 1915 and 1 July 1919. Thereafter it was used only for local freight until fully reopened on 21 November 1960 (p. 194).

After 1872 a lavish internal service of six trains an hour called at Hackney Downs. Fares were equally attractive and workmen's trains were run from Enfield at 2d for the round trip of 22 miles. Though the 1884 Act provided for one ' workmen's train from Edmonton and one from Wood Street, in 1891 the GE were running five from Enfield and six from Walthamstow alone.

In 1915 there were six '2d trains' from Enfield, two non-stop from Edmonton Low Level via Angel Road and seven from Wood Street, all leaving before 06.30. A little later the '3d trains' left, two each from Enfield, Edmonton (non-stop from Low Level) and Palace Gates and three from Wood Street. The '4d trains' and '5d trains' ran to reach Liverpool Street before 08.00.

A thirty-minute service was now provided to both Chingford and Enfield, augmented at peak periods. In the sixteen minutes between 17.18 and 17.34, eight trains left Liverpool Street for the Hackney Downs line. There were through peak-period trains from Palace Gates; otherwise there was a frequent shuttle service on the branch. There were also peripheral routes such as from Palace Gates to North Woolwich via South Tottenham.

Thus was stimulated a mass migration from the over-crowded Inner Arc and the already decaying Inner Zone suburbs of Hackney and Stoke Newington. It was the earliest such in London and for the first time the working and lower-middle classes were travelling to work by rail on a really large scale.

Through the 1870s and 1880s rows of small, jerry-built brick boxes, 'chopped off at the ends where another street crossed at distances prescribed by by-law' (R. M. Robbins), spread across Tottenham, Edmonton and the east of Wood Green. The proportion of artisans living in Enfield and Walthamstow was lower and consequently housing was somewhat better. But in the main the whole area was inhabited by lower-income groups.

The population of Tottenham doubled between 1871 and 1881 and again by 1891, when it had reached 97,174. In the same period Edmonton expanded three times from 13,860 to

36,351. Enfield, further out, developed later, increasing by only 3,000 between 1871 and 1881, to 19,104, but by 1901 it had 43,042 inhabitants. Walthamstow numbered 11,092 souls in 1871, doubling at each succeeding ten-yearly census until 1901, when there were 96,720.

By 1914 a salient of suburban development reached Enfield, Ponders End and Walthamstow, relatively further out than any other sector of Greater London except possibly at that time along the GN. But after 1930 expansion north of Enfield was halted by the high land values imposed by the intensively capitalised glasshouse industry. East of the Lea, Epping Forest interposed another barrier. However, there was some building around Ponders End and Enfield Lock, and particularly in Chingford, which grew from 9,482 in 1921 to 48,355 in 1951. In Chingford, incomes were higher and housing densities lower. After 1950 land values rose so much that horticulture retreated up the Lea valley and onto the plateau before the rapid advance of the builder. Intercensal increases, 1951–61, of 39.2 per cent were recorded in Waltham Holy Cross, 53.3 per cent in Cheshunt and 30.3 per cent in Hoddesden. Since 1970 growth has shifted even further out, to Harlow New Town, Bishop's Stortford, Ware and beyond.

Rail traffic began to decline from the inner stations after 1926, but remained heavy from the outer ones. Highams Park (on the Chingford line) is one of the less important outer stations, but in 1956, 50,000 ordinary and 1,500 seasons were sold monthly and 170 passenger trains called on weekdays. Only the Palace Gates branch experienced a spectacular decline. In 1938 there were seventy-three up trains, but by 1961 these had fallen to six. The branch was closed to passengers on 7 January 1963 and completely on 28 December 1964.

INDUSTRIAL DEVELOPMENT

The foundations of industry had been laid in the Lea valley by 1840, development being aided by the Lea Navigation, which even as late as 1960 carried 2 million tons. The railway began to play a big part after the opening of the Doncaster–March line in 1882, which turned the Lea valley approach to London into a trunk freight route. A large-scale movement of

Yorkshire coal to East London began and a northern outlet for East London industry was provided (the full story is in Vol 5).

Development accelerated after 1920, when many firms moved out from the congested East End, while many more were newly established. The whole Lea valley is highly industrialised as far as Broxbourne, factories lining the railway from Lea Bridge. Any links between these and rail were unfortunately severed during the 1960s.

A 1960 account by C. J. Allen of a trip on an express freight train, the *Lea Valley Enterprise*, introduced on 2 November 1959 between Tottenham and March, underlines the subsequent switch from rail. The train left with a single wagon, but after four stops left Broxbourne with fifty-three. Among the items conveyed were flowers, tomatoes, watercress, ventilating machinery, deckchairs, confectionery, cables, electrodes, bacon slicers, paper, roofing felt, plastics and paint. In 1957 Waltham Cross, one of the seven goods depots (all since closed) between Temple Mills and Broxbourne, dealt with 19,300 tons of sundries (mainly fruit, vegetables, fertilisers, peat and machinery), 22,244 tons of minerals and 26,610 tons of coal.

Large numbers are employed locally. In 1951 only 12 per cent of Enfield's working population travelled to the Central area and only 2 per cent from Waltham Holy Cross. From Walthamstow and Tottenham the figures were 18 and 19 per cent. Thus most journeys are short, and rail is vulnerable to loss of traffic to private transport. In 1981 only 12.4 per cent of Broxbourne District's population travelled to work by rail.

THE LOUGHTON GROUP OF LINES

It was the Blackwall Company which first had designs on the country between the Lea Valley and the Romford lines, but the powers were given to the Eastern Counties, and it was not until 22 August 1856 that the 7 miles were opened from Loughton Branch Junction on the Lea Valley to the small town of Loughton.

The district served, the flanks of the Roding valley rising to the Epping Forest ridge, was rural. Already the villages housed some wealthy businessmen and there were prospects of suburban traffic. Wanstead and Chigwell, the largest places, numbered 5,000 and 3,000 inhabitants respectively.

On 24 April 1865 the line was extended the 11.5 miles to Ongar. It ran through a remote area of low hills with a covering of boulder-clay. At first single, it was later doubled to Epping. On 1 May 1903 the 6.25 mile FAIRLOP LOOP opened from a triangular junction with the Romford line at Ilford to a south-facing junction beyond Woodford.

Compared with those over the Hackney Downs lines, services were sparse. In 1874 Loughton had 22 down trains, Epping 9 and Ongar 6, but by 1894 there had been much development at the southern end and 62 trains were now booked to pass on to the branch, 11 to terminate at Snaresbrook and 1 at Woodford; 28 went on to Loughton, 8 to Epping and 14 to Ongar. By 1920 the total had risen only to 68. Of these, 51 originated from Liverpool Street, 14 from Fenchurch Street and 3 from Stratford. In the same year the Fairlop Loop had 22 services each way between Woodford and Ilford. A shuttle ran during slack hours, but at peak periods roundabout trains were run from the London termini.

The comparatively infrequent services and more particularly the absence of workmen's facilities inhibited suburban growth and confined any there was to better-class housing. Leyton and Leytonstone grew up between 1870 and 1900, the same period as Walthamstow. Wanstead's main growth period dates from 1900 to 1914 and the houses, terrace and semi-detached, were larger.

Woodford is almost unique in the Middle Zone of north-east London, consisting largely of the detached houses of middle and upper income groups. It grew rapidly between the Wars. There was also considerable expansion around the stations at Buckhurst Hill, Loughton and Theydon Bois. Since post-war electrification, growth has continued all the way to Epping, though there is still some open country between stations. Epping's 1951–61 increase was 44.1 per cent. After 1975 the transport factor most influencing growth was the M11, but the aluminium tube trains still bounce incongruously through fields and woods.

Save where Ilford had spread out to Newbury Park, prior to 1914 there had been little development along the Fairlop Loop. Between the Wars the LCC built a large estate at Barkingside, served chiefly by trams. There was also expansion around the substantially laid-out stations beyond. This continued rapidly after 1950, the whole area having become largely built up.

THE ROMFORD LINE

An agreement between the Eastern Counties and a Stratford farmer stipulated that before construction began he could remove 'as many of the mangel-wurzel plants as may be growing on the said lands'. Market-gardens, interspersed by mansions in their parks, extended over the fertile river terraces to Romford, beyond which the line climbed into the low, wooded hills around Brentwood. Stratford, Ilford, Romford and Brentwood were the only places of consequence, strung out along the High Road to Colchester. Of these, Romford (population 5,317 in 1841) was by far the largest.

For many years the local service was sparse in the extreme beyond Stratford. Forest Gate, 1.5 miles to the east, had two trains a day and its receipts, the most meagre on the line, were so small that it closed from 1844 to 1846. But 350,000 passengers a month were using it in 1912. In 1864 there were twelve down locals beyond Stratford compared with the forty on the North Woolwich line.

By 1874 the Lea had become the frontier of Greater London, Stratford (population 23,286, in 1871) forming a sizeable bridgehead beyond. The old centre along the Broadway retained its rural charm, but Hudson Town (the appropriately named railway settlement) spread northward, grimly industrial. Here were the railway workshops, and new plants engaged in engineering, match and soap making, printing, and tar distilling. Ilford and Romford were still market-towns and growing only slowly. It was not until 1900 that rows of terrace houses began to engulf Ilford and Seven Kings. Romford was still almost unaffected, but a model estate was taking shape at Gidea Park when that station opened on 1 December 1910.

In 1894 there were 36 suburban trains for Ilford, 14 of them going on to Romford, and 8 more terminating further out. But by 1906 there were 84 suburban departures from Liverpool Street and 44 from Fenchurch Street. All the latter and 6 of the former terminated at Ilford, 57 went on to Romford, and a further 22 went beyond, mostly to Brentwood and Shenfield.

In the inter-war period building spread out to meet expanding Romford, which grew fourfold from 19,442 inhabitants in 1921 to 88,002 in 1951. North of Ilford, along the new Eastern Avenue (A12), a vast suburb grew up devoid of any rail facilities. There was even further post-1945 development in North Ilford, by now served by the Central Line, and in Romford which grew further by almost a third. On the latter's outskirts the LCC built the Harold Hill estate. By 1961 its population had reached 32,000 and it was (and is) dependent on a rather inadequate bus service.

The line had been quadrupled to Ilford in 1895, just short of Romford in 1902, to Gidea Park in 1931, and to Shenfield in 1934, after which the latter became the terminus of the intensive suburban service. Electrification of the lines beyond and population growth around the stations means that few trains now terminate there: the suburban belt is pushing rapidly outwards.

On 16 July 1883 the GE was accorded powers for a 21.25 mile branch from Shenfield to SOUTHEND. This opened to Wickford for goods on 19 November 1888 and for passengers on 1 January 1889 and on to Southend for all traffic on 1 October. Originally single, doubling was completed in 1901.

The line crossed low hills, separated from the gravel plateau on which Southend is built by a stretch of London Clay. Southend was naturally the main objective. Excursion traffic soon became important and in 1911 a business service was provided with five up fast trains in the morning and back in the evening. En route the poor soils kept land values down. This in combination with the good peak-period service created a curious form of suburban development. Outward from the stations at Billericay, Wickford, Rayleigh and Hockley spread in unplanned anarchy asbestos bungalows, huts and old railway carriages. They ranged at irregular intervals along a maze of unmade roads. Lacking normal suburban amenities such as drainage, most of the dwellings were on smallholdings of an acre or so. Too small to provide a living, the latter were cultivated by commuters as well as pensioners. With rising land values and stricter planning control, orthodox houses at higher densities have taken over, while Rayleigh and Hockley have become suburbs of an expanded Southend.

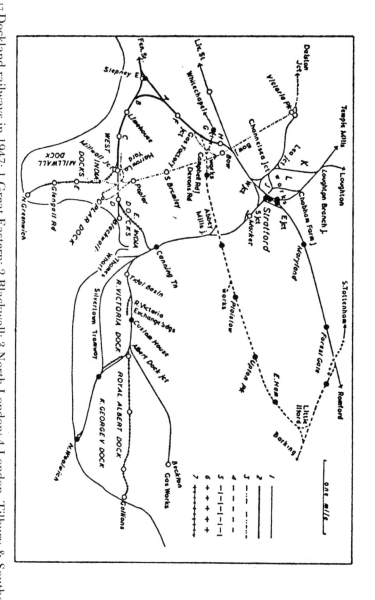

FIG 17 Dockland railways in 1947: 1 Great Eastern; 2 Blackwall; 3 North London; 4 London, Tilbury & Southend; 5 Whitechapel & Bow; 6 Tottenham & Forest Gate; 7 Port of London Authority; A Salmons Lane Junction; B Limehouse Junction; C West India Docks station; D Poplar station ; E South Dock station; F Burdett Road station; G Bow Road (W&B) station: H Bow Road (Blackwall) station: I Fork Junction.

Ever since the Northern & Eastern made its junction with the
EC in 1840, Stratford has been the key point in the railway
geography of East London. On 14 June 1847 the North
Woolwich branch was opened from Western Junction, a goods
spur being provided the same year from Eastern Junction to
Sheet Factory Junction (closed 12 March 1973). The line from
the North London at Victoria Park Junction (originally
Hackney Wick Junction) to the North Woolwich line through
the Low Level station to Sheet Factory Junction was opened
for goods on 15 August 1854 and for passengers on 16
October. At Fork Junction it joined a goods spur from the Lea
Valley line at Chobham Farm Junction (opened 1847, closed
1 June 1969). On 15 August 1854 a connection was opened for
goods from Channelsea Junction on the North London Line to
a triangular junction with the Main Line at Western Junction.
This became available for passengers on 1 September 1866. In
later years the Chobham Farm spur ran through the works,
and to avoid them a new loop was provided in 1881 from
Loughton Branch Junction to Channelsea Junction, the
layout being completed in July 1893 by a spur between High
Meads Junction and the Victoria Park line at Lea Junction,
thus forming a triangular layout.

In 1840 the EC had set up workshops at Romford, but
between 1845 and 1848 they were transferred to a site at
Stratford adjoining the locomotive roundhouse on the up side
of the Lea Valley Line. Later they expanded over the land on
the down side. In 1888 the locomotive depot was moved to a
site north of the Chobham Farm spur and in 1897 the wagon
shops were moved out to Temple Mills.

The handsome buildings of the passenger station were
erected in 1846–7 between the Lea Valley and the Romford
lines. The Lea Valley platforms have not been used since 1969
and trains rarely call at the Romford ones. The centre of
activity has moved to the new station immediately to the
west, where cross-platform exchange takes place between the
suburban services and Central Line Tube trains, which
emerge briefly at the surface. Beneath are the two low-level
platforms.

Just north of Loughton Branch Junction was a siding

adjoining a water-mill formerly owned by the Knights Templars. We first hear of Temple Mills siding in a Minute of 13 November 1877 in which the Way and Works Committee authorised an extension. Each year from 1880 to 1893 further extensions were approved and in 1930 the Cambridge 'hump' yard opened. The layout was modernised in 1954–9. In 1958 there were seventy-four daily arrivals at the south end and fifty-one departures from the north. Temple Mills yard remains open, but with the elimination of most marshalling operations it remains a pale shadow of its former self. Like all such yards it is used mainly for changing locomotives and crews.

On 4 July 1967 the London International Freight Terminal (LIFT) became operational on the site of part of the works. On the opposite side of the Lea Junction spur, on the site of High Meads sidings, the Freightliner terminal opened. Its traffic has grown greatly with the increasing importance of the Port of Felixstowe.

ELECTRIFICATION

As we have seen, the GE encouraged suburban traffic, which grew prodigiously. But the capacity limit of the approaches to Liverpool Street, set by steam haulage and semaphore signalling, had been reached. As far back as 1890 it was widely felt that north-east London required better facilities. In 1894 the London, Walthamstow & Epping Forest Railway was authorised as an electric line from Finsbury Circus. The scheme lapsed but in the 'Tube Mania' of 1891 there were two Bills, the North East London (Mansion House–Tottenham) and the City & North East Suburban (Cornhill–Waltham Abbey). Next year James Holden produced from Stratford Works a 0–10–0T locomotive tested to accelerate from rest fifteen four-wheeled coaches faster than could electricity. It was a bluff, for the track would not have stood up to such monsters. But at least no more was heard of the alternative proposals.

In 1905 the Royal Commission recommended electrification of the GE together with Tube extensions, and the 1925 London Traffic Enquiry (p. 175) echoed these recommendations. Town councils and users were continuously vociferous, and as counter-propaganda the LNE blew the dust off a 1901 GE proposal for a tube to Ilford, but it took no practical steps, maintaining that the type of traffic prevented a sufficient level of earnings to justify a large capital outlay.

The opportunity did not come until 1935 when radical improvements were decided on as part of the agreement with the Treasury which guaranteed interest on loans for capital works which would relieve unemployment (see also Vol 2, p. 190) World War II delayed implementation.

The scheme fell into three clearly marked sections: the projection of Central Line Tube trains over the Loughton group of lines; electrification of the Romford line; and electrification of the Hackney Downs group of lines.

The Central Tube was to be extended eastwards from its Liverpool Street terminus, with cross-platform exchange with the District at a rebuilt Mile End station and similarly with the LNE at Stratford. The new line would finally surface to connect with the Loughton line 0.25 miles north of Loughton Branch Junction. Tube trains would run over this all the way to Ongar and round the Fairlop Loop from Woodford to Newbury Park. But 0.25 miles to the south there would be a new Tube under Eastern Avenue (A12) back to Leytonstone on the Loughton line. Thus, at last, north Ilford would be served by rail.

Central Line trains began running to Stratford on 4 December 1946 and on to Leytonstone on 5 May 1947, when steam trains ceased to run south thereof. They were also withdrawn from the Fairlop Loop from 30 November, and on 14 December the Tube service was extended from Leytonstone to Woodford and through the North Ilford Tunnels to Newbury Park. The curve from the latter round to Ilford was disconnected immediately, but goods trains used the eastern spur to Seven Kings until 19 March 1956. The Fairlop Loop was reopened between Newbury Park and Hainault on 31 May 1948 and on to Woodford on 21 November. On that day the tube service was extended to Loughton. Epping was reached on 25 September 1949, but the steam shuttle service, retreating before the electric advance, continued to serve Ongar until 18 November 1957.

London Transport regarded the section beyond Epping through deepest rural Essex as a nuisance. To cut costs, current supply is reduced, so only a single short train can be used, necessitating a change at Epping. On 2 November 1981 Blake Hall, one of the two intermediate stations, closed, and later the service was reduced to peak only. On a 1986 census day, ninety-three passengers were counted at Ongar and twenty-five at North Weald. BR continued to provide goods services over the whole group of lines reached from Loughton Branch Junction until 18 April 1966.

Trains run out to Epping (or short thereof) and via Newbury Park to Hainault, a shuttle service connecting the latter with Woodford. In 1964 it was equipped for driverless trains as a test-bed for the Victoria Line. Traffic is heavy and posing problems. The 1986 'user' of Woodford was 3.4 million, Epping 1.2 million and Hainault 2.2 million.

Whether the method of operation, all trains stopping at all stations and formed of stock with low seating capacity and low maximum speeds, is suitable for outer-suburban work is highly questionable. The Bank, 17.5 miles from Epping, could not be reached in less than the standard time of 40 minutes in 1986, while King's Cross could be reached from Hatfield (17.25 miles) in 23 minutes and Waterloo from Walton-on-Thames (17 miles) in business hours in 21 minutes, in both cases by far more comfortable trains.

The LNE electrified the Romford Line on the overhead system at 1,500V dc. Trains began running to Shenfield on 26 September 1949, and were extended on to Chelmsford on 11 June 1956 and to Southend on 31 December. The system was converted to 25,000V ac over the weekend of 4–6 November 1961, except for the short Shenfield–Chelmsford section which was without electric trains until 20 March 1961. Electrification was extended to Colchester in 1962, where it connected with the previously converted branch to Clacton. Electric traction reached Ipswich on 13 May 1985 and Harwich a year later. Norwich was reached in May 1987.

In the last year of steam working 2.6 million ordinary passengers were carried between Shenfield and Southend/ Chelmsford. In the first year of electrification these doubled and in the second rose further to 5.9 million. Receipts rose by 117 per cent in the first year of the new working, while operating costs fell.

With electrification came growth of outer-suburban traffic

and stagnation of the inner-suburban services. In 1962 in off-peak periods 3 trains an hour left Liverpool Street for Gidea Park, 3 for Southend and 1 for Chelmsford. The 1986 pattern was 3 Gidea Park, 3 Southend, 1 Witham, 1 Clacton and 1 Manningtree which continued to Ipswich and Harwich alternately.

The Hackney Downs lines were electrified using the alternating-current system, the new services being inaugurated on 21 November 1960. Included in the scheme was the Churchbury Loop, which became the Southbury Loop. The basic service was of 6 trains per hour to Enfield and to Chingford, with 2 to Broxbourne via Southbury. At the new station the latter were divided into Bishop's Stortford and Hertford East portions. The Lea Valley Line south of Cheshunt remained diesel-operated by a shuttle from Stratford (from Liverpool Street at peaks) until electrification to Copper Mill Junction and the spur up to the line to Hackney Downs.

On 5 May 1969 a service was inaugurated of two trains an hour to Bishop's Stortford and two to Hertford via Copper Mill, connecting with each other at Broxbourne. This brought use of the Lea Valley platforms at Stratford to an end. A few trains from North Woolwich continued to Tottenham Hale via Lea Bridge, but were withdrawn with electrification to North Woolwich on 14 May 1985 and Lea Bridge was closed. Finally in May 1987 electric trains were projected from Bishop's Stortford to Cambridge. The 1986 service shows a considerable decline in the inner service, with only two trains an hour to Chingford and Enfield. The outer service remained unchanged.

The electrification scheme improved communications with the Inner Zone between Bethnal Green and Stoke Newington/Clapton, which had the worst rail service of any comparable area, and with the rapidly growing Outer Zone beyond Cheshunt (Vol 5, Chapter V), as well as the Middle Zone. But the Victoria Line, which shares Walthamstow Central with the Chingford line and intersects that to Enfield at Seven Sisters, has cut deeply into their traffic. Off-peak patronage has also fallen away generally, partly as a result of a reduction in service frequency.

Liverpool Street was opened to suburban trains on 2 February 1874 and to all traffic on 1 November 1875, when Bishopsgate was closed to passengers. It was reached by a four-road extension (increased to the present six in 1891) diverging just west of Bethnal Green and descending at 1 in 70, for the most part in a smoke-wreathed cutting in which were the platforms of Bishopsgate Low Level (opened 4 November 1872, closed 22 May 1916). Originally the terminus comprised platforms 1 to 10, now known as the West Side. The eight platforms of the East Side went into service on 2 April 1894.

Convenient situation, lavish services and low fares made Liverpool Street the busiest London station. In 1855, 2.14 million used Bishopsgate. By 1902, 65.3 million were passing through Liverpool Street. In 1897, the 2d trains carried 2 million passengers into Liverpool Street and the 3d and 4d (the 'half-fare' trains), 6 million. Workmen in caps and corduroy trousers and junior clerks in bowlers and dark suits crowded the hutch-like four-wheeled coaches. The *Illustrated London News* observed that 'the passengers by the 2d trains are not to be commended in either language or attire' but that the 'half-fare trains' were patronised by 'the better class of workmen, warehousemen, shop men and not a few poorly paid clerks'. The LCC's enquiry into workmen's services accorded the GE an accolade: 'The Great Eastern is especially the workmen's London railway – the one above all which appears to welcome him as a desirable customer.'

Between 08.00 and 09.30 the ordinary trains poured in the season-ticket holders, top-hatted and morning-coated senior clerks and executives. As yet women were conspicuously absent from these business trains.

In 1902, 90.7 per cent (59.2 million) of the passengers were travelling to and from stations less than 12 miles out; 3.8 per cent (2.5 million) were to and from stations between 12 and 30 miles out; and 5.5 per cent (3.6 million) to and from stations over 30 miles out. These figures underline the overwhelming predominance of suburban traffic. But the growth of the long-distance should not be overlooked: in total it now exceeded that of Euston or King's Cross.

By 1903, 75,000 passengers were arriving before 10.30. The

TABLE 12

SAMPLE FROM A PASSENGER CENSUS TAKEN BY THE GER
WHILE PLANNING THE 1920 'JAZZ' SERVICE

	Boarding	Alighting	Boarding	Alighting
	18.05 down		*07.40 up*	
Liverpool Street	1,241	—	—	1,022
Bethnal Green	81	2	6	35
Cambridge Heath	57	3	non-stop	
London Fields	22	2	non-stop	
Hackney Downs	62	14	33	65
Clapton	46	68	56	55
St James Street	9	551	286	0
Hoe Street	15	594	570	0
Wood Street	3	196	118	3
Highams Park	6	63	71	11
Chingford	—	49	48	—
	18.17 down		*07.03 up*	
Liverpool Street	979	—	—	1,167
Bethnal Green	65	14	10	82
Cambridge Heath	29	10	2	30
London Fields	9	18	0	25
Hackney Downs	20	41	10	44
Rectory Road	6	46	11	4
Stoke Newington	28	36	9	26
Stamford Hill	3	55	12	3
Seven Sisters	2	166	198	13
Bruce Grove	6	196	200	3
White Hart Lane	0	46	77	3
Silver Street	1	140	386	16
Lower Edmonton	13	227	236	5
Bush Hill Park	3	109	224	0
Enfield Town	—	60	31	—

comparative Paddington figure was 1,800. A total of 399 suburban and 36 main-line trains were booked to arrive daily and this total was exceeded only at London Bridge. On the nine trains from Walthamstow between 07.30 and 08.00 there were 7,400 seats and about 7,100 passengers, but the last two were uncomfortably crowded. Then as now the problem of the peak loomed large.

Over 200,000 passengers and 1,250 train movements were being dealt with daily by 1912, though trams were taking many short-distance travellers. By 1919 recovery from war was under way. Boaters were now fashionable among peak-hour crowds and World War I had turned the woman City worker into a commonplace. Traffic increases and, more importantly, intensification of the peak as a result of shortened hours were adding to the operating nightmare. But electrification of the Enfield and Chingford lines, then by far the busiest, would have cost £5 million. With the low fares dictated by statute and by road competition this was not considered economic. Instead, after a 'work study', Sir Henry Thornton, whom the GE had recruited from the USA as general manager, together with the superintendent of operation, F. V. Russell, devised an intensified service involving only minor alterations costing around £80,000.

On 12 July 1920 the 'Jazz Service' began, so called from the yellow and blue bands under the coach roofs to distinguish first and second class. By the use of engine spurs at the platform ends and turnover locomotives, platform occupation could be cut to four minutes – if the train could be loaded that quickly. In practice a train entered each platform every ten minutes. Seating was increased by 50 to 75 per cent and on the down suburban track climbing to Bethnal Green twenty-four trains an hour were scheduled, representing 20,350 passenger seats.

This has been claimed by many writers to have been more than any contemporary electric system could have dealt with. Strictly in terms of *seats* this could have been true. But in 1936 passengers were being carried at the rate of 27,000 an hour westbound through Embankment (District) and 26,000 an hour over one track of the Northern line. The GE tour de force enabled 51 trains to leave between 17.00 and 18.00, most in the charge of a diminutive, but vociferously pugnacious tank engine, 27 for the Hackney Downs line, 8 for the Loughton line and 16 for Ilford and beyond. The 'Jazz Service' represented 'the last word in steam operated suburban services' (C. J. Allen).

In 1924, 280,000 passengers a day were passing through, 40,000 in the busiest hour, which was more than many of the other London termini saw in the whole day. But the only possible improvement (short of electrification) to this, the apotheosis of steam suburban traction, was in passenger comfort. The service was still operated by sets of sixteen four-wheeled coaches. Not until 1925 did Sir Nigel Gresley start introducing his quintuplet articulated sets, two per train in peaks. And these lasted until electrification in 1960. Yet in 1925 the Metropolitan had been carrying its passengers in electric trains of bogie coaches for twenty years, while the Southern was rapidly electrifying its suburban system.

The 'Jazz Service' came to an end in 1926 when cuts in peak timetables were made in the wake of the General Strike. Further cuts were made in World War II, never to be restored. For there was a continuing decline in traffic from the Inner Zone, not fully counteracted by the increase from the outer suburbs. The Loughton-line traffic was diverted to the Central Line; much from the Hackney Downs group to the Victoria Line; and from the Romford line to the Central at Stratford. Average weekday 'user' declined to about 160,000 after World War II, but with rebuilding of the City it had recovered to 174,000 in 1958.

The census of 4 October 1960 counted 181,152 passengers passing the barriers. Though busy at all times, in the evening peak the spacious concourse became a seething lake of humanity fed by rivers converging on the station from various parts of the City and drained by others flowing through the platform barriers. A total of 43,675 (48 per cent) of the 91,013 departing passengers left between 17.00 and 18.00. The 17.46 for Chingford carried 1,289 passengers; the 14.08 carried 43.

Between 17.03 and 18.00, twenty-nine electric trains down the Romford line carried 30,530 passengers on census day, over 1,000 apiece. Incidentally, a further 6,767 passengers joined at Stratford. The peak of the peak was from 17.33 to 17.42 when six trains took out 9,743 passengers (*nearly 1,000 per minute*). As for the long-distance trains, the 1960 census showed 11,200 passengers on the fifty-two main-line departures. This was an average of 215 per train, but it varied from 613 on the 17.16 for Cambridge and 508 on the 17.45 for Harwich to 2 on the 03.20 for Clacton.

Liverpool Street acquired a rather unjustified reputation for dirt and gloom, but even in steam days it was considerably cleaner and more cheerful than Broad Street. The high roof is supported on light ornamented steel arches, in recent years tastefully painted. The rails between platforms 9 and 10 separated the two concourses, connected only by an overbridge, but in 1985 the platforms were shortened to allow circulation on the level.

In that year also work began on the extensive Broadgate

office/shop development between Finsbury Avenue and Bishopsgate and fronting Liverpool Street. It will include the whole of the site of Broad Street station, but will preserve the Italianate station frontage of Liverpool Street, a milder and less aggressive St Pancras, though not that of the hotel. It is an architecturally imaginative scheme and an appropriate one for the area. The lessons of Euston have at least been learned.

In 1986 all services, main and suburban, were on an interval basis. In 1987 all trains are electric, locomotive haulage having begun in 1985, when power to Ipswich was switched on. The longest through runs are now to Norwich and King's Lynn, though a travelling post-office does go to Peterborough via Ipswich. There are no longer through trains to Lowestoft, Yarmouth, Cromer and Doncaster.

The traffic and atmosphere at Liverpool Street accord more with those of the Southern termini. There is the problem of the peak, largely overcome by electrification and re-signalling, not to say by declining traffic.

The average daily passenger use in 1985 was 148,000, a decline of 18 per cent since 1960. The 1986 timetable shows 65 departures between 17.00 and 17.59. Only 4 left for Enfield and as many for Chingford, indicating the decline of patronage; 5 went down the Southbury loop to Cheshunt and beyond, and 10 down the Lea Valley (4 to Hertford, 4 to Bishop's Stortford and 2 continuing on to Cambridge). The majority, 40, left for the Romford line; 9 went only to Gidea Park, while 6 terminated at Shenfield. But in contrast to previous years there were 11 Southend departures and a further 1 to Southminster. On the main line 3 went to Colchester, 3 to Witham (1 through to Braintree), 3 to Clacton, and 3 to Ipswich and beyond. Finally there were 2 departures for Watford over the new Graham Road curve, superseding the former service from Broad Street (p. 87).

As at the Southern termini long-distance commuting is both traditional and, recently, growing. Southend and Clacton are the counterparts of Brighton and the Kent Coast, while the Bishop's Stortford–Cambridge line is growing in importance. There are also resorts, popular like Southend, Lowestoft and Yarmouth, or more exclusive, such as Frinton. Here there is also the continental traffic with three daily services to Harwich, though the liner specials to the Royal Docks no longer run.

CHAPTER X

Dockland and Suburbia on North Thames-side

The shores of the Thames Estuary are generally low and marshy. On the Kentish side there is firm ground at a number of places suitable for early town growth, but on the Essex side this occurs only at Grays and Southend. Thus in 1830 only Barking and Southend were of potential importance below Poplar, then on the very edge of Greater London. Barking was a market-town and small port on Barking Creek (the Roding Estuary), its fishing fleet numbering 120 smacks in 1833. Southend was a small and exclusive resort. Paradoxically the first railways on the north bank were built to serve Kent towns, but the lines soon effected such a revolution in the rural seclusion they had violated that the Kentish traffic became of very secondary import.

Apart from the Surrey Commercial Docks, London's dock system developed on the low north bank between the City and the Lea Estuary. Hard by the City, St Katharine's Dock dates from 1828 and the adjacent London Docks from 1805. Further downstream the West India Docks date from 1802 and the East India from 1806. The two last were connected with the City by the East India Dock Road of 1810, along which a ribbon of industry and housing soon spread. But southward stretched the undeveloped Isle of Dogs, while to the north fields and common land separated Poplar from Bow.

Steam vessels had further increased the heavy passenger traffic on the river. The resorts of Margate, Ramsgate and Southend received their visitors by water; the normal way from Maidstone, Canterbury and Chatham to London was by road to Gravesend and thence by water; while Woolwich and Greenwich had a frequent 'Short Ferry' service Londonward.

In the 1830s the steamers on the 'Long Ferry' to Gravesend were carrying a million passengers a year. Most of them, together with other river and cross-Channel steamers, called at Brunswick Wharf, Blackwall, for this was 6.5 miles by water from London Bridge, but only 4 miles along East India Dock Road from Aldgate Pump.

It was to speed communication between the City and Brunswick Wharf that the Commercial Railway was incorporated on 28 July 1836 to build a line from Minories to Blackwall. In 1839 its name changed to London & Blackwall when the 415yd extension to Fenchurch Street was authorised. The 3.3 miles of 5ft gauge line were opened to passengers on 6 July 1840. On a viaduct for 2 miles, it was cable-operated. A second track came into use on 3 August, allowing a fifteen-minute service.

Fenchurch Street opened on 2 August 1841, the 1846 Commission (Chapter II) being told of a 50 per cent traffic increase in consequence. Intermediate stations were provided, served by individual coaches released from the cable. But steamer passengers provided the basic revenue. In June 1844, of the 331,644 passengers landed and embarked at Gravesend, over 200,000 travelled over the Blackwall line.

In 1848–9 the line was converted to standard gauge and to locomotive haulage in preparation for the link with the EC, opened to Bow Junction on 2 April 1849 (Chapter IX). The Blackwall was turning to alternative sources of revenue, for with the development of direct rail communication with places on the Lower Thames, steamer traffic was already beginning to decline.

Other companies were encouraged to use Fenchurch Street as their City terminus. From 1850 a North London service had operated (Chapter IV), the EC began through working in 1854, and in the same year London, Tilbury & Southend trains arrived. 'Foreign' companies also used the line as access to goods depots.

Another source of revenue was the growth of docks, industry and housing in the Isle of Dogs. The West India Docks were enlarged in the 1840s and Millwall Dock opened in 1868. Housing for dock workers went up in Millwall and

Cubitt Town (laid out in 1843), while factories lined the river bank.

A railway system was laid out to serve the docks, the 'trunk' being 1.5 miles of line from Millwall Junction, on the Blackwall, to the river at North Greenwich. Built under the Blackwall's Act of 19 June 1865, ownership of the MILL-WALL EXTENSION was complex. The Blackwall had 5 chains at the north end and 31 at the south. Between, the London & India Docks had 41 chains and the Millwall Dock 52, both lengths eventually passing to the Port of London Authority.

The line to West India Dock was completed in 1867 and was opened for passengers to Glengall Road on 18 December 1871 and to North Greenwich on 29 July 1872. To reduce the fire risk, the passenger service was operated by horses until 1880. The trains, worked by three diminutive engines and primitive coaches, ran for the last time on 3 May 1926. The GE and the Blackwall had bought the ferry to Greenwich. As late as 1900, 1.3 million passengers were carried, but the ferry ceased operations in 1902 when the LCC opened the foot tunnel.

By the 1950s the line had been taken up beyond Glengall Road, the remainder being still the main line of the docks system operated by the Port of London Authority. But on 1 May 1970 it ceased rail operations. The docks gradually ran down and eventually closed.

THE DOCKLANDS LIGHT RAILWAY

The run-down and closure of the docks system left vast areas of dereliction and led to the setting up of a London Docklands Development Corporation. Radical improvement to passenger transport was considered vital to rehabilitation, but proposals to extend the Jubilee Line were deemed too costly. Instead, after careful consideration, a light-rail option was adopted, something completely new to London, although common enough in other major cities. There was a remarkably short lead time after Michael Heseltine, then Secretary of State for the Environment, rather over the head of his Transport colleague, promised the finance in 1982. In 1984 the Docklands Light Railway Act authorised the Isle of Dogs section and a 1985 Act the Stratford extension.

The system, operated by a wholly owned subsidiary of LRT, opened in July 1987 and totals 7.5 miles, with sixteen stations. It is operated with driverless railcars picking up direct current from third rail. The line starts, rather inconveniently, from Tower Gateway (Minories) and is on a viaduct paralleling the Fenchurch Street line to Stepney East. From here the right-of-way of the Blackwall and Millwall Extension is followed for the most part, a rare example of reopening after half a century. From a triangular junction on the site of Millwall Junction the former NL line is followed to Bow Road, where it swings round to end in the bay platform at Stratford provided in 1959 for an electric shuttle service to Fenchurch Street via Bow Junction which never materialised.

Already the line has had an effect on the area. In 1986 the author was told that land values rose as soon as construction started – from £300,000 per acre to £2 million. Certainly there is much development of high-tech industry and high-class housing. The possible establishment of a major financial centre at Canary Wharf has led to proposals for an underground extension to the Bank; the extension will in any case enhance the value of the line. In the future it may be extended eastward to link with the North Woolwich line and on to Beckton.

THE NORTH WOOLWICH LINE AND ITS BRANCHES

In 1844 the Eastern Counties & Thames Junction was incorporated to build 1.75 miles of line from Stratford to what became Thames Wharf on Barking Creek. Promoted by G. P. Bidder, a prominent railway contractor (p. 62), it was known as 'Bidder's Folly', passing as it did through a completely uninhabited area. The following year an Act was obtained for the 2.75 mile North Woolwich Railway to extend through roadless and uninhabited marshes to the ferry at North Woolwich.

The line was opened from Stratford to Canning Town on 29 April 1846 and on to a spacious classical terminus on 14 June 1847. R. Ruegg (*Rambles around Woolwich*, 1847) wrote that the only buildings at North Woolwich were 'a public house . . . a small house occupied by the family of a shepherd, and the terminus of the North Woolwich Railway. It is singular to hear the whistle of a locomotive . . . where twelve months since the heron, the plover and the bittern roamed.'

In 1847 the Thames Junction bought the North Woolwich and Bidder ran an hourly service until 1845, when the EC was at last persuaded to have dealings with the new line, starting a service from Fenchurch Street via Stratford. On 31 March 1858 the ABBEY MILLS SPUR (closed 1958) was opened from the London, Tilbury & Southern line east of Bromley to the North Woolwich line, and thereafter until 1940 many passenger trains used this route. In 1854 a service began over the Victoria Park–Stratford link (p. 88), worked by the NL until 1866, the GE taking over in alternate years until 1874 and altogether after that. It survived in an attenuated form until 1942.

Meanwhile Bidder had bought up the unwanted marshes and in 1850 floated the Victoria Dock Company to utilise them. 'The principal feature which distinguished the Dock from its predecessors was that it was brought into direct communication with the railways of the United Kingdom' (J. G. Broodbank).

The North Woolwich line was diverted through Custom House station on the north side of the new dock, the old line on the south side becoming the SILVERTOWN TRAMWAY (legally the 'Woolwich Abandoned Line') serving factories along the river bank. Squalid houses, crushed between factories and docks, were erected, passenger traffic increased and stations opened at Custom House (1855) and Tidal Basin (1858). In 1880 the Royal Albert Dock opened and again the line was diverted, this time into a tunnel under the waterway (the 'Substituted Line'). The original line (the 'Transferred Portion') remained part of the dock railway, carried over the waterway by a swing-bridge.

In 1870 a large gas-works was built on the marshes at BECKTON in order to use sea-borne coal. It was connected with the North Woolwich line at Albert Dock Junction by 1.75 miles of single track owned by the Gas Light & Coke Co. Opened for goods on 14 October 1872, it was leased and worked by the GE, which ran a passenger service for the workmen from 17 March 1873. In 1920 there were five services a day from Stratford, but these dwindled to one, which was withdrawn on 28 December 1940. After the coming of North Sea Gas the line was closed altogether on 22 February 1971.

To serve the Royal Albert Dock the dock company built 1.75 miles of double line from Albert Dock Junction parallel with the quayside lines to GALLIONS, opened on 3 August 1880. It was used only for passengers and parcels, a shuttle service from Custom House being provided by the owners and through trains by the GE. At Gallions an hotel and a pier were built and liner passengers landed. 'Is it Tilbury and a tender or Gallions and the Dock?' asked the hero of Kipling's *The Light that Failed.*

On 30 June 1896 the GE took over all the workings. In 1900 there were fifty-four trains, down to forty in 1920. A much attenuated service was in operation on 7 September 1940, when a stick of bombs along the line brought it to an end. The Port of London Authority, which had staffed the stations, maintained it for freight until 17 April 1966.

In 1920 there were 115 down passenger trains booked through Canning Town daily for North Woolwich and the two branches, while 17 more terminated. But competition intensified when trolley-buses were extended from Stratford to North Woolwich in 1938. Social change led to an even greater loss of traffic. Before World War II most dock and factory workers lived near their work and went home for their midday break, making four short rail journeys daily. Slum clearance, accelerated by bombing, led to the majority living as far away as Becontree or Dagenham. They ate in canteens and after work, if they had not yet acquired cars, took the bus to East Ham station on the District or all the way.

In 1939 there were still sixty down services through Canning Town, originating from Palace Gates, Stratford and Fenchurch Street. The latter ceased to run after 27 October 1940 and by 1959 there were but twenty-six down trains, and only in peak periods. In 1960, however, an hourly interval service began, strengthened at peaks. It was to be the last intensive steam-worked service in London, diesels taking over in 1962. Except for the few from Tottenham, all started at Stratford until projected to Camden Road in 1979. Electric trains with a twenty-minute service began in 1985. A new interchange with the District was provided at West Ham.

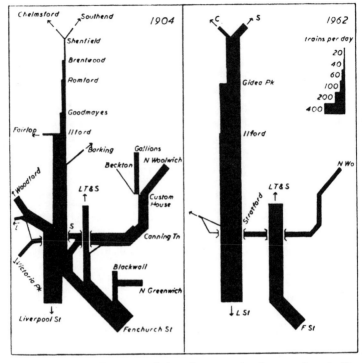

FIG 18 The decline of inner and rise of outer suburban stations in East London 1904–62. The thickness of the lines represents the number of stopping trains on an ordinary weekday.

North Woolwich has been reduced to a single dead-end, but the building has been happily taken over as a transport museum. Rehabilitation of the area is beginning and by 1986 there was significant new industry, though the process was not as advanced as in the Isle of Dogs.

The Royal Dock group was the largest in the Port of London, with 233 acres of water and 11 miles of quays. They provided the chief, but by no means the sole source of the heavy freight traffic. In 1958 there were sixty regular and six conditional freight trains booked southbound through Stratford Market station (closed 6 May 1957). Thames Wharf and North Woolwich were the main goods depots and there were private sidings on the Silvertown Tramway. As for the docks, the East India was reached by a goods branch opened in June 1848 across the Lea from Thames Wharf. The Royal Docks were served through the thirty-one-road Royal Victoria Exchange Sidings, where the blue PLA locomotives were conspicuous. Boat-trains to and from Liverpool Street were worked with decreasing frequency along the quayside by BR engines. But rail operations to all berths ceased on 1 May 1970 except for access to the heavy-lift berth in Victoria Dock. At the time of writing there are a few private sidings served by the occasional freight trip.

THE GENESIS OF THE LONDON, TILBURY & SOUTHEND RAILWAY

To meet competition from the North Kent for the Gravesend traffic, the Blackwall joined with the EC, concerned with preserving for itself the territory south of its Romford line. On 17 June 1852 they were authorised to build a line from Forest Gate Junction on the Romford line to Tilbury Fort, where two short branches to a riverside terminal made a triangle, and thence to Southend, 36 miles. On 3 July 1854 the two companies leased the line to the contractors, Peto, Brassey & Betts.

Opening to Tilbury was on 13 April 1854, to Horndon (now Stanford-le-Hope) in late 1854, to Leigh on 1 July 1855 and to Southend on 1 March 1856. East of Tilbury the line was single, and without telegraph it had to be worked as a single section. Only three daily trains each way could be operated, so the line was soon doubled. Trains carried Bishopsgate and Fenchurch Street portions joined and divided at Stratford.

To eliminate delays at Stratford and to develop local traffic west of Barking, on 7 July 1856 a cut-off was authorised between Barking and Gas Factory Junction (Bow) on the Blackwall, with running powers thence to Fenchurch Street. The new line was ready on 31 March and thenceforward all Tilbury trains ran direct into Fenchurch Street. The EC inaugurated a Bishopsgate–Barking service, GE trains running into Barking until 1918.

The proprietors of the 'Extension Shares' with which the Tilbury line was financed now worked to rid themselves of outside control and succeeded in incorporating themselves as the London, Tilbury & Southend Co. The lessees were conspicuously failing to develop traffic, but the lease did not expire until 1875, after which, failing to interest the GE, the LTS decided to work its line itself.

On 18 May 1869 the NL, having obtained running powers over the whole system, opened a spur from Bow to **BROMLEY JUNCTION**. It operated a shuttle service between Bow and Plaistow until 1916. Regular and excursion trains ran through to Southend until 1955. The spur was also used by freight trains, about twenty a day when it closed on 14 September 1959.

On 4 August 1890 the **TOTTENHAM & FOREST GATE** Railway was incorporated to build a 6 mile line from the T&HJ at South Tottenham (p. 158) to the LTS at its new station of Woodgrange Park just south of Forest Gate Junction. Built largely on viaducts, this costly line opened on 9 July 1894, and at the same time the LTS provided a spur to East Ham (closed 1958).

The T&FG had been jointly promoted by the Midland and LTS companies. It allowed the former to reach the Tilbury Docks. The latter, without a London terminus, gained entry into St Pancras, while trains could be run between the northern suburbs and Southend bypassing GE and NL metals. The Midland projected its T&HJ trains to Barking and East Ham, while the LTS operated scheduled and excursion trains from St Pancras to Southend.

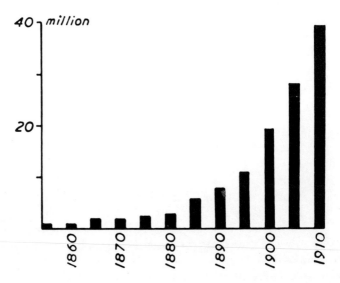

FIG 19 Passengers on the London, Tilbury & Southend Railway.

The Midland came into very close relations with the now prosperous local company and absorbed it on 1 January 1912 to the dismay of commuters who feared deterioration in the excellent service. Thus the LTS system eventually passed to the LMS and retained much of its characteristics until electrification in 1962, although control passed to the Eastern Region on 20 February 1949.

TRAFFIC GROWTH AND ECONOMIC DEVELOPMENT IN SOUTH ESSEX

When the contractors' lease expired on 3 July 1875 the LTS was in a parlous state. Commercial opportunities had been neglected and, said A. L. Stride in 1912, 'when we took over the line there was no rolling stock of any description, there was no telegraph system, there were no block signals . . .'

That this ramshackle, poverty-stricken concern was converted in thirty years into a well-run, prosperous line was largely due to A. L. Stride, engineer and general manager from 1875 to 1912. It was the continuity of his far-sighted and energetic management which raised the LTS to the top flight of railway efficiency, with such profound effects on the district served. In the first six months of 1876 the line carried 0.86 million passengers, and in those of 1912, 17 million. In the same period season-ticket holders increased from 499 to 10,892.

Because freight did not flow in any quantity from Tilbury Docks until after 1910 or from industry until after 1930, the line was largely dependent on passenger traffic, residential and holiday. This it successfully stimulated by a frequent and reliable service, comfort and, above all, low fares. In the early 1920s bogie stock was commonplace when four-wheelers were the GE standard.

SOUTHEND

Among the far-reaching consequences of LTS policy was the phenomenal growth of Southend as both resort and outer suburb. The low gravel hills of South Essex sweep eastward from Brentwood to reach the river as low cliffs between Benfleet and Shoeburyness. Around a break in these grew up a hamlet, South End in Prittlewell Parish, which had fifty-one houses in 1801 and was already something of a sea-bathing resort. By 1848 'quiet, dull Southend' extended over a mile of sea front and straggled up the High Street to where Central station now stands. In 1859, three years after the coming of the railway, Brassey laid out Cliff Town among cornfields and New Town was started. In 1863 three hotels opened and day visitors were becoming more numerous. The Scratton Estate, south of the railway, was sold for building, but there was no contemporary development north thereof.

Soon after opening in 1856, six trains a day to London were provided, one of them a fast business service. But the early importance of Southend as a residential suburb must not be exaggerated. The population of Prittlewell Parish grew only from 2,359 in 1851 to 8,009 in 1891, while in 1889 there was still only a single business express.

On 24 July 1882 a cut-off was sanctioned from Barking, through Upminster and over the Laindon Hills to rejoin the original route at Pitsea, thus avoiding the detour through Tilbury. This opened throughout on 1 June 1888 and brought Southend to 32.25 miles from Fenchurch Street, a saving of 7.75 miles. Fast trains now took only fifty minutes and the service was considerably increased.

Southend grew fourfold in the twenty years to 1901 and doubled again to reach 70,767 in 1911. In the 1880s the town spread north of the LTS line along the newly made-up Victoria Avenue, though even in 1898 the GE station was on the northern edge of the town and Marine Park (now the Kursaal) the eastern. After 1910 expansion continued rapidly, Westcliff grew up and the old village of Leigh developed fast. The Chalkwell Hall Estate dates from 1900–5.

The 1882 Act also authorised the LTS extension to Shoeburyness, where the school of gunnery had been established in 1859. The line was opened on 1 February 1884. On it Thorpe Bay was started as a high-class residential resort after the station opened in 1910.

The coming of the GE in 1889 brought still more trade, partly through the intense competition which followed. The GE line led to the northward expansion of Southend, the built-up area taking in Prittlewell, Rochford and Rayleigh. In the area as a whole there has been a continuous spread of building since 1920. From Leigh to Shoeburyness is now a single conurbation with a 1981 population in Southend District of 157,083.

In 1876, apart from Southend and Gravesend, the only source of traffic for the LTS was the district between Stepney and Barking. In Bromley and Plaistow, factories were springing up among mean houses. Plaistow, where the LTS established its workshops, numbered 6,669 in 1871. The potato fields and the sheep grazing the Lea marshes were disappearing fast. 'The fields changed into streets which lead nowhere and which are left unfinished and fragmentary and lined with mean little tenements', said Thorne in his 1875 guide.

In contrast, East Ham merely 'straggled for a mile along the lane from Little Ilford to North Woolwich' (Thorne), the surrounding market-gardens being noted for pickling onions. Barking, population 5,766 in 1871, had a 'large corn mill on the site of the old Abbey Mill'. Below it were barges loading local onions and potatoes for London and 'fishermen lolling about'.

East Ham grew from 9,713 inhabitants in 1871 to 69,758 in 1901, but the main period of expansion was the next twenty years and in 1921 the borough numbered 143,246. A gridiron of streets was laid over the market-gardens, and terraces of small houses were erected, as superior to those of Plaistow as they were to be inferior to those of Becontree. A similar fate overtook Barking.

It was not possible to enlarge Fenchurch Street to deal with the consequent traffic increase. Accordingly a relief route was provided by the WHITECHAPEL & BOW Railway, authorised in 1897 to extend the District line from Whitechapel 1.75 miles to join the LTS at Campbell Road Junction. Opened on 2 June 1902, it was jointly owned by the LTS and the District and was worked by the latter, its trains mostly terminating at East Ham.

The increased service forced the LTS to quadruple the Campbell Road–Barking section, a work completed to East Ham in 1905 and the rest in 1908. In 1903 it was estimated that 13.5 million of the LTS passengers used Fenchurch Street, 2.4 million the Whitechapel & Bow, 230,000 St Pancras and 35,500 Liverpool Street.

District electric trains ran to East Ham from 20 August 1905 and to Barking from 1 April 1908, being allocated the northern pair of tracks. The District also used its electric locomotives on through Ealing–Southend trains, with the change to steam at Barking. Inaugurated on 1 June 1910, this service lasted until 1 October 1939. In 1938 there were four daily trains each way.

East of Barking the great Becontree Estate, with a 1960 population of 90,800, was laid out by the LCC 1925–35 to rehouse East Enders. A 1929 survey covering 37,000 wage-earners on the estate found 60 per cent still working in London and a further 8 per cent in places between. The need for additional transport facilities was therefore urgent. Two additional tracks, chiefly for the use of District trains, were opened between Barking and Upminster on 12 September 1932 and five new stations were provided on the 7.75 miles. One, Heathway, booked 2.25 million ordinary passengers in 1955 and sold 62,000 seasons.

In 1938 there were 301 eastbound District trains daily through Campbell Road Junction, 166 for East Ham or Barking, 38 for Dagenham and 97 for Upminster. By 1960 a higher proportion continued beyond Barking, there being a ten-minute off-peak service to Dagenham East, alternate trains continuing to Upminster.

The improved service encouraged speculative builders in Hornchurch and Upminster, Hornchurch Urban District growing from 17,489 in 1921 to 104,092 in 1951 and 128,127 in 1961, when growth had tailed off. Meanwhile the Laindon Hills had become covered with a chaotic chicken-farm-cum-bungalow growth, similar to that described on page 188 and centred on Laindon and Pitsea stations. Between these last two the New Town of Basildon was founded to clean up the area. In 1981 the District numbered 152,185 inhabitants. In spite of the line passing through the business centre of this large town, in 1961 the general manager of the Eastern Region made the astonishing statement that it was not worth while to provide a station. Looking back, the defeatism of BR in those days was scarcely credible. Eventually the station opened on 25 November 1974, soon becoming one of the busiest on the line. Benfleet is rail-head for Canvey Island, disfigured by caravans and shacks since the motor-car enabled holidaymakers and rate-dodgers to occupy sites remote from railway stations. Beyond this the Southend complex begins.

To fend off the GE from Tilbury two short single-line branches were sanctioned on 20 August 1883, from Upminster to GRAYS and ROMFORD. The former opened on 1 July 1892 and the latter on 7 June 1893. They have pursued a placid existence, the Romford line surviving closure threats to be electrified in 1986. The Grays branch was converted in 1962 along with the main line.

In 1912 the Midland on taking over the LTS undertook to electrify as soon as possible. The LMS failed to avail itself even of the 1935 Treasury Agreement. In 1950 the British Transport Commission announced that it was next on the conversion list, but the expectations of the long-suffering commuters, riding in ageing coaches behind worn-out steam locomotives, were constantly disappointed until 18 June 1962, when electrification was completed, half a century after it was first considered vital. The same system was used as on the Liverpool Street lines and the Gas Factory–Bow Junction (now singled) and Barking–Forest Gate links between the two networks. Until 14 May 1985 they were used for stock transfer and emergency working, but then early and late trains were diverted from Fenchurch Street to Liverpool Street over the latter.

The LTS and LRT pairs of tracks have been completely segregated, Barking becoming the main interchange station, there being no other LTS-served station between Stepney East on the London side and Upminster on the Basildon line. In 1900 Barking had two platforms at a level-crossing, but was rebuilt with quadrupling and again modernised in 1932. By 1958, 2.5 million tickets were being sold together with 75,000 seasons, while 15,000 passengers a day were changing trains. Between 1959 and 1962 the station was again entirely rebuilt, and to enable better exchange facilities the up LRT line was brought by flying and burrowing junctions outside the Basildon lines. A further flyover connects the Forest Gate with the Tilbury lines to enable freight trains to cross the complex clear of other traffic.

THE DOCK AND INDUSTRIAL TRAFFIC

A 3.75 mile single line was opened on 7 June 1855 from

Mucking on the Tilbury–Pitsea section to THAMES HAVEN. Steamers for Margate called and trains ran in connection, while the LTS tried unsuccessfully to encourage the import of cattle from the Continent, though there was some general cargo which ceased when Tilbury Docks opened. No passenger trains have run since 1880 except for workmen. Since World War II two oil refineries have been built and freight traffic has proliferated. Numerous trains of petroleum products and chemicals keep the branch busy.

Mention should be made of the 2 mile, independent CORRINGHAM LIGHT Railway across the marshes to the north, which operated an isolated passenger service until 1952. Its eastern end became part of the internal system of one of the refineries.

The sprawling settlement (hardly a town) which is Tilbury dates only from 1886, when the first houses for dock workers were built. Previously the only traffic at Riverside station was in connection with the Gravesend ferry. Until 1880 the LTS could only carry rail passengers, but by purchase and lease it then gained the monopoly of the ferries, together with the use of West Street pier. The vehicular ferry closed with the opening of the Dartford Tunnel in 1961 and the foot ferry was transferred to West Street from the Town Pier, which had all the appurtenances of a station, but with a boat waiting beyond the ticket barrier. Through bookings to Gravesend were issued from all LTS stations.

Tilbury Docks were the outcome of severe inter-company rivalry and were built by the East & West India Dock Co. to intercept traffic from upstream docks. They came into operation in 1886 when the North End exchange sidings went into service. Tilbury Town station had opened on 15 June 1885 as Tilbury Docks. Because there were few warehouses in the new docks, the owners leased the new LTS Commercial Road goods depot and agreed special freight rates to and from Tilbury.

Development was slow until the Port of London Authority was created in 1909, after which trade rapidly expanded. Until 1939 there was no road access and 87 per cent of the traffic was railborne. But by 1959 this had declined to 35 per cent, though, in 1961, 250 loaded wagons were forwarded daily. Then from 25 July 1969 all rail traffic destined for the general cargo berths ceased.

Tilbury was selected as the London container terminal and by 1969 six berths were ready or building, and since then they have been added to by the Northfleet Hope development. Tilbury docks are now the only PLA dock system. As far as rail is concerned, they are served by two freightliner terminals and a rail-connected grain terminal.

On 16 May 1930 the landing-stage, used by liners to land or embark passengers, was opened. A new customs hall and Riverside station were designed as an integrated unit. The station had four passenger platforms and two for baggage. In 1955, 500 liners called and as many boat-trains ran, carrying 147,298 passengers, 942,024 tickets being sold to local passengers. Until electrification trains also ran to liners at their berths. But all this ceased in the 1960s.

At Purfleet an outcrop of chalk approaches the river, and a lime and cement industry was established in the eighteenth century. The marshes were also sufficiently isolated for powder factories. But otherwise there was little industrial development until in 1930 the Ford Motor Co. started on its vast Dagenham plant. Since then the Essex shore from Barking to Thames Haven has become highly industrialised. The LTS section thus became a major freight carrier. In 1953 there were twenty-three booked freight trains through Barking and in 1960 1.75 million tons originated on the LTS section. Increasing freight traffic overwhelmed the LTS yard at Little Iford, now the electric depot at Barking, and in 1937 Ripple Lane Yard began to be laid out between Barking and Dagenham Dock. Modernised in the 1950s, it had fifty-one sorting sidings and a daily capacity of 2,000 wagons. Its use declined with the growth of block trains, but much of it has been taken over as rail-served container, inland clearance, and general freight depots. Eastward the line still has a concentration of private sidings unusual in Greater London since 1960.

This is one of the few areas of Greater London where rail freight traffic has actually increased over the years. By 1983 some fifty freight trains were booked to pass Barking daily. Analysis of 1985 traffic showed fifteen trains leaving the Thames Haven branch; three were Speedlink services carrying chemicals and the rest block trains of petroleum products.

Destinations of the latter included Kingsbury (West Midlands), Thame, Staines West, Micheldever, Dunstable and Watton-at-Stone. Freightliner trains left Tilbury for Glasgow, Garston (Liverpool), Leeds and Willesden. There were also freightliners from Ripple Lane to Southampton and from the Dagenham Storage Company to Stratford. In addition three block trains of parts were run between the Ford plants at Dagenham and Halewood, as well as car-delivery trains to destinations such as Wrenthorpe (Wakefield). There was a service for edible oil from Bromborough to Purfleet. East and West Thurrock Junctions were the origin or destination of a number of Speedlink services.

In contrast, the cement production has been concentrated on Northfleet (Kent) on the other side of the river. West of Barking freight traffic has ceased. Originally there were five goods depots served by short branches from the 1.6 miles of main line between Stepney East and Fenchurch Street. These were (opening and closing dates in brackets) Goodman's Yard (1 February 1851–1 April 1951), Royal Mint Street (1 August 1858–1 April 1951), East Smithfield (17 June 1864–1 July 1966), all owned by the GE, Haydon Square (12 March 1853–2 July 1962), LNW, and Commercial Road (1 July 1886–3 July 1966), LTS. There was also a branch to the wool warehouse in St Katharine's Dock.

FENCHURCH STREET

The Blackwall Railway opened Fenchurch Street in 1841, probably with two platforms, and enlarged it in 1854 to accommodate the EC and NL traffic. The Blackwall service, though frequent, soon became but a minor part of the station's activities. The NL operated a fifteen-minute service from 26 September 1850, but ceased to be interested when it opened Broad Street, though a shuttle service from Bow lasted to 31 December 1868. For the EC it was the only City terminus from 1854 to 1874, when Liverpool Street opened. But the GE still ran a frequent service to Ilford and to North Woolwich, supplemented by business trains to Romford, Ilford and even Southend. Until 1894 it was the only London terminus for the LTS and it was always its principal one.

Thus, until 1900, Fenchurch Street, with its heavy traffic to and from the Inner Arc and Inner Suburban Zone, was one of the busiest London stations. As early as 1861 it was used by 7 million ordinary passengers and 1,286 season-ticket holders. In 1903 passenger 'user' had grown to 32.9 million, 13.4 million by LTS trains and 10.5 million by those of the GE; 223 trains arrived daily, 79 before 10.30.

But traffic declined thereafter. The Whitechapel & Bow diverted many LTS passengers, traffic over it increasing from 2.4 million in 1903 to 9.4 million two years later. Electric trams ate into the short-distance traffic, while the telephone replaced messengers between city offices and ships in the docks. Fenchurch Street was also inconvenient for the growing West End traffic. On a census day in 1913, 48,386 passengers used the station, representing an annual rate of about 17 million. On the other hand the LTS service frequency had increased; there were 560 train movements, involving some 280 arrivals.

The Blackwall service ceased in 1926 and all other LNE trains had been withdrawn by November 1949, leaving LMS trains in sole possession of this LNE station. Yet such had been the growth of the Middle and Outer Zones that the 175 trains using the station daily in 1955 carried in total some 45,000 passengers. This represents a much greater passenger comp-lement per train than in 1913. Delay in electrification in favour of the GE route to Southend led to a fall in traffic to 37,700 on the 1960 census day. But the 1962 census, after elec-trification, recorded 51,700. In 1962 there were 265 trains a day, an increase of 90 over the steam service. The thinning of off-peak frequencies and the diversion of early and of late trains meant a decline to 251 in 1986, when some 45,000 passengers used the station daily.

Fenchurch Street is convenient for the City, but suffers from being with Holborn Viaduct the only London terminus without an Underground station. It suffers too the familiar problem of increasing numbers travelling in ever contracting periods. In the 1960 census 19,059 departing passengers were counted; 10,569, or *56 per cent*, left on the thirteen trains between 17.04 and 18.03. There were 15,060 seats on those trains. Only the 17.23 was badly overcrowded. The four Tilbury-line services carried only 2,308 passengers, as traffic with Central London has always been small from below

Barking. Outside 16.00 to 19.00 the passenger complement exceeded 200 on only two trains.

The station has a severely plain but pleasant façade, spoiled by the neurotic zigzag of the GE canopy. The office block erected over the station in 1986 is not visible from street level behind. At a high level are the two island platforms. In 1935 these replaced five platforms, two very short and only No 4 of any great length. In 1913 this was the only one available for LTS trains and 12 departed between 16.57 and 18.07. In 1986 all four platforms were used to despatch 23 trains between 17.00 and 17.56 (18 between 17.02 and 18.00 in 1962). It is now purely suburban in function, even if it were ever anything else. With nationalisation the LTS line at last got its own London terminus.

This chapter has largely been the story of the LTS, a compact, intimate and largely self-contained system with a tradition of good management. In 1958, when BR was sliding, through the combined shortcomings of government policies and of its own, into financial chaos, the 90 route miles of the LTS and its sixty-two stations earned £4.25 million from passenger traffic and £2.75 million from freight. This represented over £75,000 per mile, and provided an operating surplus of £300,000.

This was before electrification swept shabby and outmoded steam trains into unregretted oblivion. South Essex was given a service of unprecedented frequency and speed. In 1986 in off-peak periods there are 5 trains an hour from Fenchurch Street, 1 fast and 2 stopping to Shoeburyness via Basildon, and 2 to Southend via Tilbury Town. Since 1983 these have missed Riverside, leaving that imposing memorial to the past only with the hourly service from Upminster.

But though brought to the peak of modernity in 1962, the line, like so many others, has suffered the stop-go in investment forced on BR by successive governments. Twenty-five years later, with little or no improvement, it has once more started to lag behind and is in need of new rolling stock, better signalling and modernised stations.

CHAPTER XI

Railways and Megapolis: A Conclusion

London's development since 1840 has far exceeded that of all the previous centuries. It is no coincidence that the period has been that of the Railway Age and the Motor Age, for this development has resulted from the growth of trade, commerce and industry, in turn fostered by developments in transport and communications, among which the railway has been prominent. But the spectacular growth of population and, especially, the even more spectacular growth in area since 1900 is, even in recent years, almost wholly the consequence of concurrent developments in rail transport.

Without the suburban railway the almost complete separation of work and residence, a fundamental social change of the last 150 years, could not have taken place. The railway is, as yet, the only possible mass mover on the scale necessary to allow this. Its technological and economic characteristics make such journeys possible at a cost in time and money that is socially acceptable and with minimal damage to the environmental fabric of the city, its suburbs and rural surroundings.

R. J. Smeed (then of the Department of Scientific and Industrial Research) demonstrated the complete dependence of London in its present form on its railways. One person, travelling at peak hours, occupies 1sq ft if travelling by rail, 3sq ft if walking, 4–10sq ft by bus and 50–80sq ft by car. While the City has 0.14 square miles of roadway, if 335,000 commuters arrived by car they would need 0.65 square miles, with parking extra. Even the 1963 Beeching Report left Greater London virtually unaffected by its long list of recommended closures. In 1978, 40 per cent of all person-trips within Central London were by rail, as were 51 per cent of the radial trips to and from the centre.

Without railways twentieth-century London might or might not be a better place to live in; it certainly would be a different one. The problem has been a public and private reluctance to recognise that, just as the present shape of Greater London is due largely to continuous transport development, the future of transport depends on the future shape of the conurbation.

Separation of work and residence has permitted a constant rise in living standards in general and housing standards in particular. An ever greater range of choice of where to live has also been made possible. But communities have become less close-knit and all too many people no longer identify themselves with either their place of residence or their place of work.

The indisputable fact remains that, for good or evil, the railway has been and is the instrument of growth. The problems of Greater London are thus those of its railways. Just as one of London's major problems is the journey to work, so one of the railways' major concerns has always been the problems of commuting. The 'Problem of the Peak', a phrase once used by P. A. White, formerly of the Southern Region, is an apt description of the basic problem of London's railways over almost the whole of their history. The result of the peak is the inevitable overcrowding and the inflation of cost to such an extent that the community must choose between subsidy or decay of transport facilities, for to provide for the car involves as great a subsidy element. Successive governments vow they will reduce subsidies when newly elected, but their policy quietly changes as the next election looms.

Nevertheless, while there has been an underlying theme, attitudes have changed through the years. The first London railway, the London & Greenwich (1836), was essentially a suburban line and set the pattern for that form of operation. That pattern was followed as a matter of policy by the southern lines and the GE, and by a more ambivalent GN, but was avoided by the other northern lines. Virtually all, however, sought the main prizes, access to the City and the West End, and, for freight, a water outlet. Suburban growth began in earnest after 1860, and among other factors was stimulated or hindered by railway company policy.

The Metropolitan of 1863 was the first urban line with a function of relieving street congestion. Apart from the District, development was held back until the introduction of electric traction in about 1900. This led to the split between the 'rapid-transit', metro-style, Underground lines, which eventually surfaced and reached out into the expanding suburbs, and the 'main lines', which engaged in long-distance passenger and freight carrying as well as suburban working. The latter were occasionally converted to electric working.

In this period there was little government intervention, and so little overall planning. Although Parliament vetted proposals for new lines it initiated none. However, some of its policies were positive, such as the insistence on workmen's services where property was demolished by railway extension, a policy which eventually brought the separation of work and residence at least for artisans.

The inter-war period saw radical new developments, the main one being the great period of rehousing which affected all classes and which led to the phenomenal outward spread of the urban area. By 1939 separation of work and residence had become universal among all classes, while Greater London had become the country's industrial growth area. All this was coupled with an outward spread of rapid-transit lines and the electrification of the Southern's system. The other main lines suffered stagnation through lack of investment. At the same time there was more active intervention by government, setting two important precedents: the creation of the LPTB, bringing the rapid-transit lines as well as buses and trams into public ownership; and in effect introducing public funding by guaranteeing interest on capital works at a time of declining rail profitability. This led to the widespread takeover by rapid transit of main-line suburban routes.

The immediate post-war years saw nationalisation of all London's public transport, but saw rather less integration, not only between LT and BR, but between LT rail and road. They also saw the completion of the 1935 Plan, and additional electrification projects on Eastern Region by 1962.

By that time public transport was incurring increasing losses and the period since 1960 has been marked by a lack, displayed by all political parties, of coherent government policy towards subsidy and investment. This has increased management difficulties, chiefly because new schemes have been allowed to stagnate rather than receiving incremental investment. Southern and Eastern Regions have both suffered badly as far as their shorter-distance services are concerned.

The period since 1960 has seen movement of population and industry away from Greater London. At first this was with government encouragement, but later it was in spite of government efforts to prevent it. At first it affected only the inner area, but from 1970 there was a steady decline in employment in the Central area and the decline also began to affect the Outer Zone as well. The rapid development of the 'Outer Metropolitan Area' beyond Greater London, coupled with the piecemeal improvement of outer-suburban services and a growth in disposable incomes all led to the growth of long-distance commuting, from stations of hitherto unheard-of distances from London. This was coupled with a decline in commuting from the Inner Zone and stagnation in the Outer.

The 1968 Transport Act at last put the criteria for capital investment in rail infrastructure on an equal basis with that for urban roads, ie on social cost-benefit grounds rather than on narrow profit-and-loss grounds. The Minister of Transport was also given powers to make 75 per cent grants toward rail investment in urban areas. This later led to the Transport Policies and Programmes method of funding by the Department of Transport of balanced road/public transport plans agreed with the local authorities. In London this did not affect BR which was subsidised through the Public Service Obligation Grant.

The 1969 London (Transport) Act brought LT under the GLC, which was also the road authority. At first the GLC tended to be road-oriented but in 1974 Labour won an election in which an issue was the proposed 'motorway boxes'. From then until abolition in 1985 the GLC's policy became ever more public-transport oriented, as we have seen. This culminated in the 1983 'Fares Fair' proposals to peg fares and increase subsidy. The scheme was declared illegal by the House of Lords, but it led to the introduction of the intermodal 'Travelcards'. For the first time LT rail and road fares were really integrated, and, in the form of the 'Capital-card', this was extended to BR within the LT area in 1984. By the end of 1985 there were 80,000 Capitalcard users.

While the policy of winding down integrated transport planning since 1980 has affected provincial conurbations, this has not been applied to Greater London, where for the first time there has been integration of planning by LT and BR with the setting up in September 1984 of the London Passenger Transport Group. Apart from Capitalcards a small sign is the publication of maps showing both networks. Meanwhile in both these organisations government pressure has led to greater cost-effectiveness and labour productivity. At the same time labour relations must permanently recover from the lows of which the major consequence was inconvenience to commuters, the major market. The apparent death wish of the major rail unions and senior management was at one time quite remarkable.

The period since 1960 has seen a catastrophic decline in BR's freight carryings. This has been due to the decline in the consumption of industrial and particularly of domestic coal together with the extinction within Greater London of port activity. But it is also true that the effort put into developing freight traffic has not matched that given to the Inter-City sector. There are now surprisingly few freight terminals in the whole of Greater London.

The same period has seen the decline of commuter traffic from the Middle Zone, balanced by unprecedented growth in long-distance traffic. That this was due to fares for most of the period rising more slowly than disposable incomes has already been mentioned. Another factor has been the traditional 'taper' in season-ticket rates. Thus the season-ticket rate to Rugby (82 miles) is only some 30 per cent more than to Bletchley (40 miles) and this could be offset against lower house prices. Finally, while the time available to the commuter is fixed, train speeds have constantly increased.

At the time of writing there are appearing on the horizon some more hopeful pointers for the future than were present when the book was last revised in 1971. In 1986, BR, having separated commercial functions from the Region and set up the London & the South East Sector, inaugurated 'Network South East'. This is a massive exercise in the creation of a new image. It is too early to judge its success, but the name of the driving force behind the venture, Christopher Green, may become one of the great names in the history of London's railways. A uniform house style and a greater uniformity of trains (and of their passengers) has led to the decline in the idiosyncracies of the London termini, so clearly visible even in 1963. For the first time the main-line suburban services of Greater London have been given a uniform identity.

The trend toward unification of London's rail system has been extremely slow. It began with the creation of London Transport in 1933 and the integration of the Metropolitan into the rapid-transit system of the former UndergrounD group lines. But the various sections of British Rail for long preserved their historic identities. Even on the Southern Region the services over the three Divisions, South Eastern, Central and Southern, showed a remarkable independence of each other. It is too early to ascertain the consequences of the 1983 abolition of the Divisions. Integration of the Underground and BR has also been very slow until very recently.

Another point of significance is that Network South East covers an area even wider than that of the Outer Metropolitan Area. Meanwhile travelcards and other measures have led to a 46 per cent increase in passengers on London Underground in the period 1982–5 to 762 million in 1985, exceeding the previous record year, 1948. There are also indications of a reversal, however temporary, of the downward trend of Central area employment. In addition the decline in numbers of commuters on BR has shown an upturn between 1983 and 1985, while the Underground ridership has increased even more significantly.

In spite of constant governmental hankering for economic viability in public transport, it must recognise that the latter has a social basis. A great city and its public transport are inseparably linked. To ignore the social, economic and environmental implications of railways for 'Megapolis' is dangerous in the extreme. Their importance to Greater London is as great now than at any time in the past.

The central theme of this study, in which limitations of space have meant so many aspects have perforce been neglected or at best summarily dealt with, is the fact that over a million people are moved into the 6.5 square miles of Central London and then out of it again each working day, the majority by rail.

Bibliography and Acknowledgements

Only a small selection of the vast bibliography covering Greater London and its railways can be given here to serve as a starting point.

ORIGINAL SOURCES

These fall into a number of groups:

1. The reports of enquiries into London's transport, including the 1846 Royal Commission on London Traffic, the 1865 Select Committee on Metropolitan Communications, the 1892–8 LCC Reports on Workmen's Trains, the 1901 Select Committee on London Underground Railways, the 1903–5 Select Committees on Workmen's Trains, the 1905 Royal Commission on the Means of Locomotion in London, the 1925 Report of the Home Counties Traffic Advisory Committee, the 1949 London Transport Executive Travel Survey, the 1959 Nugent Committee on the Future of Public Transport, the 1962, 1971 and 1981 Greater London Travel Surveys (by the GLC), the 1973 London Rail Study (GLC) and the 1981 Monopolies and Mergers Commission Report on BR London Commuter Services.
2. Local Acts of Parliament and associated Committee Papers.
3. Reports and minute-books of railway companies, and annual reports of the LPTB, LTE, LTB and LRT.
4. Working and public timetables.
5. Press files: (a) the nineteenth-century railway press mainly for investors, including *Herapath's Journal, The Railway News*; (b) the twentieth-century technical press, particularly the *Railway Gazette International, Modern Trans-*

port, Modern Railways and the *Railway Magazine*; (c) house journals; (d) the *Illustrated London News, The Times* and local newspapers.

6. Statistical returns of the Census of England and Wales, Board of Trade, Ministry/Department of Transport.
7. Maps by G. F. Crutchley (1825–43), various editions of the Ordnance Survey, and Railway Clearing House maps and junction diagrams.

In the preparation of a book such as this there is no substitute for fieldwork and hundreds of miles were covered by train, bus and foot. A car is useless in Greater London.

SECONDARY SOURCES – GENERAL

There are a number of geographical descriptions of Greater London, including *Greater London* edited by J. T. Coppock and H. Prince (1964). Social history is dealt with by R. J. Mitchell and M. D. R. Leys in *A History of London Life* (1958), while A. A. Jackson's *Semi-Detached London* (1973) is best for suburban growth. Industry is dealt with by D. H. Smith in *Industries of Greater London* (1962). R. M. Robbins's *Middlesex* (1955) was of particular value. Of early guide-books the most useful were J. Thorne's *Handbook of the Environs of London* (1875) and D. Lyson's *The Environs of London* (1896).

J. G. Broodbank's *History of the Port of London* (1920) and J. Bird's *Geography of the Port of London* (1957) cover the port aspects to that date. The best source for the general transport history is T. C. Barker and M. R. Robbins's *A History of London Transport – Vol 1: The Nineteenth Century* (1963) and *Vol 2: The Twentieth Century* (1974).

SECONDARY SOURCES – RAILWAYS

Only a selection of the numerous publications can be included here. Files of the *Railway Magazine* and the former *Railway and Travel Monthly* contain numerous local studies, many of a high order of scholarship, on which the author was greatly dependent. H. V. Borley published a series of articles on the railways of the Inner Zone in the *Journal of the Railway & Canal Historical Society* (1957–60). Of major books, mention must be made of E. A. Course's *London Railways* (1962), A. A.

Jackson's *Rails Through the Clay* (1964), *London's Termini* (1969), and *London's Local Railways* (1978), Charles Klapper's *London's Lost Railways* (1976) and, particularly for its photographic material, R. Davies and M. D. Grant's *London and its Railways* (1983). For individual lines particular mention must be made of R. H. G. Thomas's *London's First Railway: The London & Greenwich* (1972), C. H. Grinling's *History of the Great Northern Railway* (1898, but still a classic), J. N. Young's *Great Northern Suburban* (1977), D. Edwards and R. Pigram's *Metro Memories* (1977) and *The Final Link* (the GW&GC line) (1982), A. A. Jackson's *The Metropolitan Railway* (1986), C. E. Lee's *The Metropolitan District Railway* (1956), C. F. Dendy Marshall's *A History of the Southern Railway* (1936), H. D. Welch's *The London, Tilbury & Southend Railway* (1951), R. M. Robbins's *The North London Railway* (1953) and T. B. Peacock's *The Port of London Authority Railways* (1952). There are a number of local monographs; E. A. Course's *The Bexleyheath Railway* (1979) and G. F. A. Wilmot's *The Railway in Finchley* (1976) are good examples. Finally, H. V. Borley's *Chronology of London Railways* (1982) is fundamental and the author depended heavily on it.

The outward expansion of suburban services means that this volume of the 'Regional History of the Railways of Great Britain' series must be read in conjunction with the volumes covering adjoining areas: Vol 2, *Southern England* (H. P. White), Vol 5, *The Eastern Counties* (D. I. Gordon) and Vol 13, *Thames and Severn* (R. Christiansen). The author gratefully acknowledges the MSc (Econ) thesis (Univ. of London, 1954) *Some Aspects of the Recent Industrial Development of West London* by B. A. Bates as the source of statistics on traffic at West London goods depots.

The author also wishes to place on record his gratitude for help given in preparing the 1963, 1971 and 1986 editions. Those to whom he is indebted include the Archivist of the British Railways Board, for permission to publish material, and his staff, for assistance in gaining access to it; Mrs Southgate and Mrs Woolley, Librarians of the Chartered Institute of Transport; the public relations officers and their staffs who freely made available so much statistical data, Messrs M. B. Thomas (Eastern Region), R. W. Crawshaw (London Midland Region), F. D. Y. Faulkener (Southern

Region) and C. J. Rider (Western Region); Mr C. Austin, London and Regional Planning Manager, Network South East; Mr M. Webster, London Underground Ltd; Mr S. Jolly, Docklands Light Railway; and the then Director of Housing, LCC, for information on the Council's estates. To Mr R. M. Robbins the author owes a very special debt both in his former capacity of Commercial and Public Relations Officer, London Transport Board, when he so generously furnished facilities for research, and also as transport historian for encouragement in the early stages of planning the book.

So many individuals have helped with information and discussion that they cannot be listed here, only gratefully thanked. But the author must make individual mention of Professor M. J. Wise; Dr J. Martin (for suggesting the term 'Inner Arc'); Mr J. Westergaard (for the concept of the 'job ratio' – the ratio between daytime employment and night-time residence amongst the economically active); Mr B. N. Nunns for tireless assistance in fieldwork and obtaining illustrations; Mr G. F. A. Wilmot for placing at the author's disposal his unique knowledge of the Finchley area; and Dr E. A. Course and Mr J. G. Spence for their comments on the South London chapters. The author is of course responsible for any errors. Thanks are also due to Professor J. A. Patmore for help and advice in preparing both the second and this the third edition. Last but by no means least, sincere thanks are due to Mr D. St J. Thomas for his constant help and encouragement over more years than either of us would probably like to think.

Index

Bold type is used to indicate pages giving the opening date of a section (not individual stations except in the case of main-line termini). Branch openings are indexed at the station at the farthest end (from Central London). Popular names of lines are listed as well as those of the promoting companies. Towns known by compass points are listed under these, but stations are listed under the town name: thus, 'West Drayton' but 'Croydon, West'.

Abbreviations: elec, electrification; tfc, traffic.

Abbey Mills spur, **204**
Acton, 117, 118, 137, 138; —— Gate
    House Jct, 138; —— Main Line·
    Yard, 159; —— North Jct, 122, 123;
    —— South, 141; —— Town, 140,
    141; —— Wells, 137, 138
Addiscombe (Road), **54**, 70, 101
Addison Road, *see* Kensington
Ahrons, E. L., 46, 90
Albany Park, 20
Aldenham Works, 176
Aldgate, 97, 101
Aldwych, **109**
Alexandra Palace, **172**, 174;
    —— (formerly Wood Green), 73,
    109, 167, 169, 182
Aldersgate (Street), *see* Barbican
Amersham, 146, 147, 151
Anerley, 30
Angel, **105**; —— Road, 179, 180, 181,
    182
Angerstein Wharf, 56
Architecture, 35, 37, 41–2, 46, 47, 49,
    57, 87, 114, 120, 125, 126, 143, 152,
    155–6, 162, 176, 218
Archway (Highgate), 106, 173
Arnos Grove, 19, **176**
Ashstead, 69
Aylesbury, **143**, 146, 150, 151, 152;
    —— & Buckingham Rly, **143**

Baker Street, 90, 91, 100, 101, 108, 142,
    143, 144, 146, 147, 152; —— &
    Waterloo, **107**
Bakerloo Line, 26, **107–8**, 129, 146, 152
Balham, 61; —— Jct, 40
Bank, 51, 105, 112, 193
Barbican, 90, 91, 92
Barking, 18, 20, 27, 158, 200, **207**, 208,

210, 212, 213, 215, 216, 218;
    —— Creek, 200, 203
Barkingside, 186
Barlow, P., 103
Barlow, W. H., 156
Barnes, 63, 64
Barnet, 18, 20, 168, 173; ——,
    Chipping, 171; ——, High, 169, **172**,
    174; ——, New, 166, 167, 169
Barrington Road Jct (Brixton), 57
Basildon, 21, 212, 213, 218
Battersea, 17; —— Park, 67, 68
Beazley, S., 33, 52
Beckenham: —— Hill, 58; —— Jct, 39,
    54, 70, 72; ——, New, 54
Beckton, **204**
Becontree, 18, 205, 211
Beddington Lane, 62
Bedford, 95, 117, 160
'Bedpan', 108, 160
Beeching Report, 87, 219
Belgravia, 27
Bellingham, 47
Belmont, 131
'Belt line', 80, 159
Benfleet, 212
Bermondsey, 16, 30; ——, South, 33
Bethnal Green, 16, 18, 27, 178, 180,
    181, 194, 197
Bexley, 18, 20, 75
Bexley Heath Rly, 55
Bexleyheath, 55; —— line, 55, 70, 72,
    73, 75, 77
Bickley, **39**, 58, 59
Bidder, G. P., 62, 203, 204
Billericay, 188
Birmingham, Bristol & Thames Jct
    Rly, 131
Bishop's Road, *see* Paddington

Bishop's Stortford, 184, 194
Bishopsgate, **179**, 195, 207; —— goods, 180; —— Low Level, 195
Blackfriars: (BR) **45**, tfc 46–7, 72, 95, 139; —— goods, 45; (LT). **95**, 139
Blackheath, 12, 16, 52, 55, 74; —— Hill, 58
Blackwall, **201**, 217; —— Rly, 82–3, 179, 185, **201–2**, 203, 207, 216
Blake Hall, 193
Bounds Green Depot, 159, 167; Bounds Green (LT), 176
Brassey, T., 210
Brent Yard, 157, 159
Brentford, 63, 124
Brentwood, 12, 29, 187, 188
Bricklayers' Arms, **32**, 52; —— Jct, 33
Brill, 152
British Rail, 15, 23, 87, 218, 221, 223, 224
British Transport Commission, 95, 114, 213
Brixton, 61; —— East, 67; —— Hill, 28
Broad gauge: (7ft), 40, 88–9, 94, 117, 119, 124, 134; (5ft) 178, 201
Broad Street, **84**, 85, elec 86, tfc 87, 110, 129, 134, 165, 167, 173, 180, 198–9, 216; —— goods, 84
Broadgate development, 199
Bromley: (by Bow), 204, 211; (Kent), 13, 20, 54, 75; —— Direct Rly, 56; —— Jct, 39, 204, **208**; —— North, **56**, 70
Brompton & Piccadilly Circus Rly, 108
Brookmans Park, 169
Broxbourne, 179, 194
Brunel, I. K., 119, 120
Brunel, Marc, 101
Brunswick Wharf, 201
Buckhurst Hill, 186
Bushey, 131; —— Heath, 176

Camberwell, 27, 43
Camden, 81, 83, 127, 136; —— Bank, 127; —— goods, 128; —— Road, **82**, 87, 160, 205; —— Town, (BR) 13, 27, 28, **82**, 84, (LT) 105, **107**
Campbell Road Jct, **211**, 212
Canning Town, **203**, 205
Cannon Street, **36**, tfc 37, 38, 70, 72, 97
Canonbury spur, 85, 86, 109, 164, **165**
Carpenders Park, 13, 130
Capitalcards, 222
Caterham, 70, 71

Catford, 58, 70; —— Bridge, 70; —— Loop, 46, **58**, 70
Central Line, 188, 192, 198
Central London: definition, 15; —— Rly, **105–6**, 110, 112, 122. 123
Chalfont & Latimer, 143
Chancery Lane, 111
Channel Tunnel, 550
Charlton, **55**, 77, 79
Chaplin, W. J., 66
Charing Cross: (BR) **29–38**, tfc 37–8, 46, 50, 79; (Embankment) 107, 197; (Strand) 106, 107, 111; ——, Euston & Hampstead Rly, **106**
Cheam, 68
Chelmsford, 193, 194
Chesham, **143**, 146, 152
Cheshunt, 182, 184, 194, 199
Chessington, 20; —— South, **72**
Chigwell, 12
Chiltern Hills, 11, 23, 143, 144, 153; 'Chiltern Line', 151
Chingford, 158, 181, 184, 185, 194, 197, 198, 199
Chipstead Valley Rly, **62**
Chislehurst, 12, 13, 18, **54**; —— & Sidcup UDC, 75–7
Churchbury, *see* Southbury
City, the, 12, 14, 27, 28, 43, 61, 71, 80, 84, 89, 91, 96, 98, 105, 109, 122, 128, 129, 134, 137, 179, 198, 217, 220; —— & South London Rly, 92, **103–5**, 107; —— Line, (LCD) **43–7**, 51, (Metropolitan & District) 97, 98, 101; road space in, 219

Clapham, 28, 57; —— Common, 104, **105**, 107, 133, 135; —— Jct, 47, 49, 59, 64
Clapton Jct, 181
Claygate, 68
Cobham, 64
Cockfosters, 19, **176**
Colnbrook, **124**, 125
Commercial Rly, 201
Commissions and Committees of Inquiry, 15, 28, 66–7, 95, 103, 118, 175, 191
Copenhagen Tunnel, 164, 165, 166, 168
Corbett's Lane Jct, 30
Corringham Light Rly, 214
Copper Mill Jct, 181, **182**
Coulsdon North, 68, 69
Cricklewood, 137, 157, 158, 160
Crofton Park, 70

Cromwell Curve, 97
Croxley Green, **131**
Croydon, 18, 23; —— & Oxted Joint
  line, 56; ——, East, 39, 59, 71, 72, 79;
  ——, West, **30**, 60, 62, 71
Crystal Palace, 33, 38, 39, 40, 58, 59,
  60, 61, 68, 70; —— & South London
  Jct Rly, **58**
Cubitt, L., 162
Cubitt, T., 40
Cuffley, 169
Custom House, 204
'cut and cover', 103

Dagenham, 205, 215; —— East, 212;
  ——, Heathway, 212
Dalston: —— Jct, 84, 87; (Kingsland)
  82, 87, 88
Dartford, 52, 55, 74; —— Jct, 55; ——
  Loop, **55**, 70, 72, 73
Denham, 122, 148
Denmark Hill, 12, 57, 74
Deptford, 17; —— Wharf, **62**
District Rly, 22, 25, 63, 64, 68, 71, 90,
  95–102, 106ff, 134, 138, **139–42**,
  205, 211, 212, 220
Docklands: —— Development
  Corporation, 202; —— Light Rly,
  202–3
Docks, 80, 81, 82, 84, 199, 200, 201,
  202, 204, 205, 206, 208–9, 214, 215,
  216
Dorking North, 69
Dudding Hill loop, 137, 138
Dulwich, 16, 43, 61

Ealing, 12, 20, 99, 117, 118, 139; —— &
  Shepherd's Bush Rly, 122, **123**, 133;
  —— & South Harrow Rly, **141**, 150;
  —— Broadway, 123, 124, 140, **141**;
  —— West, 123
Earl's Court, 99, 108, 134, 135, 139,
  140, 141
East & West India Docks &
  Birmingham Jct Rly, 81
East Anglian electrification, 193–4
East Coast Main Line, 12, 170
East Ham, 205, 208, 211, 212
East London Rly, 101
Eastcote, 20
Eastern Counties Rly, 178, 179, 185,
  201, 207, 216; Eastern Counties &
  Thames Jct Rly, 203
Edgeware, Highgate & London Rly,
  171

Edgware, 19, 28, 108, 135, 146, 166,
  171, **172**, 173, 174, **176**; —— Road,
  27, 28, 146
Edmonton, 28, 180, 183; ——, Lower,
  180, **182**, 183
Effingham Jct, 69
electrification, 23, 24, 25, 37, 51, 66–74,
  86, 94, 95, 101–2, 105, 129, 131, 134,
  138, 140, 141, 146, 160, 170, 191–4,
  205, 213, 221
Elephant & Castle, **45**, 47, 104, 108
Elmers End, 54, 56
Elmstead Woods, 54
Elstree, 157, 160; —— Tunnel, 153
Eltham Park, 55
Enfield, 13, 20, **169–70**, 179, 180ff, 194,
  197, 199; —— Lock, 184; —— Town,
  182
Epping, 186, 192, 193; —— Forest, 12,
  180, 181, 184, 185
Epsom, **62**, 63; —— Downs, **62**, 70
Erith, 52, 75; ——, North End sidings,
  53
Euston, 12, 81, 105, 117, **125–7**, tfc 127,
  129, 195, 199

Factory Jct, 40
Fairlop Loop, **186**, 192
'Fares Fair', 222
Farnborough extension, **39**, 40, 54
Farringdon (Street), 43, 45, 88, 91, 95,
  162
Fay, S., 139, 149
Feltham Jct, **63**; —— yard, 159
Fenchurch Street, 82, 84, 97, 108, 111,
  158, 159, 179, 186, 187, **201**, 204,
  205, 207, 210, 211, 216–18, tfc 217
Ferme Park yard, 159, 167
Ferries, 202, 203, 214
Finchley, 12, 18, 19, 171, 172; ——
  Central, 172, 174; —— East, 172,
  173; —— Road, (Met) 106, 143ff,
  (Mid) 159, 160
Finsbury Park, 92, 109, 110, 111, 164,
  166–8, 172ff; —— yards, 167
Forbes, J. S., 96, 99
Forest Gate, 213; —— Jct, 208, 213
Forest Hill, 30, 61
Freightliner, 88, 121, 157, 167, 191, 215,
  216

Gallions, **205**
Gas Factory Jct, 207, 213
Gas Works tunnel, 163ff

Gatwick Airport, 43, 95, 135
Gerrards Cross, 150
Gibb, G., 112
Gidea Park, 187, 188, 194, 199
Gloucester Road, 90, 97, 139
Golders Green, 106, **107**, 128, 173
Gordon Hill, 170, 175
Gospel Oak, 80, 158, 159, 161
Graham Road curve, **87**, 199
Gravesend, 52, 200, 201, 207, 214
Grays, 200, **213**
Great Central Rly, 121, 143, **149–52**
Great Eastern: —— Rly, 23, 87, 101,
    158, 178, 179, 197, 207, 209, 210, 213,
    216, 218; —— Metropolitan Station
    & Rlys, 179
Great Northern: —— Railway, 88, 89,
    92, 109, 110, 153, 155, 159, **161–75**,
    184; —— & City Railway, 109–10;
    '—— electrics', 24, 45, 86, 94, 95,
    170–1; —— & Strand Rly, 109; ——,
    Piccadilly & Brompton, **109**
Great Western: —— Rly, 23, 40, 45, 94,
    117–25; —— & Brentford Rly, **124**;
    —— & Great Central Joint
    Committee, 121–2; —— & Uxbridge
    Rly, 124
Greater London Council, 13,18, 87, 95,
    115, 222
Greathead, J. H., 103
Green Belt, 10, 72, 174
Green Park, 111
Greenford, 121ff; —— Loop, **123–4**
Greenwich, 55, 200, 202; —— Park, **58**,
    72
Gresley, N., 173, 197
Grove Park, 18, 54, 56, 77
guide books, 30, 64, 203, 211
Guildford, 64; New Guildford Line, 63,
    64–5, 68, 69
Gunnersbury, 137, 138

Hackney, 16, 82, 183; —— Central, 87;
    —— Downs, 181, 182, 183; Hackney
    Downs lines, 186, 192, 194, 197, 198;
    —— Wick, 87
Hammersmith, 12, 27, 68, 101, 109,
    122, 137, 140, 141; —— & Chiswick
    Rly, **138**; —— & City Rly, 99, 118,
    119, **122–3**, 133, 134, 137, 138; ——
    Broadway, 139; —— Extension Rly,
    139; —— Jct Rly, 140
Hampstead, 12, 13, 171; —— Heath,
    158; —— Junction Rly, 80, **83–4**, 87,

129, 133; —— Road, 84; ——, South,
    129; —— Tube, 85, 105, **106–7**, 176;
    ——, West (LT) 159, (Mid) 160,
    (Met) 95, **142**
Hampton Court, **65–6**, 68
Hanwell, 117
'happy afterthought', 84
Harlesden, 128, 129
Harringay spur, **159**
Harrow, 13,19, 23, 128, 129, 131, 134,
    144, 146, 150, 168; —— &
    Rickmansworth Rly, 143; —— &
    Stanmore Rly, **131**; —— & Uxbridge
    Rly, 99, 147; —— on the hill, **143**;
    ——, South, 141, 143
Hatfield, 12, 166, 169, 170
Hatton Cross, **141**
Haverstock Hill, 159, 160; —— tunnel,
    153
Hawkshaw, N., 36
Haydons Road, 66, 71
Hayes: (Kent) 12, **56**, 154; (Mdsx) 117,
    118
Heathrow: —— Airport, 12; ——
    Central, **141**; Terminal Four, **141**
Hendon, 20, 107, 159, 160; ——
    Central, **172**
Herne Hill, 12, **45**, 51, 57, 59, 70, 92;
    —— Sorting Sidings, 45
Hertford: —— East, 194; —— Loop,
    167, **169–71**, 175, 182
High Beech, 180, 181
Highams Park, 184
Highbury, 111
Highgate, 12, 13, 171, 172, 174; ——
    Road, **158**, 161
Hinchley Wood, 69
Hitchin, 153, 161
Hither Green, 35, 54, 55; —— yard, 71,
    159
Hoddesdon, 184
Holborn (Viaduct): (BR) 28, **45**, tfc 47,
    58, 69, 71, 72, 217; (LT) 95, 108, 109,
    111
Holloway, 13, 16, 18, 158, 165, 168;
    ——, Upper, 159
Homerton, 87
Hornchurch, 20, 212
Hornsey, 17, 165, 166, 168, 175
Hounslow, 20, 68; —— & Metropolitan
    Rly, **140**; —— Barracks, 141; ——
    Central, 140; —— Loop, **63**, 68, 136;
    —— Town, 140; —— West, **140**

Ickenham, 147
Ilford, 12, 186, 187, 188, 192, 197, 216
Inner Arc, 15, 18, 23, 84, 183
Inner Circle, 88, 91, 95, 101, 102, 103, 108, 139, 141, 146; —— Completion Co, 96
Inner Suburban Zone, 16, 18, 35, 46, 74, 164, 183, 194, 198, 217, 222
Inter-City, 43, 95, 135, 223
Isle of Dogs, 200, 201, 202, 206
Isleworth, **63**, 64
Islington, 16, 18, 27, 28, **81**

'Jazz Service', 195, 198
Jubilee Line, **111**, 146, 152

Kempton Park, 66
Kennington, 27, 105, **107**
Kensal Green, 117, 130
Kensington, 18, 27, 133, 134, 135; ——, Addison Road, 134, 137, 138, 139; ——, High Street, 97, 99, 135, 139; ——, Olympia, 135; ——, South, 90, 95, 97, 101, 109, 139
Kentish Town, 16, 92, 155, 158, 161
Kew, 13, 137; —— Bridge, 136, 137
Kilburn, 28, 130, 146
King William Street, 104, 105
King's Cross: (BR) 46, 81, 89, 91, 92, 101, 105, 110, 153, 156, 161, **162–4**, tfc 164, elec 164, 165, 167, 168, 170, 193, 195; (Met) 89, 173; —— goods, 153, 166
Kingsbury & Harrow Rly, **142–3**
Kingston-on-Thames, 63–4, 68; —— & London Rly, 64; —— Loop, **64**

Ladbroke Grove, 122
Ladywell Loop, **54**
Laindon, 12, 212; —— Hills, 212
Lambeth, 27; —— North, **108**
Landmann, G., 230
Latchmere Jct, 40
Latimer Road, 122, 123
Lea Valley, **180–5**, 199; —— line, 180; Lea Bridge, 181; 'Lea Valley Enterprise', 185
Leatherhead, 69, 72
Lee Jct, 55
Leicester Square, 112
Leigh-on-Sea, **207**, 210
Lewisham, 17, 18, 52, 54, 72
Leyton, 17, 186
Leytonstone, 186

Liverpool Street: (BR) 50, 86, 102, 105, **179**, 183, 186, 187, 191, 195–9, tfc 198–9, 211, 213; (Met) 90, 94, 96, 101, 102; (LT) 87, 90
London: —— & Birmingham Rly, 81, 125, 127, 131; —— & Blackwall Rly, **201**; —— & Croydon Rly, **30**; —— Greenwich Rly, 29, **30**, 32, 33, 52, 220; —— & North Eastern Rly, 152, 165, 173, 175, 176, 192, 193, 217; —— & North Western Rly, 23, 45, 81–6, 121, 125–37, 143, 155, 165, 171, (New Lines) **128**, 129, 131; —— & South Western Rly, 39, 40, 47, 63–6, 68, 107, 109, 133, 134, 138; ——, Brighton & South Coast Rly, 30, 33, 38, 41, 57, 59–63, 67–8, 101, 133; ——, Chatham & Dover, 39, 40, 41, 43, 45, 91, 92, 133, 156, 162, (Metropolitan extension) 40, 46, 69; —— Bridge, **29–38**, tfc 35, 39, 52, 59, 60, 62, 67, 68, 70, 72, 74; —— County Council, 18, 67, 113, 126, 130, 168, 195, 202; —— County Council estates, 20, 47, 58, 71, 74, 130, 186, 188, 212; —— Midland & Scottish Rly, 160, 173, 217; ——, Tilbury & Southend Rly, 22, 97, 159, 201, 204, 207–18; —— Transport, 15, 51, 102, 110, 143, 148, 173, 174, 176, 192, 221, 223, 224; —— Transport Board, 114; —— Transport Executive, 114; —— Passenger Transport Board, 113–14, 221; —— Passenger Transport Group, 223; —— Regional Transport, 112, 115–16, 138, 203, 213
Longhedge Jct, 40, 65
Loughborough: —— Park, 43, **62**; —— Junction, 57
Loughton, 185, 186; —— Branch Jct, **185**, 190, 192; —— lines, 185–7, 192, 197, 198
Ludgate Hill, 43, **45**, 46, 51, 56, 57, 66, 95, 138
Luton, 160

Maiden Lane: (North London) 83, 88; (GN) 161, 168; —— spur, **164**
Maidenhead, **117**, 119
Mansion House, **95**, 96, 98, 108, 134, 139, 140
Marylebone: (BR) 25, 121, 122, **149**, 150–1, tfc 151, 152; (LT) **108**

Maze Hill, 55, 74
Merton, **66**
'Metroland', 144–5, 168
Metropolitan: —— Rly, 22, 25, 43, 45, 81, **88–102**, 110, 119, 121, 131, 132, 138, 162, 165, 198, 220; —— & Great Central Joint Committee, 145; —— & St John's Wood Rly, **142**; —— Rly Extension, 85, 107, **142–7**; —— Rly Country Estates, 144, 148
Mid Kent: line, 70; —— (Bromley to St Mary Cray) **39**, **54**
Middle Circle, 137
Middle Suburban Zone, 18, 20, 23, 74, 164, 186, 194, 217, 223
Midland: —— Rly, 45, 83, 92, 94, 137, 138, 143, 153–60, 162, 172, 176, 208, 209, 213; '—— City', 160
Mile End, 192
Mill Hill, 160; —— East, 172, 174
Millwall: —— Extension Rly, **202**, 203; —— Jct, 82, 202, 203
Minories, 95, 201
Mitcham Jct, 59, 60, 70
Moorgate (Street), 28, 90, 91, 92, 94, 98, **105**, 109, 110, 134, 156, 160, 167, 170, 173
Morden, 71, **107**
Motorways, 81, 135, 186
Motspur Park, 69
Mottingham, 55
Muswell Hill, **172**, 173, 174; —— Rly, **172**, 182

Neasden, 144; —— yard 151; —— to Northolt line, **150**
Neele, G. P., 126, 128, 131, 136
Network South East, 73, 224
New Cross, 52, 54, **101**; —— Gate, 62, **101**
New Malden, 64
New Towns, 21, 169, 184, 212
Newbury Park, 186, 192, 193
Nine Elms, 47
Noel Park (Green Lanes), 182
North & South Western Junction Rly, 80, 84, 125, 129, **136–8**, 141
North Greenwich, 202
North Kent: —— Rly, 32, 33, **52**, 54, 55, 69, 70, 207; —— East Jct, 32, 52
North London Rly, 22, **80–8**, 125, 136, 138, 164, 165, 201, 203, 204, 208, 216
North Metropolitan Rly, 88
North Woolwich, 18, 87, 183, 187, 190,

194, **203**, 211, 216); —— line, 203–7; —— Rly, **203**
Northern & Eastern Rly, 179, 190
Northern City Line, 173
Northern Heights, 92, 128, 167, 171–5, 178; —— freight tfc, 177
Northern Line, 92, **106**, 108, 173, 174
Northfields, 141, 142
Norbiton, 74
Norbury, 61
Northolt, 123; —— Jct, 121, 156
Norwood: —— Jct, 30, 39, 61, 68, 71; —— extension, **39**
Nunhead, 58, 70, 71

Oakwood, 19, **176**
Ockenden, 12
Old Oak: —— Common, 121; —— Jct, 83
Ongar, 12, 22, 112, **186**, 192
Orpington, 18, 23, 46, 54, 59, 69, 70, 75, 95
Outer Circle, 134, 137, 139; Super ——, 138
Outer Metropolitan Area, 221, 224
Outer Suburban Zone, 20, 23, 194, 199, 217, 222
Oxford & Aylesbury Tramroad, **152**
Oxford Circus, 111, 112

Paddington: (BR) 12, 25, 64, 81, 88, 90, 98, 107–8, 117, **118–21**, tfc 122, 123, 130, 148, 151, 196; (LT) 108, 129; ——, Bishop's Road, 89, 90, 94, 118; ——, Praed Street, 90
Palace Gates, **182**, 183, 184, 205
Park Royal, 121, 141; —— goods, 121
Peckham, 61; —— Rye, 57, 58, 59, 67, 68, 74
Penge Jct, 40
Peto, Brassey & Betts, 207
Petts Wood, 20
Piccadilly Line, 19, **108–9**, 112, 140, 141, 149, 175–6
Pick, F., 114
Pimlico, 27, 39
Pinner, 18, **143**
Pitsea, **210**, 212, 214
Plaistow, 208, 211
Plan for Transport (1935), 146, 173, 192, 213, 221
Plumstead, 52, 53, 55, 56
Ponders End, 184
Poplar, 18, **82**, 184, 200

Population density and change, 9, 14, 16, 18, 20, 21, 52, 53, 75–7, 130, 144, 147, 148, 168, 183, 200, 210–11
Port of London Authority, 214, 215; —— Rly, 202, 205, 207
Potters Bar, 166, 167, 169, 175
Pouparts Jct, 40
Prestons Road, 82
Primrose Hill, **82**, 88, 129, 155; —— tunnel, 128
Prittlewell, 209, 210
'problem of the peak', 220
Purfleet, 214
Purley, 13, 62, 68
Putney, 16, 65; —— Bridge, 65, **140**; ——, East, 64, 65, 68

Quainton Road, 143, 149
Queen's Park, 129, 130
Queen's Road (Peckham), 67
Queenstown Road (Battersea), 49

'rapid transit', 25, 112, 145, 224
Rayleigh, 188, 210
Rayners Lane, 20, 147, 148, 149
Raynes Park, 63
Richmond, 13, 47, **63**, 64, 87, 131, 133, 134, **137**, 138, 140; —— Rly, 47, 48, 86, 87
Rickmansworth, **143**, 146, 148, 152
Ripple Lane yard, 80, 215
Road (tram and bus) competition, 23, 24, 46, 61, 63, 67, 69, 85–6, 160, 182, 205
Rochford, 21, 210
Romford, 12, 13, 20, **178**, 179, 187, 188, 190, 192, 198, 207, 216; —— line, 187–8, 193, 199
'roundabout services', 60, 71
Rotherhithe, 27, 101
Royal Oak, 118
Royal Victoria exchange sidings, 207
Ruislip, 20, 147, 148; —— Gardens, 139; ——, West, 112, 122, 150

St Albans, 12, 131, 155, 160
St James's Park, 113
St John's Wood, 27, 142
St Helier, 18, 71
St Pancras, 46, 49, 138, 154, **155–7**, tfc 156, elec 156, 158, 159, 160, 199, 208, 211; —— goods, 153, 157, 159; —— Jct, 83; ——, St Paul's Road Jct, 153, 156

St Paul's, *see* Blackfriars
Sanderstead, 18, 72, 95
Scott, Gilbert, 155
Sekon, G. A., 12, 108
Selhurst, 50, 59, 61
Selsdon (Road), **54**, 56, 72
Seven Sisters, 182, 194 (*see also* Finsbury Park)
Sevenoaks, 46, 95
Shenfield, 24, 188, 193, 199
Shepherd's Bush, 102, **105**, 112, 118, 122, 149
Shepperton, **66**, 68
Shoeburyness, 209, **210**, 218
Shoreditch, 28, **101**, 102, 178
Shortlands, 18, **39**, 70; —— & Nunhead Rly, 58
Sidcup, 13, 18, 55, 77–9, 169
Silvertown Tramway, 204, 206
Slade(s) Green, 55, 59
Sloane Square, 100
Slough, 21, 118, 120
Smithfield Market, 28, 83, 89
Snaresbrook, 186
Snow Hill, 45, 92, 95
Somers Town, 155; —— goods, 157
South Eastern: —— Rly, 30, 39, 52–6, 92, 95, 101; —— & Chatham, 36, 59, 69, 92
South Herts Plateau, 12, 128, 153, 161, 171
South Lambeth goods, 41, 48
South London Line, 33, 57, 60, **62**, 67, 101
Southall, 13, 40, 118, 124, 134
Southbury Loop, **182**, 194, 199
Southend, 158, 182, **188**, 193, 194, 199, 200, 207, 208, 209–11, 212, 216, 217, 218
Southern Rly, 42, 59, 69, 71, 72, 73, 178, 198, 220
Southwark Depot, 35
Speedlink, 215–16
Spitalfields, 28, 180
Staines, 71; ——West, **124**
Stanford-le-Hope, **207**
Stanley, A. (Lord Ashfield), 112
Stanmore: (LNW) **131**; (Met) 20, 146, **152**
Stepney, 16, 27, 82, 179, 211; —— East, 213
Stevenage (Langley Jct), **169**
Stewarts Lane, 40
Stockwell, **104**

Stoke Newington, 28, **181**, 182, 183, 184
Stoneleigh, 20
Stratford, 12, 87, 88, 158, 179, 180, 182, 186, 187, 190, 192, 193, 194, 198, 204, 205; evolution of layout, **190**; —— Market, 206; —— extension (DLR), 203
Streatham, 43, 59, 61; —— Hill, 60
Stride, A. L., 209
'suburban opportunity' and 'suburban incubus', 121
Sudbury, 13, 142
Surbiton, 19, 64
Sutton, 18, 20, 23, 28, **59**, 62, 64, 69, 71
Swiss Cottage, 16, **142**
Sydenham, 28, 38; ——, Lower, 53

Tadworth, 70, 71
Tattenham Corner, **62**, 71, 73
Teddington, 73
Temple Mills, 190; —— yard, 80, 189, 190, 191
Thames: —— gravels and terraces, 11, 12, 25, 46, 117; —— Haven, **214**, 215; —— Link, 95; —— side, 13, 53, 54, 82, 192; —— Tunnel, 101; —— Valley Rly, **66**; —— Wharf, 206
Theydon Bois, 186
Thornton, H., 197
Thornton Heath, 61
Thorpe Bay, 210
Tilbury, 13, 159, 204, 210, 213, 214, 215; —— line, 217; —— Riverside, 218; —— Town, 218
Tite, F., 48
Tolworth, 72
Tooting, 28, 61, 66
Tottenham, 17, 28, **158**, 159, 183, 185, 205; —— & Forest Gate Rly, 158, 159, **208**; —— & Hampstead Jct Rly, **158–9**, 160, 182, 208; —— Hale, 180, 194; —— North Jct, 159; —— South Jct, 80, 158, 159, **182**, 183, 208
Tower: —— Gateway, 203; —— Hill, 97; —— Subway, 103
Tubes, 25, 26, 51, 71, 85, 92, 99, **103–16**, 128, 129, 164, 173, 174, 175, 191, 192, 193
Tulse Hill, 59, 61, 68, 69
Turnham Green, 27, 140, 141
Twickenham, 13, 64

Underground, 15, 23, 46, 49, 58, 126, 217, 221, 224; —— Electric Rlys, 106; UndergrounD, 11–13, 224
unification, 224
Union Street spur, **46**
Upminster, 19, 210, 212, 213, 218
Uxbridge, 12, 20, **124**, 140, 141, **147–9**; —— & Rickmansworth Rly, 148; ——, Belmont Road, 149; ——, High Street, **148**; ——, Vine Street, **148**

Vauxhall, 49
Verney Jct, **143**, 146, 151
Victoria, 33, **38–43**, tfc 42, 45, 46, 56ff, 60, 67, 68, 70, 71, 72, 92, 100, 134; —— Line, 43, **110–11**, 174, 193, 198; —— Station & Pimlico, **40**
Victoria Park, 204; —— Jct, 88, 190

Waddon Marsh, 62
Waltham Holy Cross, 184, 185
Walthamstow, 13, 180, 181, 184, 185, 186, 196; (Vic Line) **111**; —— Central (Hoe Street), **181**, 194; ——, Shern Hall Street, **181**; ——, Wood Street, 181, 183
Walworth, 27, 28
Wandsworth, 18, 64; —— Common, 39; —— Road, 57
Wanstead, 185
Wapping, 27, 101
Warren Street, 111
water outlet, 25, 62, 220
Waterloo, 39, 43, **47–51**, tfc 50, 120, 126, 134, 137, 193; —— & City, **49**, 51, 107, 109; —— Jct, 36
Watford, 12, 26, 84, 86, 87, 128, 147, 199; ——, Met & L.N.E, **152**; —— & Rickmansworth Rly, **131**; —— High Street, 131; —— Jct, 129, 131; —— South Jct, 146
Watkin, E., 96, 97, 99, 143, 144
Welham Green, 169
Welling, 77
Welwyn Garden City, 169, 170, 171
Wembley, 144; —— Park, 146; —— Stadium, **152**
West Brompton, **139**
West Coast Main Line, 11, 13, 88, 122
West Drayton, 117, 118, 124, 148
West End, 12, 28, 37, 38, 42, 51, 61, 89, 98, 107, 110, 134, 167, 217, 220; —— of London & Crystal Palace, **39**
West Ham, 17, 205
West London: —— Rly, 45, 80, 84, 123,

125, **131–6**; —— Extension Rly, 40,
131–6; —— Jct, 133
West Wickham & Hayes Rly, **56**
Westbourne Park, 118, 121, 122
Westminster, 14, 27, 95
White City, 123
Whitechapel, **99**, 101, 211; —— & Bow
Rly, **211**, 217
Whitton, 63
Wickford, **188**
Widened Lines, **91–5**, 99, 163, 165;
—— goods depots, 92
Willesden, 85, 88, 128, 130, 131, 134,
135, 136, 144; —— Green, **142**, 146;
—— Jct, 129–30
Wimbledon, 57, 64, 65, 71; —— &
Croydon Rly, 62, 66; —— & Dorking
Rly, 63; —— & Sutton Rly, 66

Windmill Bridge Jct, 40
Windsor, 71, 119, 140; —— Line, 47,
50, 63, 137; ——, Staines & South
Western Rly, 48, 63
Wood Green, 161, 183 (*see also*
Alexandra Park)
Wood Lane, 105, 123
Woodford, 13, 186, 193
Woodside, 54, 56; —— & South
Croydon Rly, **56**, 72
Woolwich, 18, 52, 53, 55, 92, 200; ——
Arsenal, 56, 69
Worcester Park, 69
Workmen's trains, 43, 77, 118, 130, 185
Worship Street, 87
Wyatt, M. D., 120

Yerkes, 106, 109, 112